1∿3388   /⟨∿ ⎯

CW01500715

'ᴏ

The spectacle of nature

THE SPECTACLE OF NATURE

Landscape and bourgeois culture in nineteenth-century France

NICHOLAS GREEN

Manchester University Press

Manchester and New York

distributed exclusively in the USA and Canada by St. Martin's Press

Copyright © Nicholas Green 1990

Published by Manchester University Press
Oxford Road, Manchester M13 9PL, UK
and Room 400, 175 Fifth Avenue,
New York, NY 10010, USA

Distributed exclusively in the USA and Canada by
St. Martin's Press, Inc.,
175 Fifth Avenue, New York, NY 10010, USA

British Library cataloguing in publication data

Green, Nicholas
    The spectacle of nature: landscape and bourgeois culture in nineteenth-century
France.
    1. France. Urbanisation, history
    I. Title
    307.7′6′0944

Library of Congress cataloging in publication data
Green, Nicholas, 1954–
    The spectacle of nature: landscape and bourgeois culture in nineteenth century
France/Nicholas Green.
        p. cm.
    ISBN 0-7190-2843-4
    1. Cities and towns—France—History—19th century. 2. City planning—
France—History—19th century. I. Title.
    HT135.G74 1990
    307.76′0944′09034—dc20   89-12647

Reprinted in paperback 1992

ISBN 0-7190-3909-6 *paperback*

Printed and bound in Great Britain by
Biddles Ltd, Guildford and King's Lynn

Contents

Illustrations

Acknowledgements

This book developed out of my PhD thesis, begun in 1978 and completed in 1986 for the CNAA. My first acknowledgements are due to the supervisors of that project, Griselda Pollock and Adrian Rifkin, who guided me in the right direction, and to the external examiner, Jacques Rancière, for his stimulating responses.

Research was primarily carried out in Paris, at the Bibliothèque Nationale, the Archives Nationales and the Bibliothèque Historique de la Ville de Paris. However, I would like to express a special debt of gratitude to the staff of the Archives Départementales, Melun, and the Bibliothèque Municipale, Fontainebleau, who helped me uncover some of the most interesting archive material. Particular thanks are also due to Georges Gendreau, former librarian at Fontainebleau, who, at an early stage, drew my attention to useful texts on the forest and inspired me with his great enthusiasm.

The book has taken a number of years to research and write, and has undergone various mutations. During that time, it has been discussed and endured by numerous friends, relations, students and colleagues. I would like to thank the following for their support, encouragement and good advice: Jane Beckett, Rod Brookes, Deborah Cherry, Jane Collins, Annie Coombes, Alain Cottereau, Mike Foster, Jo and Peter Green, Sheila Henderson, Patrick Llompart, Neil McWilliam, Lynda Nead, Richard O'Leary, Michael Orvicz, Roy Peters, Lisa Tickner, Trevor Wadlow, Christine Weedon and Tim Winter. In addition, a special mention is due to Peter Green and Sheila Henderson for their assistance in checking and typing parts of the manuscript.

Finally, I owe more than I can say to Frank Mort, who has lived this project almost as intensely as I have. Without the rigour of his intellectual interventions and his continued emotional support it would have come to nothing. The book is dedicated to him.

INTRODUCTION

I am looking through the train window. The view is, for me, hypnotic: the sky a deep impenetrable blue; open fields receding in gentle undulations, equally intense under the slanting beams of a low January sun; the bare branches of an occasional tree spreadeagled against the sky, fingering the blue. In the distance, the black line of a dense copse seems precisely placed to frame and close the panorama, while above a flock of birds – rooks perhaps – wheel and circle, following the line of some invisible tractor. It is not just the vividness of the colours, the clarity of form peculiar to the winter sunshine, that is so gripping. It is the way the whole thing I am experiencing keeps changing shape and definition. By which I mean that it represents both a deep, physical, almost visceral space – a space to be measured by the eye, to be tramped, if only metaphorically, by the feet – *and* a carefully-ordered pictorial composition, an 'image' of nature. As if the glass of the window becomes the two-dimensional surface of a picture on which are traced the lines of successive planes. As if nature itself becomes the means of its own objectification. In that oscillation between two quite distinct modes of representation lies something of the intensity of sensation procured by this innocent and transient perspective.

To begin with such a conceit is not just to acknowledge my own prior engagement with something called the countryside (and landscape art) but to stake out the framework for some of the big issues pursued in this book. The picturing of nature is central. Usually the question of the relation between landscape imagery and what lies out there 'through the train window' is posed in terms of a debate about realism. This all too easily slides into a sterile discussion of which forms of representation are more or less 'realistic'. The problem is the casual assumption not only that some modes of discourse *can* approximate to the 'real' but that there is a 'real' – out there – to be approximated to. My reading of the view through the window suggests that the sense to be made of something called nature is already shaped by a complex network of expectations and interpretations grounded in social experience. Thus, though the issue of realism may rear its head from time to time, the questions we shall be addressing are of a different order. Such as: what is implicated in the exchange between pictorial and spatial codes in the visualisation of nature? How are ways of seeing active in the production of social reality? And, most important, how can such a seemingly transparent dialogue become the vehicle for powerful social articulations?

Yet this is primarily an historical book. It is about the ways the countryside was imagined and experienced in early nineteenth-century France, and the effective appropriation of the category *nature* to describe these sensations. For if nature could mean, and had meant, many things – God's creation, the rationalist human nature of Jean-Jacques Rousseau, the classificatory systems of natural history – it was in the nineteenth century that it was hegemonised by a definition of the external world as scenery, views, perceptual sensation. In that sense, the object *nature* is taken here not as some pre-existent given, not as some idea in the mind of man to be reinterpreted according to the 'spirit' of the epoch, but as a social and cultural construct specific to a particular material situation. It is its historical *specificity*, as against any notion of transhistorical continuity, that will be frequently reaffirmed.

What is distinctive to early nineteenth-century France is the extra-ordinary proliferation of texts and practices – from illustrated books to theatrical spectacles, from jokes to country houses – that evidence interest in the countryside. Of course, many commentators on literature and art of the period have noted the prevalence of images of nature, explaining them as a key facet of romanticism. What they have rarely tried, though, is to set the production and circulation of such literary and pictorial codes in articulation with other, perhaps more mundane, processes of leisure and pleasure, as part of the uneven field of discourses constituting nature. Viewed more sociologi-cally, from the point of view, say, of the tourist excursion, the 'image' of nature looks somewhat different from that in Lamartine's meditative poetry or Turner's fiery sunsets. It is with mapping the 'common argument' linking these apparently disparate phenomena into a coherent cultural frame, pinpointing the material conditions by which it was sustained and pursuing its ramifications and effects, that much of this account is concerned.

The argument, then, stems methodologically from Michel Foucault's dictum that social reality is constituted in and through historically specific languages and forms of knowledge;[1] that, moreover, discourses are never free-floating in a vacuum but take on meaning only in so far as they are inscribed in material practices and institutions. *Discourse* here designates a coherent pattern of statements across a range of archives and sites that sets the terms for the operation of both truth and power in any field of knowledge. From which it follows that the discourse on nature has to be analysed in terms of its *systematic relations* rather than the properties and characteristics of any particular text or image. The point needs emphasising because this meth-odological insistence has brought the project, somewhat brutally, into confrontation with the preconceptions and methods of one of the dominant cultural approaches to occupy the field; that is, art history. Since a body of visual images usually claimed for art makes up a major component of the historical archive on nature, and since recent developments in 'radical' art history have offered powerful arguments about the complexity of visual ideologies, it seems useful to indicate briefly where the differences and disagreements arise.[2]

The sticking-point is the retention by art history, even radical art history, of a set of texts designated *art* as the fulcrum for cultural analysis.

3

This, it may appear, shares common ground with much historical and contemporary analysis – what do most historians start with but texts! By *textual* analysis, however, I mean something quite precise. Namely that certain highly wrought and codified objects – whether oil-paintings, banners, cathedrals, 1950s furniture or critical writing on art – provide not only the way into research but its touchstone. Methodologically, the procedure goes something like this. We move from the given set of texts (visual or otherwise) outwards to the wider historical structures within which they are seen to be produced and circulated. In doing so, we cast the net much wider than the received wisdom of art history, to draw in the state and its institutions, family patterns, professional groupings, and so on. From there, armed with such knowledge, a number of conclusions can be drawn out about the connections between texts and social relations. There need not be an explicit return of the repressed. However, it is the spirit of the text which always gives the argument its *raison d'être*.

An implicit circularity, then, takes us from text to social conditions and back again, reproducing a figure-on-ground, black-on-white relation between something called 'the text' and what may be called history, conditions of production, readers or audiences. The route is by no means confined to art history. It characterises all forms of cultural analysis which work with such textual procedures, notably deconstructive literary criticism and certain types of film and media studies. For art history, though, it has very definite implications indeed.

What is meant by this? Given the route just mapped, the text-based approach can easily smuggle back in something called art, not now aesthetically but *epistemologically*. Built into the paradigm is the central importance of those initial highly-coded objects/texts for defining the field of study, fixing the limits of visibility. The thing comes ready-packed in a certain order of knowledge. Art still stands as the *métalangue* for how culture as a whole is to be envisaged. That is to say, what is on offer is a tightly-specified field of texts, products and genres which marginalises all those processes that cannot be handled in a textual way, that cannot be neatly frozen or framed. Deep down here is a root disagreement about culture. There is no question of waging a vendetta against those studying art practices, but when the art-derived method foreshortens the cultural agenda, then the cutting-edge of radical theory is in danger of getting blunt.

This book attempts to push for a more interdiscursive approach to the visual – as part of an interlocking series of histories which involve multiple relations and dependencies across a range of social domains. The question is no longer one of analysing an internal field of images in its relation to a set of external determinations – art *and* society, art *and* nature – but of grasping the interdependence of cultural practices along with their mutually reinforcing results. The method is intertextual in that it holds on to objects, relations, readers and audiences *in process*. One inference to be drawn from all this is that the pictures and prints of landscape churned out in such quantities in early nineteenth-century France may not be quite what they seem. Their obviousness – to our eyes – as art is overdetermined (historically) on the one hand by their production and circulation as commodities on the Parisian luxury goods market, and on the other by their integration into the cultural *spectacle* of the metropolis as a way of life. In which connection, another inference is that the visual can now be articulated according to distinct modalities, as much a structure of perception organising and ordered by space as the property of pictures themselves.

The question of *space* is crucial. Urban historians and geographers have frequently directed attention to the role played by space in ordering the social relations of the city.[3] And at one level Paris has been taken as the classic model. This is germane to the argument of the book. Space, here, is seen to carry powerful ideological resonances – constructing particular subjectivities and modes of perception. These dimensions did not just register material economic and political change; they were *active* in shaping urban social relations. Moreover, it was in and through the type of modern urbanism crystallised in 1830s and 1840s Paris that the conditions for a new discourse on nature were laid down. *The spectacle of nature* weaves together those urban conditions and their ideological readings of space with the range of practices – rural visits and excursions, the diorama, country houses – through which they were played out.

But why nature? Why spend years researching and writing on a topic which hardly warrants a flicker of interest in the weighty tomes of economic and political history? Is this not a purely antiquarian enterprise? What has nature, after all, to do with politics and power? There are a number of ways to respond. The most obvious is to make the point that all discourse is political in the broadest sense, in that it shapes the kinds of cultural map we carry in our heads and act out in our day-to-day lives. The difficulty, though, with such a stance is its totalising relativism, whereby everything seems reduced to the same level of significance. This can be a real problem for Foucauldian analyses where concentration on the microphysics of discursive power (around sex, education, the psychological individual) dissolves away any broader categories of class, gender and the state.[4]

The second response is more precisely historical. It is to claim that in early to mid-nineteenth-century France nature did play a significant role in the securing and maintenance of a certain kind of bourgeois hegemony. This is not to say that nature reflected or expressed the ideas and feelings of the rising bourgeoisie in any simple sense. Class relations, as we shall see, were not quite like that in the French context. Rather, metropolitanism – of which nature formed a subset – exerted a magnetic pull over a spectrum of economic class fractions and political affiliations. In drawing them into identification with the city and its pleasures (including nature), this formation cut across and reworked economic class lines, relocating class in cultural terms. More of this in a moment.

And then there is a third, more general response. Which is to see nineteenth-century French nature as a case study within a wider argument about the structures of civil society. Nature has largely to do with leisure and pleasure – tourism, spectacular entertainment, visual refreshment; it occupies a 'space', physical as much as metaphorical, apparently on the margins of big structures like the state and class struggle. A major ambition of this book is to challenge the kind of *a priori* hierarchy which pushes the quiet and modest practices of civil society to the peripheries of historical attention. To reiterate, space is never a neutral vacuum but involves ways of reading and structures of experience which, even when they seem most private and personalised, are in fact profoundly social.

It follows from what has been said already that tackling the power of the countryside means getting to grips with the cultural dimensions of class formation. To bridge the gap, as it were, between Foucault's image of power as fluid subject positions located within discourse and the marxist tradition. Of least help here have been those economistic accounts, both theoretical and historical, which set the agenda for class analysis in purely economic terms.[5] In the most deterministic variant, the bourgeoisie is set up as the expressive agent of the developing capitalist system, with subdivisions and fractions of capital – financial, commercial, industrial – preponderant at different moments in the nineteenth century. Not only does this reading run into the familiar problem of how to explain the class location of groups like professionals with little obvious economic rationale; it also fails to grip on a cultural formation, like ours, which is not reducible to economic conditions and interests. Metropolitan culture cannot be ascribed to any one economic class grouping; it has no 'class belonging' as such. Yet that is not to deny its considerable social power, its ability to forge a broad-based identity of interest.

Far more useful have been the insights of structuralist marxism associated with Louis Althusser and recent rereadings of Antonio Gramsci.[6] Gramsci's notions of power bloc and hegemony make any understanding of ruling-class power more complex, teaching us to look for the diversity of social strands and the ways they are unevenly worked together in any dominant social formation. While the Althusserian concept of relative autonomy has transformed the way marxists think about class. For Stuart Hall, classes are 'complexly constituted at each of the levels of the social formation – the economic, the political and the *ideological*' (my emphasis).[7]

In other words, the languages and practices of ideology are now credited with a productive and, in some sense, independent role in the shaping of class. Recently, marxist historians like Gareth Stedman Jones and Jacques Rancière have pushed the orthodoxy to its limits.[8] In *La Nuit des prolétaires* (1981) Rancière eschews the well-worn narratives of economic conditions, strikes and workplace struggle, delving instead into those discourses of journalism and poetry, those negotiations of bourgeois intellectual philosophy, those aspirations, dreams, songs which filled 'proletarian nights'. Polemicising against the over-identification of working-class consciousness with production, Rancière argues for the constitution of the class through a complex dialectic between the denial of work – its moral and physical degradation – and the affirmation of the dignity of labour.[9] Dressing, speaking, thinking *not* like waged labour was, paradoxically integral to 'being' working-class.

Implicit in Rancière's historical and linguistic analysis is a challenge to the fixity of the conceptual schema even of complex marxism. Through the focus of 'proletarian nights' and the way the languages of radicalism construct identity, what is brought into question is the necessary priority of the economic over other determinants in the shaping of class. This comes close to the position occupied by the following account. Here, too, the concern is with the social personas produced in and through discourse, but without losing sight of their articulation with economic categories. More than that, drawing on Althusser's theory of interpellation, I seek to show how – through what mechanisms and with what effects – the ideology of nature was *lived out* at the level of personal identity.[10] Far from being anti-marxist, the aim is to bend the 'spirit' of historical materialism in new directions.

Framed by such debates, this is obviously going to be an academic book. Given the current position of intellectual knowledge in this country it could hardly be otherwise. Yet in the writing of it, the text has often come alive for me in the unfolding of particular narratives – tales of individuals and places. In retelling some of these modest stories, I also hope to have conveyed some of the pleasure to be found in the rich texture of history.

PART ONE

The metropolitan gaze:
Parisian urbanism, 1820-1850

Introduction

> What a magnificent spectacle this fashionable boulevard presents when at dusk the café waiters light the gas-lamps and torrents of light instantly flood forth, pure and white as the moon! These fashions, these thousand carriages of all shapes and sizes drawn up along the street, these fiery horses just kept under control by grooms covered in gold brocade, the Café de Paris and Tortoni's whose open windows display by the light of a thousand chandeliers a crowd of men and women eating cream and glazed fruits . . . this murmur of conversation, these adorable particles which drift from all those dresses and costumes scented ten times a day by the art of Tessier and Chardin; these tables under the trees adorned by fresh and modest beauties, among which glide other beauties equally fresh but much less chaste . . . that is something of the essence of the Boulevard des Italiens.[1]

Auguste Luchet, a young republican journalist, evoking Paris's grand boulevards in the late 1820s. Glossy surfaces and showy pleasures, idle conversations and conspicuous idleness, these are the things that catch his eye. It is a world where overt consumption has become a complex cultural ritual for those with the economic power and ample leisure to enjoy it. For, as he sternly remarked of the adjacent Chaussée-d'Antin:

> It is not the *people* who govern here; here, to the contrary, the people are despised. The Chaussée-d'Antin is the haunt of those speculators who make up the proudest élite of all – the aristocracy of wealth. Industry was robbed of the capital which raised up these splendid mansions, which paid for these magnificent furnishings, these carriages and horses. It was the stock exchange and its loathsome game of chance which gave 200,000 a year and endless leisure to the sort of character who, in earlier days, was a shoeshine in a second-class hotel of the Rue de Richelieu.[2]

Luchet's, of course, was a politically committed critique, written in the harsh climate of repression and censorship that triggered the July revolution of 1830. Following well-known prototypes, he worked with modes of investigation which were at once historical, sociological and anecdotal to reveal the contrasting quarters of the city.[3] His radical, if coded, attack on the contemporary political order was projected through the sharp polarities of current social relations: divisions between rich and poor, the leisured and the labouring, the artificial and the natural. What particularly aroused his wrath was the blatant antithesis between the glamorous *flâneurs* on the boulevards and the robust artisans of the Rue de Temple or the bustling Rue Saint-Martin.[4] His proletarian heroes enjoyed their leisure roughly but honestly in the drinking-halls of the suburbs. Theirs was the hard-won respite from daily toil. On the boulevards, by contrast, artificiality reigned supreme. It stuck like glue to the idle yet shrewd merchants of finance capital. It was proudly paraded as the essence of modernity in the spectacular consumption of fashion, perfume and glazed fruits. Indeed, for Luchet, the invasive *immorality* of speculation (sweeping the streets like a sudden fever) could not be disentangled from images of the modern city; from the artificiality punctuating urban space, from the glittering carriages and the paraphernalia of personal appearance to the very fabric of buildings and streets.

Why begin a book on nature with such exotic urban spectacles? The quality of city life, of Paris specifically, is in fact central to our argument about the discursive relation of nature to bourgeois culture. But this city is not set up as the counterpart to some natural 'other'. Rather, it is the material and cultural fabric of the metropolis which is seen to set the terms for the social production of the countryside – what will be termed natural nature or *natura naturans*. In short, such a vision of nature was deeply bound into the crystallisation of a powerful metropolitan ideology. What Luchet does is point us to the development – much earlier than we usually think, and well before the elaborate urban programme of Haussmannisation – of a self-consciously modern formation of Paris, centred around a specific topography.

More important still, look again at the language through which he characterises the boulevards. The literary rhetoric guides us from the moon-like glow of the gas-lamps to the gilt-embroidered grooms, the exquisite fashions and the equally exquisite refreshments of Café Tortoni. On one level this descriptive cornucopia can be read as a standard feature of contemporary French literary discourse – a Balzacian 'realism' obsessed with the continuous piling-up of significant detail. But look instead at the way the vocabulary works to convey the social character of the scene through *visual* signifiers. The spatial layout of 1820s Paris is imbricated with social meaning. These meanings are not just ideas about Paris carried as content in written texts like Luchet's. They are visual objectifications underpinned by certain ways of looking and spectating. Indeed, it is through a precise repertoire of looks and glances that a 'physiology' of the city, moral as much as physical, is mapped out. The visual ordering of space has become a vehicle for articulating cultural values. Which directs us to the very heart of the project. For it is the urban apprehension of space that, more than anything else, points the way to understanding the relationship between *natura naturans* and the formation of French bourgeois culture.

Nineteenth-century Paris stands as a classic paradigm for studying modern urban development. Existing interpretations, though, tend to pre-scribe both the chronology and the form of change in terms of their own methodological focus. The problem is that in most cases the period of the early nineteenth century is rendered virtually invisible. For social historians and urban sociologists the massive transformations initiated by Baron Haussmann, Prefect of the Seine under the Second Empire, mark a definitive metamorphosis from medieval city to modern metropolis.[5] And who can deny the impact (even on us today) of the imposing arterial boulevards dissecting yet co-ordinating the city, or the acres upon acres of uniform yet luxurious apartment blocks? Add to that the extension of the city's boundaries at the end of the 1850s, the new sewerage and water systems, and the parks and gardens of Vincennes, Boulogne and the rest, and it all amounts to a formidable urban package. Not surprising then that urbanism and capitalism have been seen to be inextricably linked. Decisive change in the contours of the city, it is argued, exemplified the generalised take-off of industrial capitalism from the early 1850s, liberated from earlier constraints by Napoleonic dictatorship. Broad, straight streets facilitated the circulation of commodities (Paris as industrial entrepôt), together with the military deployment of troops to keep down a potentially insurgent working class. In Walter Benjamin's classic account, the spectacular format of city culture revealed a fetishism of commodities symptomatic of the 'high era' of capitalism.[6]

Urban and planning histories also recognise the dominance of the Haussmann epoch, though they adhere to a different historical trajectory.[7] Put simply, the city's development is seen to observe an inexorable process of evolution towards a rational and coherent urban plan. From the seeds of Louis XIV's boulevards in the seventeenth century, it moves via the abortive Artists' Plan of the Revolution to full realisation under Haussmann. What are consistently privileged are those moments of government initiative and action, conceptualised through the modern problematic of state *planning*. According to the rubric of both interpretations, changes located in the period from the 1820s to the 1840s appear insignificant, or, at worst, go completely unseen. On the one hand, early nineteenth-century Paris is portrayed in relation to a decaying medieval past – a gloomy, enclosed and rat-infested place. Evidence from the 'gothic' literature of Victor Hugo or Eugène Sue looms large here, alongside the condemnatory rhetoric of later Napoleonic panegyrists like Maxime Ducamp.[8] On the other hand, those 'limited' modernising schemes that were implemented from the 1820s are dissolved into the much broader panorama of urban progress and, consequently, dwarfed by Haussmann's grand plan.

And yet, looking at the situation from the perspective of both economic *and* cultural developments, I have more than a suspicion that these histories are missing out on a vital dimension. Too preoccupied on the one hand with the urban relation to capital and on the other with the autonomy of the 'plan', they fail to grasp the dynamic configuration around metropolitanism forged between the 1820s and the 1840s. This coherent regime of city life spanned civil society and state. It was underwritten by a combination of economic conditions, official policy, and professional and cultural practices. Though forms of investment capital and commodity consumption played a major role in its making, they did not take precedence over other conditions. Nor, more important, did these economic factors dictate the terms in which the city was ideologically shaped. Metropolitan ideology preceded the full-scale emergence of French industrial capitalism. And yet the culture of the city was active in generating some of the key structures of modern French society – nowhere more so than in the production of class languages and subjectivities. All of which is essential for unpicking the role of nature as conduit of cultural power and identity. Moreover, it is the urban complex which underpins our argument about the place of the visual. For, in so far as the construction of natural nature involved looking through metropolitan eyes, it also meant participating in a visual and spatial dialogue productive of distinct cultural personas. The social power caught up in those personas lies at the core of this enquiry.

Modern Paris, then, was in part a symbolic category – a pattern of representations that addressed specific urban publics. Yet it also had a literal topography, located materially in the landscapes of the city. In his evocation of spectacular artifice, Luchet conjured up one leading quarter. The glazed fruits of Tortoni's and the scented dresses of Tessier and Chardin were to be found in the second (now the second and ninth) *arrondissement*. The area stretched north and south of the grand boulevards and, in particular, of the prestigious Boulevard des Italiens. Close by were the stock exchange, a dense nexus of finance houses, the opera in the Rue Lepeletier and fashionable cafés. To the south, a concentration of deluxe industry such as fashion in the Rue Vivienne and, further off, the declining gambling rooms and antique stalls of the Palais-Royal. While to the north and north-west were spreading a series of newly-planned complexes of streets. Some were already built or in the process of construction, others only laid out in anticipation of future speculative development. It is by making a foray into these new quarters, or rather by probing what was specifically new about them, that we shall begin.

[*facing*] Road plan of the city of Paris, by Herisson, geographer, 1828.

[*overleaf*] New plan of fortified Paris, 1847.

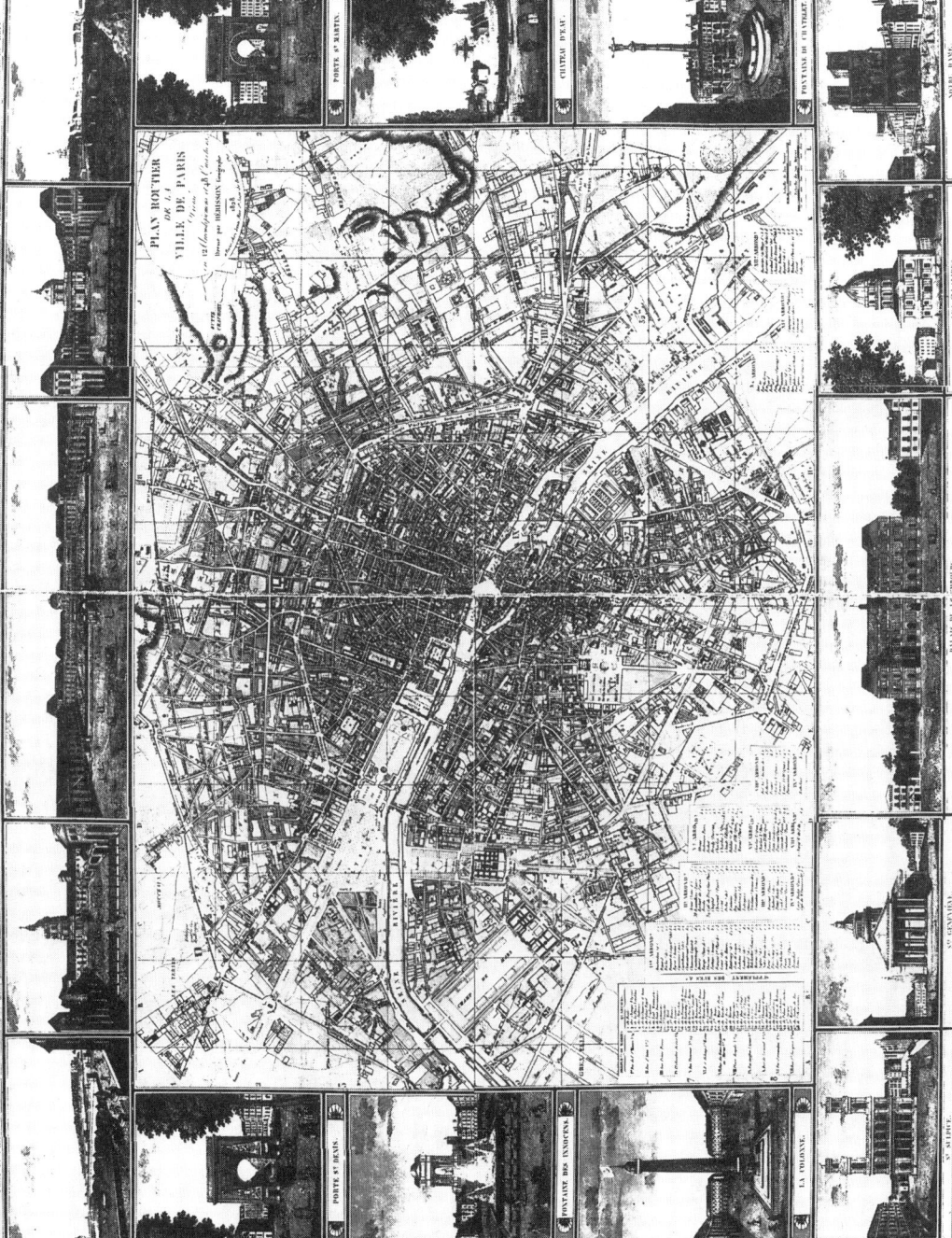

PLAN ROUTIER
DE LA
VILLE DE PARIS
1828

PORTE ST MARTIN.

CHATEAU D'EAU.

FONTAINE DE L'ENTREPOT.

NOTRE DAME.

LES INVALIDES.

PALAIS DE LUXEMBOURG.

STE GENEVIÈVE.

PORTE ST DENIS.

FONTAINE DES INNOCENS.

LA COLONNE.

ST SULPICE.

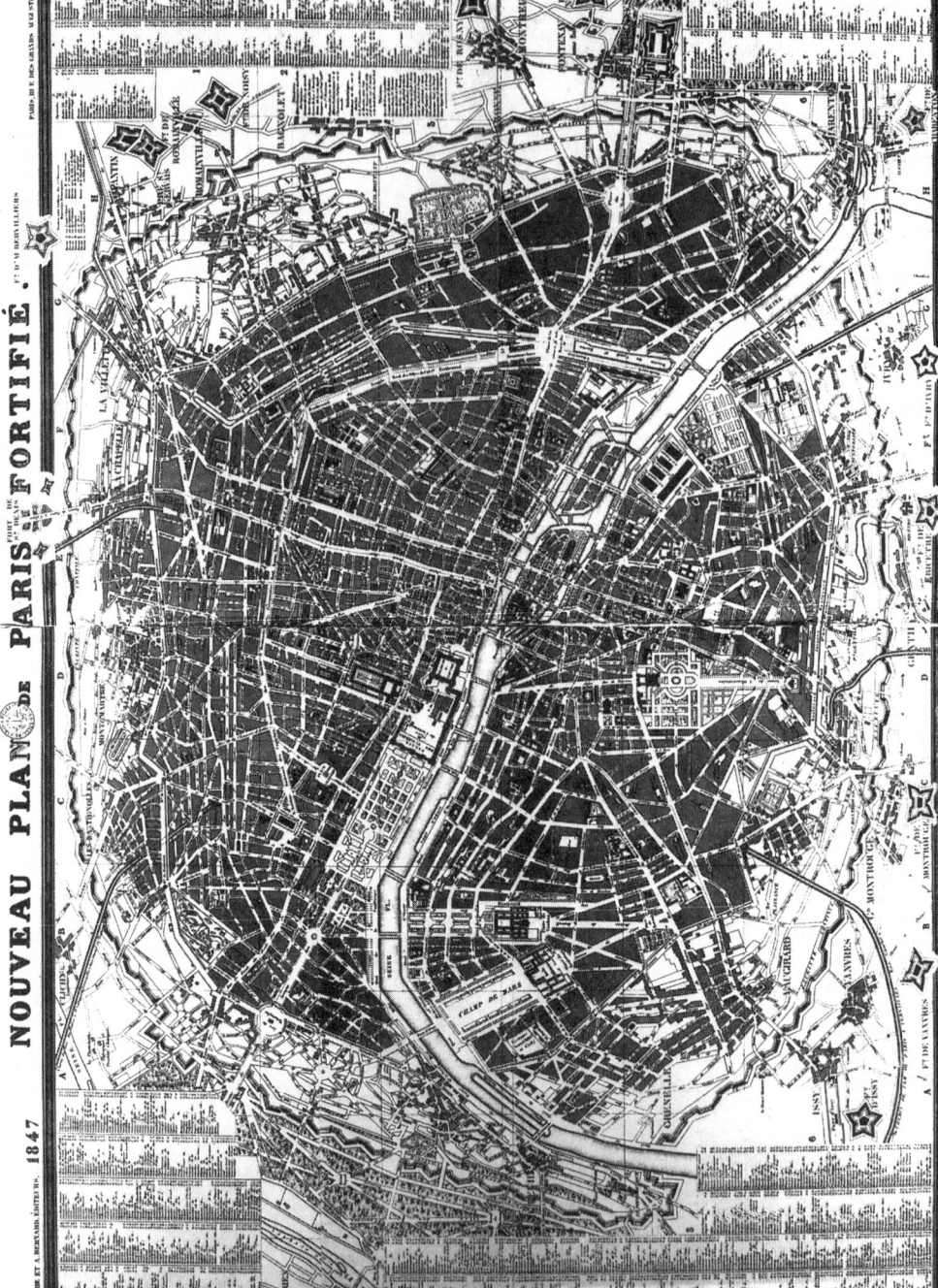

NOUVEAU PLAN DE PARIS FORTIFIÉ.

1847

The modernity of Paris

1   **Building the new quarters**

In common with a number of major French cities – Bordeaux, Nantes, Lyon, Mulhouse – Paris experienced a dramatic building boom in the first half of the 1820s.[9] Investment capital, now released from the constraints of the Napoleonic wars, found an outlet in land speculation and construction projects. Professional speculators like Alexis-André Dosne (father-in-law to the leading Orleanist politician and historian Adolphe Thiers) and bankers such as Jacques Laffitte made, and in some cases lost, fortunes through their financial involvement. Unlike Haussmann's later developments, the 1820s building boom was not initiated by state intervention into road construction and associated facilities. Primary stimuli came from private enterprise and financial pressure over land speculation. Yet the state, embodied in the activities of the Prefecture of the Seine, was to play an important part through regulating the width of streets and quality of construction, and through specifying the provision of urban embellishments.[10] Though perhaps the junior partner in this collaboration, state involvement was by no means absent. It was especially active in sponsoring features like gas lighting and bitumen pavements that were to become emblematic of Parisian modernity. Official statistics, for instance, charted a spectacular rise in pavements from only 267 metres to 6,145 metres between 1822 and 1827.[11] Provisions such as these laid down the infrastructure for a public parade of promenading and spectating.

There were five major sites of building activity to the north and north-west of the old city centre, and outside the grand boulevards. The scale of the enterprise can be partly gauged by the dramatic increase in workers (mainly building workers) migrating to Paris, a rise from 30,000 in 1824 to a peak of 45,000 in 1826.[12] The areas swept away by construction were mainly market gardens, surburban plots and the commercial pleasure parks of Tivoli and Beaujon. Further in, but in the same general direction, mansions were demolished to make way for tightly-knit five or six-storey apartment blocks organised around interior courtyards.[13] This was, nonetheless, deluxe housing and, even on the upper floors, relatively expensive. Although the working-class population of the city was expanding rapidly, the new quarters bore little or no relation to their requirements.

By 1826, overinvestment of limited financial resources, an endless cycle of speculation that led to vastly inflated land prices, together with insufficient take-up by builders and consumers alike, culminated in a massive slump in the Paris building industry.[14] All of which took place against the backdrop of a more general industrial and agricultural crisis. Some of the more grandiose projects had hardly got started and were not to be fully developed until after mid-century. On the plain beyond the Champs-Elysées a desolate semi-urban sprawl of new roads, rubble and the occasional finished house was a potent reminder of the volatility of speculative capital. In a not untypical fluctuation, by the 1830s the area had become identified as a dangerous breeding-ground for thieves and brigands.[15]

Smaller schemes fared better, and building activity was quietly sustained throughout the following decades. Look, for example, at two adjacent developments just to the north of the Boulevard des Italiens: the Quartier Saint-Georges, splayed out around the church of Notre-Dame-de-Lorette (completed in 1826), and the Quartier Nouvelle Athènes – so called because of long-standing associations with literary and theatrical characters.[16] Under the Empire these had still been on the city's fringe, with a characteristic conglomeration of economic and cultural activities. Market gardens, windmills, limestone quarries and popular drinking-halls jostled with the remains of aristocratic and religious estates and a number of newly-built individual houses. Modest *pavillons* rather than grand mansions, such properties were favoured by rising financiers, writers and actors. Eighteen-twenties expansion first involved the laying-out of new streets and a further growth of small urban *hôtels* for individual clients. Dosne, one of the major backers of the Saint-Georges project, had a house built in the main square to his own specifications. Then, during the 1830s, construction work moved in the direction of terraces. Typical was the Square d'Orléans (1830–1842), an homogeneous sequence of integrated apartments ranged around a central

[*facing, at head*] Notre-Dame-de-Lorette from the rue Laffitte.

[*at foot*] Rue Saint-Lazare from Notre-Dame-de-Lorette.

Passage de l'Opéra, photographed in 1870.

[*facing, at head*] 26, place Saint-Georges, built 1843.

[*at foot*] The *maison dorée* on the corner of the Boulevard des Italiens and Rue Laffitte before 1839, with Café Tortoni on the ground floor.

garden.[17] Looking to English models, like Nash's Regent Street, and designed in a sober neo-classical style, the square offered up-to-date accommodation with all the material connotations of prestige and luxury – the carriage archway, the portico frontage, and the rest. As so often, one immediate consequence of the process of gentrification was the removal of the last vestiges of light industry and working-class culture. The neat pattern of broad streets, with their modern lighting and bitumen pavements, projected an exclusive uniformity. And, as we shall see later, it was as much through this ordering of space as through architectural and technological motifs that the image of the modern city, twinning novelty and exclusivity, was actively generated.

2   Consuming passions

The presence of finance capital, embodied in the material fabric of the nearby banks and stock exchange as in the rapid expansion of these new streets and apartments, was a major determinant in the production of modern Paris. But it was not only investment capital that counted. In the area just slightly to the south, there was also the marked concentration of leisure, luxury and service industries.[18] Luxury trades and shops marketing clothes, personal accessories and domestic trifles, together with the entertainment and service sector of theatres, cafés and restaurants – these swarmed around the stock exchange and boulevards, capitalising on the profits of speculation and the pleasures of leisured *flâneurs* and tourists. Here was a burgeoning market in deluxe commodities for which Paris was becoming internationally famous. Indeed, the dymanic of consumer capitalism stood in a direct relation to the economic and ideological possibilities opened up by buoyant finance capital.

One obvious focus for commentary has been the prominence of theatres, from élite to popular, from the Opéra to the Variétés. On all sides, entrepreneurial initiatives were turning theatrical spectacles into big crowd-pullers. The *succès de scandale* of Victor Hugo's *Hernani* in 1829 was mythologised as the flashpoint for the 'romantic revolution'.[19] More to the point, it launched a whole genre of commercially successful historical dramas by the likes of Alexandre Dumas *père*. During the same period, the Opéra, directed by the shrewd cultural entrepreneur Dr Louis Véron, alternated between the flamboyant spectaculars of Meyerbeer and the 'romantic' ballet of Maria Taglioni, danced to increasingly fantastic sets and lighting.[20] At the other end of the spectrum, Frédéric Lemaître, master of low comedy, forged an epic reputation with his portrayal of the distinctively contemporary rogue Robert Macaire.[21] Lovable yet despicable, Macaire was a peculiarly metropolitan invention, displaying all the skills of a con-man attuned to survival and success in the city.

Before or after the theatre, a stroll on the boulevard – itself a long-established pastime for the wealthy, leisured and curious – would undoubtedly take in a restaurant and café or two. No one could claim to be a true Parisian, vaunted Véron retrospectively, who was unacquainted with the many restaurants flourishing since the 1820s and offering a sumptuous service day and night.[22] Tortoni's, with its glittering ambience, figured time and time again in current accounts as the Parisian café *par excellence*.[23] Significantly, it also developed during the 1830s and 1840s as an informal but thriving black market for shares.[24] At such sites, business and pleasure, speculation and consumption went hand in hand. There was no rigid differentiation between the economic domain of work and the cultural domain of leisure. To the contrary, they formed part of an integrated series of public and often frenetic activities.

As for shopping, listen to the Vicomte Charles de Launay, writing a gossip column in the daily *La Presse* of 1836. Even in the snowy depths of winter, marvelled the writer, Parisians were out and about:

> But then doesn't everyone have to go out at this time of year? The new year's gifts are hanging over us, duty compels us to pay a call at Lesage, or Giroux, or Susse; like everyone else our reason forces us to choose something not too dear while regretting all those seductive items beyond our scope . . . the shops are full to overflowing, you can neither get into Susse nor get out again.[25]

Shops like these sold a whole gamut of quality trifles and *curiosités*, from paperweights and dolls to miniature bronzes and oil pictures. Their cornucopia of fancy goods is implicitly depicted here as an almost erotic feast for the eyes, titillating the audience with that which is financially just out of reach. The new year's duty call is given a distinctly novel gloss, now turned into the compulsion to spend.

Of course, it is all too easy to claim these forms of consumption as totally new, to see here the birth of consumerism and its related cultural process, the fetishisation of commodities. That was not necessarily the case. There is evidence to suggest that both restaurants and deluxe shopping were already familiar by the 1800s. One sardonic commentator, the anonymous Hermit of the Chaussée-d'Antin, writing during the late Empire, dated the shift from *table d'hôte* caterer (*traiteur*) to *à la carte* restaurant to the mid-1770s.[26] In order to impress tourists and foreigners, he drawled, try establishments like Véry's near the Tuileries, whose 'brilliant salons' were exquisitely arranged for 'the pleasure of the eyes'.[27] In this explicitly Parisian mode, visual display was already set up as integral to the process of public consumption. Equally, the Hermit had a keen eye for fashionable ladies who descended from their carriages in the Rue de Richelieu to make choice purchases of cloth, hats or perfume.[28] By 1812, at least, when he was writing, women from sections of

23

the new Napoleonic gentry and *haute bourgeoisie* were becoming active consumers, incorporating deluxe shopping into their round of social pleasures.

But, if not new to the 1820s, the network of consumption did play a seminal role in the orchestration of a modern Paris. This was a question both of geographical sites and changing technologies. First, the leisure and luxury market was now crystallised by its close association with the newly-built quarters and the dynamism of finance capital and stock-exchange speculation. In material terms, there was a dramatic migration of small businesses away from their traditional sites of production – the old centres, the Marais and the left bank – to the perceived focal point of consumption. One example was the silk industry. By 1840, thirty-eight of the capital's silk enterprises had gravitated towards the Bourse.[29] An ironic observer complained that the Chaussée-d'Antin, formerly the exclusive preserve of grand political seigneurs like Mirabeau and Cardinal Fesch (Napoleon's nephew), was now being infiltrated by finance and commercialism – what was derogatorily termed a clutter of apothecaries, drapers and grocers' shops.[30] The magnetic pull of the new quarters gave rise to rather different anxieties in official circles. Repeated reports emanating from the city council from the late 1830s onwards bewailed the 'displacement' of the business population which ruptured the traditional economic balance of the capital.[31] The left bank, abandoned by commerce and segregated from Paris's thriving heart, was turning into a sleepy provincial town.

At the same time, the culture of consumption was being transformed by new marketing technologies. Certainly, by the Restoration the shop had ceased to be either the antechamber to an artisanal workshop or the market-style stall piled high with assorted goods. Its physiognomy was now changing in apparently contradictory ways: one, via the bazaar, towards the open layout and fixed-price goods of the department store; the other, more immediately, into the elegant displays of the élite boutique.[32] Capitalising on the increase in pavements, the luxury shop trade exploited glass shop-windows (*vitrines*) and with them window displays to entice the passer-by. Visual allure was intensified by strips of mirror, often decorated, set to either side of the window, which cast flattering reflections on the strolling viewer/*flâneur*. Such devices were especially suited to the arcades that proliferated in the period. In the early 1840s, anecdotal accounts talked not only of the Passage de l'Opéra as a 'bazaar of deluxe industry' and 'scintillating shops' but also of the 'coquettish public' in the Passage du Panorama.[33] Free from the nuisance of traffic, beggars and streetsellers, these elegant covered walkways lined with shops were a positive paradise of mutual display for the leisured and the leisurely, and particularly women.

Since Benjamin, the arcades – so glamorous and so very up-to-date –

have often been singled out as a graphic expression of Parisian commodity capitalism.[34] But what is more revealing for our argument is the way their spatial organisation stimulated a series of links between parading on the boulevards, looking and acquiring. Commercial developments involved more than economic production; they carried an ideology of personal consumption operating through specific cultural rituals. One aspect was the visual emphases which fed into a distinctive mode of experiencing the city. This Paris, it seems, was a sequence of spectacles to be grasped in the pleasure of a gaze that structured the flow between promenade, theatre, café and arcade.

It was these two factors – the geographical reorientation of luxury businesses and a new shopping technology – which inflected the formation of Paris as a modern city. Both were graphically played out in the case history of one specific form of cultural industry which was to be crucial in the marketing of nature – dealing in contemporary pictures and other luxury goods.

3   Dealing and retailing: the case of the art dealer

Previously, shop-based art traders and print sellers had been concentrated in two areas. Either they clustered round the long-established artists' quarters of Saint-André-des-Arts and the Ecole des Beaux-Arts on the left bank.[35] Or they were scattered through the old commercial centre just north of the river, stretching from the Marais to the Louvre. Art *dealers*, on the other hand, were a rather superior breed. Posing as connoisseurs and sensitive middlemen, they had little use for shop premises since they usually worked on a one-to-one basis with individual collectors or through public auctions.[36] Men like Jean-Baptiste-Pierre-Lebrun, himself a painter and married to the successful portraitist Vigée Lebrun, flourished up to and during the Revolution. He moved skilfully between selling reputable 'old masters' and marketing contemporary material by friends and protégés. As freelance advisers to the noble and wealthy, these operators eschewed base connections with trade.

In the 1820s, a different kind of art dealer became visible. Building on the localised proliferation of luxury consumption in the new quarters, they dealt in a whole range of decorative products and related services. Contemporary art – especially the smaller and cheaper 'minor' genres like landscape – figured as one element. The Giroux firm, singled out by de Launay as one of the most renowned luxury shops in Paris, is a case in point.[37]

Set up in 1801 by Alphonse Giroux, former pupil of the leading history painter Jacques-Louis David, the establishment gradually eased across from restoring and copying to permanent displays of old and modern paintings for sale. Quick to exploit the possibilities of visual publicity, they advertised the collections with an album of engravings in 1819. In 1826, the family set up a commercial society for the sale of 'pictures, stationery and curios', publishing an inclusive catalogue of their art stock the following year. When, in 1830, Alphonse Giroux retired to make way for his sons, he auctioned off a good deal of his picture stock.[38] It seemed that the Giroux sons were more interested in the stationery and decorative dolls side of the business. Prices at the auction were low, partly owing to the absence, as yet, of a market in modern work sold at public auction.[39] But this also suggests that, in the context of the dealers, art products functioned as relatively low-cost consumer articles little different in status from children's toys or the elegant trifles offered as new year's gifts.

The Giroux enterprise embodied two major characteristics of early nineteenth-century dealing. On the one hand there was the artisanal route from copying and restoring into selling pictures for modest but steady returns; on the other, the marketability of contemporary art as a minor *article de luxe*. The cachet here was, at least in part, its up-to-date and modern connotations. The artisanal tradition was at work in the careers of the majority of operators who graduated into dealing from trades such as gilding, framing or selling artists' materials and stationery.[40] Many continued to offer such services. A skilled trade provided economic security in periods of financial slump, when luxury consumption was quick to suffer. Jules Berville, of the Chaussée-d'Antin, advertised in the 1842 *Almanach Bottin du commerce* an 'exhibition of modern paintings and drawings, for sale and rent', as well as 'all equipment necessary for painting and framing'.[41] Binant, also listed as a restorer, offered a 'continual exhibition of paintings and drawings in every genre of the modern school available for renting' alongside a 'collection of miniatures and mannequins'.[42] Most up-market were Susse Brothers, just opposite the Bourse, who reflected all the demands of the new luxury market. Their fashionable and prestigious establishment sold a wide variety of decorative items, encompassing a 'rich collection of paintings and modern drawings for sale and for rent, engravings, lithographs, bronzes, religious books, keepsakes, artists' models, frames, daguerrotypes, export business'.[43] Note that all three suppliers hired out pictures, a practice which had disappeared from the dealer's repertoire forty years later. Indeed, the prevalence of works for hire is some intimation that in this mode of consumption possession was less significant than appropriation through looking. It was appearances that mattered!

What also mattered was location. The Giroux enterprise was situated in the Rue Coq Saint-Honoré, part of the old commercial centre. During the 1830s, as competitors multiplied, they inched their way towards the stock exchange and boulevards, following the general trend of deluxe business migration. This was the third strand in dealer development. By 1842, about a third of the traders listed in the commercial dictionary were orientated towards the new quarters.[44] The cultivation of a good site and maximum visibility for the right kind of clientele became the key marketing practice.

The history of the Durand Ruel firm is instructive.[45] Chief employee at a stationer's shop in the university district of the left bank, Durand married its young proprietor Mademoiselle Ruel in 1825 and took control of the business. Though the firm retained her name, she was to play no active part in its expansion; the gendered relations of capital underpinned here by a Catholic ideology of separate spheres.[46] Durand moved almost immediately into trade in artists' materials and pictures, concentrating, as did most traders, on small-scale genre works and landscapes. Images of nature, as we shall find at a later point, were a recurrent component in the retailing stock of luxury goods. At the same time, he continued to sell stationery and related materials. The steady turnover from this secure branch of the trade helped tide him over crises like the slump following the 1848 revolution. In 1833, an employee was left in charge of the shop on the left bank, which was hardly 'favourable to the luxury trades due to its distance from the rich quarters of Paris', and a new branch opened in the Rue des Petits Champs on the right bank.[47] Solely given over to artists' materials and pictures, the new outlet was nicely positioned between the Rue Saint-Honoré, focal point for the Orleanist aristocracy, and the new wealth of the boulevards and stock exchange. Ten years later, Durand was on the move again, north and west to the Rue de la Paix. This turned out to be a mistake. Though the premises incorporated two spaciously-proportioned salons, it was out of the way, losing the crucial benefit of visibility. Within three years he recouped the loss, making his most ambitious leap yet – to the Boulevard des Italiens: 'the place most frequented in all Paris, in the path of stockbrokers and visitors to the city'.[48]

These economic and cultural migrations were charted retrospectively by his son, Paul Durand-Ruel, a dynamic dealer in his own right.[49] What his memoir recorded was the absolute centrality not just of being in the right place but of capitalising upon a direct visual engagement with potential customers. It is interesting, for instance, that Durand *père* tried to minimise the disadvantages of the concealed Rue de la Paix site by publishing a two-volume catalogue of his stock, entitled *Galerie Durand Ruel: Spécimens les plus brillants de l'école moderne* (1845). The frontispiece carried an engraving of the major gallery space.[50] The room was represented as spacious, elegantly furnished and virtually empty of visitors. Come and stroll around the space, enjoy the paintings as if in a private collector's gallery – this seemed to be the tacit invitation. The imagery reworked the theme of the public promenade while contrasting sharply with the push-and-shove of competing shops. Connotations were élite rather than popular, promoting the aristocratic ambience of the leisured connoisseur. All in all, staking out an ideal field of visibility was paramount. Like the arcades and shop-window displays, such sophisticated commercial tactics plugged luxury consumption into the pleasures of promenading and looking.

4   Decoding modernity

Private capital and state intervention; dynamic speculation and luxury commerce; new building and urban pleasures – the integration of all of these promoted a special 'topography' at the modern heart of Paris. It was this formation which was so characteristic of the 1820s–1840s. Back in 1812, the caustic Hermit of the Chaussée d'Antin may have identified bankers with the street of that name, feminised shopping with the Rue de Richelieu or promenading with the boulevards, yet there was no sense in which such images and activities articulated together as a coherent whole. Here, then, was not simply a shift in the geographical-cum-social organisation of the capital. Such conditions worked to produce metropolitan modernity in terms of a quite novel pattern of representations which, by implication, projected their own structures of experience – of what it meant to *be* in the city.

How to decode this particular construction of modernity? So far we have been looking at conditions of existence. But conditions do not, in and of themselves, deliver the rules of the discourse. What were its dominant themes? Where and how was it experienced? And was it constitutive of specific social and class groupings within the metropolis? One way in is via the plethora of contemporary journalistic and semi-literary texts which took Paris as their explicit focus – as object of consumption, whether for the tourist or the Parisian. They included a whole sub-genre of *Physiologies* such as the *Physiologies parisiennes*.[51] More substantive were *Les Français peints par eux-mêmes* of 1840–1842 (of which five volumes were devoted to Paris), the *Diable à Paris* (1845–1846) and Louis Lurine's edited *Les Rues de Paris* (1844). In handling the new quarters, the most obvious feature was the stress on rapid urban change and the dynamism of finance capital. All of them registered the variety of consumer delights twinned with the fickleness of speculative fortunes. But, where earlier accounts like that of the eighteenth-century commentator Louis Mercier or the Chaussée-d'Antin Hermit had evoked metropolitan existence by means of contrasting quarters, social constituencies and distinct class populations, now it was as much the surfaces, objects and appearances colouring urban space that carried the cultural resonance of the new city.

Luchet spied out speculative corruption in the very fabric of the glamorous new apartment blocks. For him, the lines of carriages with their gold-brocaded grooms were immorality personified. Similarly, from quite different perspectives, technological novelties like bitumen were richly invested with meaning. As one poetic encomium thrilled in 1844:

> By this boiling lava from volcanoes snatched,
> Which flows and hardens with time's despatch,
> Our public places and our pavements
> Once arid now become resplendent.
> And he who compares the old and the new
> May wonder indeed at Paris renew'd;
> Thus, all is made grand for the honour of France:
> This is a new era and our Louis has begun it.[52]

The toadying doggerel offered up servile tribute to the Orleanist regime. 'A man of letters' was how the author, Pluchonneau (*aîné*), described himself; though the range of his work – a dithyramb on the death of the King's son, a topographical tract on Saint-Helena and a gothic 'physiology' of freemasonry – reveal a modest hack with an eye for the main chance.[53] But the point is that it was *gleaming bitumen*, the product of civil society, as much as state planning or politically-inspired projects, that stood as his distinctively contemporary monument. Bitumen brought together multiple social images. First, as with Luchet's evocation of the moon-like glow of gas-lamps, the comparison to volcanic eruptions served to point up its artificial, unnatural character – a counterfeit of nature thrown up by modern production. Then, the essence of the commodity was less solid object than covering or packaging, flowing and hardening as a sheeny coat wrapped around the city. Written into the panegyric to renewal was a notion of theatrical transformation. In fact, there is in the language here a sense of the inherently unstable, even illusory, nature of capitalist production and commodity forms. At a moment before industrialisation had quite set the parameters of social experience, such images and objects oscillated between tangible evidence of progress and a chimera transfixed as spectacle.

Take another poem by Pluchonneau, where gas was the theme of his eulogy:

> But what is this great torchlight
> Image of pure day so lovely and bright?
> Man from God has ravished it in all its might,
> A reflection of the sun which must ignite.
> From the aerial fluid, from the effluvial gleams
> Clustering before our eyes such numbrous beams;
> And gas upon Paris, the initial splendid sight,
> Pours nocturnal in long shafts the arrows of its light.[54]

Again the trite rhetoric plundered natural analogies to generate a feeling of wonder before this ingenious addition to urban technology. The apprehension of progress was refracted through the excitement of invention and discovery. Similarly, the rich significance of the commodity as 'sign of the times' lay in its peculiarly visual qualities, both in appearance and effect. Here was an image of shafts of light adorning the city; a decorative accessory, like sheeny bitumen pavements, to the ordered display of the new quarters. Equally implicit was the fantasy of theatrical illusion, as gaslight irradiated its own artificial day. The fluid play on different forms of visual perception and consumption was what conjured up Parisian modernity.

Lurine's *Les Rues de Paris* deciphered urban surfaces and spaces in different, though related, terms. The ploy of the book was to personify and personalise the streets as seen through the eyes of an initiated *flâneur*. A large proportion of the essays were devoted to the new quarters and boulevard area, registering their pull on definitions of Paris *per se*. Historical anecdotes being largely absent here, it was the observable correlatives of architecture, inhabitants and public activities which spelt out character. Meet the Rue Notre-Dame-de-Lorette, for instance, a playful combination of 'wit, intrigue and charming coquettishness'.[55] If the presence of 'poetic' artists living in garrets and elegant ladies of leisure fostered that reputation, it was also materially exhibited in the bitumen pavements glowing in the heat and the proliferation of small two-storey *hôtels* – 'the last word in small-time speculative luxury [*luxe boursicotier*]'. All the charms of the street were concentrated at the Square Saint-Georges; here was its 'eden, its oasis, the jewel in the crown'. The components: 'a fountain with naiad as guardian, several elegant *hôtels* and a house which seems, I would not say built, but embroidered by the hands of fairies . . . I do not know if the divine chisel of the great artists of the Renaissance has ever shaped a diamond whose form was more svelte, gracious and pure'.[56]

These are not, of course, serious or weighty texts, any more than the verses by Pluchonneau could be said to lay claim to consideration as poetry. Indeed, they were not meant to be taken seriously. Like de Launay's gossip column *Les Lettres parisiennes*, they rifled a broad repertoire of humorous styles – irony, parody, gentle caricature – to lace information and anecdote with lightweight entertainment. But they were important historically, as elements in the discursive construction of forms of leisure and enjoyment that not only targeted a broad, literate audience in a new manner but also initiated novel definitions of what leisure meant. A focal point was the circulation of images of the metropolis. And, in that context, what matters for us is their sensitivity to urban surfaces, the way that modernity was consistently located in certain visual objectifications. Thus, Albéric Sécond, author of the Notre-Dame-de-Lorette sketch, shuffled his metaphors. The Square Saint-Georges was now precious jewel, now fairy fantasy; now luxury commodity, now vivid spectacle. As with Pluchonneau, the contemporaneity of urban experience seemed to hinge on pleasures and desires stimulated by intersecting modes of consumption and spectatorship.

Written into the textual characterisations was the same dynamic as in the visual format of arcades or dealer galleries; that is, a distinctive structure of cognition. To read the streets meant to adopt codes of looking that could single out, sift and move across the meanings of public space. All of which suggests an individualisation of vision, a fragmentation of earlier, more totalising social panoramas into a picture built up from individuated objects and images. The elaboration of such codes was underpinned by some of the cultural rites we have touched on: theatrical spectacle, the boulevard promenade and, crucially, the desiring gaze of the consumer. Through that process the most unlikely objects were drawn into the same perceptual plane. Glazed fruits at Tortoni's, fashionable dresses on the boulevards and the phantasmagoria of toys, paperweights and pictures in Susse or Giroux formed a continuum with the showy novelty of bitumen pavements and fancy architectural detail around Notre-Dame-de-Lorette. Whether it was the public stare by which strollers appraised the streets or each other's appearance and behaviour, whether it was the longing glance cast over choice items in the shops or the narcissistic reflection back from the mirror surrounds, these were the rules that structured participation in the game. But they were, of course, rules that were gender and class-specific.

So who was endowed with this specular power? In the world of objectified appearances, people were by no means absent. Indeed, modern Paris had its own specific social constituencies. In part, these were themselves put into discourse as components of the metropolitan 'semiotic', decorative accessories to the 'personalities' of the streets. Yet 'textual' constructions also gestured towards the broader economic and cultural categories that made up the metropolitan audience.

Focus in on three of the most visible groupings associated with the new quarters. First, the agents of finance capital so despised by Luchet – financiers, brokers and speculators. One end of the spectrum was typified by the Rothschilds. During the 1840s they owned three *hôtels* on the Rue Laffitte, which ran north from the Boulevard des Italiens and was depicted as the haunt of 'commerce, the arts and pleasure'.[57] A traditional finance house – dating back to the late eighteenth century – they seemed to mix easily with the political notables of the Orleanist regime. Famed for philanthropic gestures, they were equally admired for their resplendent balls and luxurious apartments.[58] 'It is a palace', one commentator gasped, 'where you find astonishing gilt decorations, magnificent silks, superb furniture, royal carpets'.[59] Yet the Rothschilds' extravagant display was always calculated on the basis of sober enterprise and careful accounting. Part of their traditionalism meant that they steered well clear of innovative or risky investment projects. A more graphic exemplar of current dynamism was Jacques Laffitte. A major beneficiary of the 1820s building boom, he claimed a fortune of twenty million francs before 1830.[60] When re-elected opposition deputy in 1827, he held open court, illuminating his mansion (again on the Rue Laffitte) and firing gun salutes in the courtyard.[61] The July revolution saw him playing an important negotiating role. Laffitte, it was claimed, virtually offered the crown to Louis-Philippe. But dynamism had its pitfalls. Within a year or two, his political career was in ruins and he was more or less bankrupt, only to rise again, more modestly, in the later 1830s with further radical schemes for co-operative financial investment.

At the other end of the scale were the brokers and speculators – the gamblers in stocks and shares. The image ranged from that of elegant yet ruthless young men who lived out aristocratic pretensions in houses 'full of fine furniture and costly antiques' and 'went hunting or entertained charming young ladies', through to minor crooks (*volereaux*) eking out a modest livelihood through petty cons and trade-offs.[62] Lemaître's Robert Macaire character, especially as reworked by Honoré Daumier's cartoons published in the popular *Charivari*, combined elements of both.[63] At Daumier's hands, Macaire became the archetypal modern villain, typifying the widespread corruption of the Orleanist regime. Whether as lawyer, doctor, journalist, beggar or bookseller, financial speculation was at the root of all his personas. Dapper but seedy, he was the professional fast-talker, forever setting up the next profitable deal. Built into the enduring appeal of the character – a genuine anti-hero of the period – was the power of the speculative dream. During the first railway boom of the mid-1840s, one Parisian recalled, if with obvious hyperbole,

> the speculative fever became almost hysterical; people chased after shares or the promise of shares; people queued at the doors of bankers and brokers of all kinds ... From workers and servants to *grands seigneurs* one thought dominated all, to get hold of shares. It was madness, delirium. The ladies were particularly noticeable for their bold schemes and intrigues. In shops, in salons, in the foyer of the theatre, at the ball, everywhere and at all times, it was the only thing talked about.[64]

The share craze swept in, invading all the social spaces of the new Paris, an instant obsession defying rationality. In decoding modernity, what is so significant is the way the image of finance capital recurs as the ether breathed by so many publics from different social constituencies.

Alongside the dynamism of financiers went the glamour of intellectual and artistic personalities, especially in the Nouvelle Athènes. George Sand held court in the Square d'Orléans for some years in the 1830s, while nearby neighbours included the painters Eugène Delacroix and Ary Scheffer, tutor to the royal family, and writers like Pierre-Jean de Béranger and Théophile Gautier.[65] Young and aspiring artists, littérateurs and journalists all flocked to the right bank, where they could take over the upper and cheaper storeys of new apartment blocks *and* be close to the centre of cultural consumerism and public entertainment. In addition, 'high' culture and 'high' finance were increasingly perceived to be closely aligned. Writers such as Dumas *père* and Alphonse de Lamartine ran their literary careers with the flair of ambitious entrepreneurs.[66] Equally, the Rothschilds, and later the Pereire brothers, were lavish art collectors, while Laffitte patronised struggling writers.[67] Both were high-risk enterprises, and both could be defined in terms of dynamism and progress but also instability, sudden failure and even moral corruption. Most important, the growth and concentration of artistic professionals related to the economic and cultural clout of the expanding press and publishing industries, also loosely based in the same area. Developments in the print business, as will become recurrently clear, were themselves a major element in Paris's thriving cultural economy and generated a proliferation of journalistic and literary careers and genres.

The broadly-defined 'artistic' community continually slid across between a self-conscious command of metropolitan ideology and the objectified object of its gaze. On the one hand, writers were a potent force in disseminating Paris both inside and outside the city. They were the guide – the all-seeing eye – for the uninitiated, for provincials and tourists. On the other hand, it was by means of their own visual appearance and behaviour that certain artists, often extravagantly-publicised examples, began to mark out a special status for themselves. There was Sand, for example, with her 'manly' attire, or the flamboyant little group of poets and writers gathered around Hugo from the late 1820s. According to Gautier, long hair and/or moustaches were *de rigueur*, together with outrageous clothes like his own bright-red waistcoat.[68] Let one example of this romanticism in action suffice. At a soirée given by the Italian nationalist Princess Belgiosjoso in 1835, the attaché to the Austrian ambassador, Count Apponyi, was dismayed at the behaviour of Alfred de Musset.[69] Not only did the writer smoke cigars in front of the ladies, but he rolled around on the sofas and put his feet up on the table. Written as it was by a diplomatic representative of one of the most rigid regimes in Europe, Apponyi's intimate memoir was rooted in political circles and aristocratic codes somewhat distanced from metropolitanism. This caveat apart, the point still carries that such little niceties of transgression only made their impact though visibility at society salons, as well as circulating on the streets, or in the press.

Finally, equally connected with the new areas and equally ambivalent in their significations was a third grouping – those elegantly-dressed and fragrant ladies who glided along the boulevards or descended upon arcades and boutiques. 'The boulevards are in flower', hymned de Launay in spring 1837; 'it is the season of pretty women, pretty dresses, every costume is a bouquet'.[70] Women's fashions had long since abandoned the informality of the Empire line. Leg-of-mutton sleeves now exaggerated the width of shoulders as tightly-laced stays pulled in the waist to emphasise slimness and delicacy.[71] Encased in this highly stylised shape which heightened gender difference, women were presented as elegantly-wrapped delicacies – as much *objets de luxe* as the decorative commodities on offer in the shops.

Yet it would be a mistake to see fashionable women as entirely passive – the unwitting focus of male objectifications. They were, as we have already seen, *active* as consumers; while some of the new breed of society hostesses, like the formidable Sophie Dosne (mother-in-law to Thiers), were a force to be reckoned with politically as well as socially.[72] Even participation in the tortuous contours of fashion could carry positive pleasures and identities for women. Around 1830 there was a vogue for the *toque à creneaux*, a medieval-style bonnet with, it was thought, a touch of Joan of Arc about it. Like share speculation, here was another craze to sweep the boulevards! One young lady, Anaïs Gerfaut, writing to a friend outside Paris in 1831, recounted how when out walking she came across at least twelve ladies similarly attired:

> Can you believe old Madame S. parading around with that on her old yellow wig? It was enough to make one die laughing . . . Her daughter Mathilde was at her side, very lovely this afternoon, and also wearing the same object on her beautiful blond hair . . . Really my dearest, we must decide to do like everyone else since it is all the rage.[73]

Another, Louise de B., commented to her mother that she wore a *toque à creneaux* – which suited her very well, all the gentlemen said – when visiting her friend Clotilde. Hardly had she arrived for the visit when in trooped four others, all sporting the same headgear: 'When the third appeared, we looked at each other in surprise; with the fourth, we fell about laughing. We looked like soldiers on parade.'[74] In the intimate and feminine languages shared among wealthy women, a sophisticated rapport with fashion novelties functioned most obviously as a sign of metropolitan exclusivity, a demonstration of the requisite cultural knowledge as well as economic power to consume. But there was another and less literal script acted out here whereby the spectacle of fashion was read ironically or at one remove, part of a spirited comedy of manners. Far from taking it all seriously, our youthful correspondents laughed not only at old Madame S. but at themselves and their own objectifications. A self-conscious play on and with appearances and identity hints at a discourse of ironic detachment, as coolly urbane as it was gendered.

Where public perceptions were altogether more problematic, and where gender divisions were at their most acute, was in the visual ambiguity between moral and 'immoral' women. For, as that stern republican moralist Luchet remarked, among the fresh and modest beauties 'glide other beauties equally fresh but much less chaste'.[75] Along with the economic and social developments shaping the new quarters, the intensification of consumerism worked to reorder male sexual definitions of women in public space. Typical was the construction of the *lorette*, who carried within her persona all the connotations of urban display and luxury consumption. Coined around 1840 by journalist Nestor Roqueplan to characterise the middle ground between street prostitute and the *grande dame* of commercial sex, the courtesan, *lorette* became an umbrella term for the kept woman set up discreetly in a private apartment by businessman, professional or wealthy student.[76] The physiognomy of this largely literary and press creation was most graphically delineated in Paul Gavarni's many cartoons.[77] Always elegantly dressed, the *lorette* peeps out coyly from a theatre box, engages in *double entendre* with male admirers at a masked ball, displays herself while enjoying the view from her apartment window. Jeanne Duval, mistress of Charles Baudelaire, was one example who fitted the image; while Apollonie Sabatier, his poetic 'muse', represented the upper end of the scale.[78] Illegitimate daughter of a vicomte, she was taken up by a wealthy Belgian businessman, Alfred Mosselman, and installed in the elegant Rue Frochot, right at the northern tip of the new quarters. Here, she presided over a circle of male admirers, mainly artists. The location is relevant. The particular habitat of the *lorette* was perceived to be the many well-appointed modern apartments which building entrepreneurs had failed to rent or sell to the limited market of speculative or professional clients. Indeed, it was the supposed proliferation of such 'respectable' mistresses in the streets around Notre-Dame-de-*Lorette* that gave rise to the tag.

Like more glamorous courtesans such as Alice Ozy, who was known to be linked with one of the King's sons, the Duc d'Aumale, the *lorette* slid imperceptibly across the boundaries of acceptability and social stigma. Taken up by wealthy or aspiring metropolitans – from speculators and entrepreneurs to state officials and aristocrats – and pulled into all the cultural rituals of the modern city, she was simultaneously cut off from her own, usually lower-class, roots and milieu. On the boulevards, she was virtually indistinguishable in costume and appearance from the more fashionable among her lover's female relations. And, in a sense, for men she was a quintessentially *public* property – to be admired, discussed, acquired. Anecdotes about Ozy's exploits, business acumen and wit were a staple of male after-dinner conversation; she was put into circulation, metaphorically as well as literally, as object of titillation and fetishised fantasy figure.[79] Yet no 'honourable' man, of course, could introduce her to his family, and it was a moot point whether he could even indulge in a discreet salute in the street, if accompanied by women relatives. In other words, there was a radical mismatch between the social and moral codes marking out the *lorette* within

[*at head*] First view of the Salon of 1843, engraving from *L'Illustration*, 1843.

[*at foot*] Frontispiece by Charles Daubigny to Durand Ruel's *Spécimens les plus brillants de l'Ecole Moderne,* 1845, showing the dealer's main showroom.

[*facing, at head*] The parade outside Café Tortoni on the Boulevard des Italiens, from *Les Rues de Paris*, ed. L. Lurine, 1844.

[*at foot*] Advert for the musical comedy *Le Passage de l'Opéra*, designed by Paul Gavarni.

LE PASSAGE DE L'OPÉRA.

BLUETTE

PAROLES DE MARC CONSTANTIN

Musique de

ALFRED QUIDANT

Prix 2 F

DU MÊME AUTEUR:

Une Scolette — Une Voisine
Cara Enfance — L'Auberge du Diable

à Paris, chez BERNARD-LATTE, Editeur, Boulevart des Italiens, 2

LES BOULEVARTS

Parfois, être savant c'est deviner le moyen de découvrir la science où elle se trouve, où elle se cache. Près de toucher, du bout de ma plume, à l'histoire des boulevarts de Paris, je compris qu'il me fallait savoir bien des choses : comment faire pour venir à bout de mon embarras qui était extrême, de mon ignorance qui était complète ? Je résolus d'aller frapper à la porte d'un homme qui sait tout quand il s'agit de la grande ville ; je me promis de feuilleter tout à mon aise, les pieds sur les chenets, un véritable livre vivant qui se laisse entr'ouvrir par tous les amis intimes de la maison, pourvu que les amis consentent à flatter la curieuse faiblesse de ces monomanes que l'on appelle des *collectionneurs*. Le savant, le livre animé dont je vous parle, se nomme Pierre Lambert : il est bien connu dans Paris ; il demeure sur le boulevart Poissonnière ; c'est le marquis de Carabas du *bric-à-brac* et de la curiosité.

Il serait difficile de rien imaginer

1824.   *Costume Parisien.*

(2244.)

Modes de Paris.

[*left*] Parisian costume, 1824.   [*right*] *Le mercure des Salons* – town dress, 1831.

[*facing, at head*] *Une loge au Théâtre Italien* – the 'lorette' with her admirer – by Paul Gavarni.
[*at foot*] Carnival dress – the 'lorette' in *débardeur* costume – by Paul Gavarni.

'respectable' Parisian society and the way she gained public representation in the spectacle of the metropolis.

Given such visual confusions, public space was becoming potentially traumatic for the respectable lawyer's wife, the banker's well-dressed daughter and even the self-confident aristocratic *grande dame*. In the eyes of men, a consumerist objectification of female appearance as flowers or decorative trifles could also be laced with sexual voyeurism. For them, the streets resonated not only with the excitement of spectacle but with sexual temptation and, perhaps, the thrill of possession. By the 1850s another stern republican moralist, the historian Jules Michelet, was warning against allowing women to travel about the city alone, for fear of such awful misconstructions:

> How many irritations for the single women! She can hardly ever go out in the evening; she would be taken for a prostitute. There are a thousand places where only men are to be seen, and if she needs to go there on business, the men are amazed and laugh like fools. For example, should she find herself delayed at the other end of Paris and hungry, she will not dare to enter a restaurant. She would constitute an event, she would be a spectacle. All eyes would be fixed on her, and she would overhear uncomplimentary and bold conjectures.[80]

Alone in public, it seemed, women were subject to multiple readings which defied and disrupted the ordered hierarchies of class and morality. For Michelet, playing up these dangers was very much part of an explicit polemic for a gendered ideology of domesticity – woman as the complementary partner, her delicacy protected by male strength.

There are some more general conclusions to be drawn from these narratives. In the cultural regime of early nineteenth-century Paris, modernity was conveyed in an interconnected flow of visual objectifications. These were male as well as female. But the issue at stake is the differential power relations inscribed in gendered spectatorship, the way that male sexual power was now institutionalised in public space through its novel integration with modes of spectacle and luxury consumption characteristic of the new quarters. The effect was partially to disenfrachise women as a public presence or voice. It was to position the metropolitan gaze primarily in relation to the priorities and pleasures of men. To take a case in point, our gossip columnist de Launay was neither count nor man but – Delphine Gay, a well-known poet and novelist in her own right, and married to the newspaper magnate and editor of *La Presse*, Emile de Girardin. To take up a position on the streets and convince her audience of her observations, Gay had to adopt a male persona and perspective – a paradox to be returned to.

Further, it is clear that a reciprocal dialogue existed between the construction of modernity and the audiences most immediately addressed by it. To be a metropolitan, to participate in those codes of looking, equally meant to become an object of that gaze. Yet such typical groupings – the agents of finance capital, cultural professionals and 'fashionable' women – can also be used to point the argument outwards. They raise questions about the much wider constituencies of interest which could – to a greater or lesser degree and in ways that were transient, fragmented and contradictory – ideologically buy into 'metropolitanness'. There was the consumer of Parisian literature as much as the active participant in the press and publishing industries; or the occasional stroller on the boulevards between café and theatre – a 'tourist' from other quarters as much as from out of town. What about the small investor anxious over share-price fluctuations; or the provincial notary's wife scrutinising fashion plates and magazines for the latest developments in style? These heterogeneous personas do not, of course, add up to anything as solid as a class constituted in economic and political terms. But they do begin to suggest the components of a culturally-defined bloc, a bloc within which disparate economic fractions and social interests could be brought together under the rubric of a shared vocabulary. The success of metropolitan ideology was to articulate, from the 1820s onwards, a vision of social power that fitted with the aspirations and experiences of groups otherwise finding little grounds for coherence. How potent a force this was in providing the elements of a social cement we shall explore with more precision in the analysis of the consumption of nature.

5   Beware the thorns from the flower seller's roses: modernity's other face

For those inside this urban culture, modern Paris was the Paris that counted. One of the obsessions of Gay's column was the elision between the world of elegant boulevards and salons and the capital as a whole. In the autumn of 1836, she charted the seasonal cycle of social migration with evident relish: 'The fashionable world returns, that is incontrovertible; the theatres and the boulevards have changed their appearance. The streets of Paris have become Parisian again.'[81] Yet it would be over-simple to argue that other spatial dimensions and social constituencies were just written out of court. In fact, the manner in which they were set up with and against the images of modernity formed an integral part in the production of the metropolitan repertoire.

Take the representation of the established aristocracy. On one level, Gay, along with other commentators, was both ecstatic and reverent towards the traditional round of political and society salons in the Saint-Germain and Saint-Honoré quarters. She luxuriated in accounts of summer retreats on distant country estates. Through her assumed persona she set herself up as an experienced, if not cynical, aristocratic witness, someone in the know about élite society gossip. All of that indicates a desired identification with the customs and values of the pre-Revolutionary nobility, an explicit display of social deference. However, in the codes of popular journalism, stories of 'high society' were pulled into the all-encompassing framework of anecdote and entertainment. More to the point, the narrative was hardly addressed to the established gentry, and it was even less founded on their priorities and concerns. What was important for Gay were those aspects of aristocratic life-style that could be annexed to metropolitanism. In other words, the aristocracy – their carriages, their salons, even their love-affairs – were offered up to her audience as yet another object of luxury consumption.

More significant was her handling of a different cultural otherness – that of the urban poor. For the identification of Paris and the Parisians with the new quarters was implicitly played off against the presence of a very different city, a sort of underbelly, that was simultaneously marginalised and yet obsessively referenced at every instant. Listen to the 'Vicomte' again in 1844:

> For a month I've heard nothing but talk of nocturnal attacks, of ambushes and audacious thefts . . . what is so terrifying about these assaults is the noble impartiality of the assailants; they attack rich and poor indifferently, they are as intent on frisking the badly dressed as the fashionable.[82]

Nothing could be better calculated to strike terror into the hearts of her readers; neither anonymity nor lack of display would protect the law-abiding. Theft, so it seemed, was essentially egalitarian. In other cases the threat was less straightforward, more insinuating. In 1839, with a combination of comedy and gothic menace, she wrote on the hazards to 'respectable walkers' from streetsellers and the like who got in the way.[83] Beware the thorns from the flower seller's roses, the barking dog of the butcher's boy, or the heavy load of the coalman. This was harmless farce, yet it deftly played on the sinister threat potentially posed by the dangerous classes inhabiting the same urban space.

Similar themes surfaced in the popular texts dealing with the physiology of the city. Notable within the genre were the contributors to Lurine's *Rues de Paris*. The Rue Lescot, in the old business quarter, was summed up by just four words, 'murder, theft, destitution and prostitution' – crime and vice had been its prerogative throughout the ages.[84] The writer graphically depicted seedy lodging-houses where itinerants slept on the floor, separated only by pieces of card, and were regularly subject to official check-ups on identity papers. To compound the *frisson*, he added a vignette of the night prowler-cum-assassin (*rodeur*), finally tracked down and ambushed by the police at a *rendez-vous* with his mistress. Another essay conjured up the Ile de Cité. Full of streets that were narrow, stinking, horrific, it was depicted as a dangerous and alien world that you would enter at your peril.[85] And again, take Roger de Beauvoir's image of the Rue de la Harpe, close by the university quarter: 'The road is ugly, filthy, with here and there some feeble attempts at gas lighting and a few hotels and cafés roughly renovated by a slap of paint; but it is clear to see that mud and misery, shady drinking-halls and argumentative eating-houses won't be got rid of easily.'[86]

Journalistic narratives of this kind touch on a quite specific theme within metropolitan culture, a series of apparently oppositional definitions of the city as disease-ridden, vicious and politically menacing. Though primarily identified with the older and more decaying urban quarters, paradoxically such definitions were as modern as the parade on the Boulevard des Italiens. Modern, first, in that they were shaped by a distinctively novel alliance of official discourses and professional knowledges. Modern, too, because they took the new quarters as a key point of reference – the standard for comparison and contrast. Investigating these themes is germane to our enquiry. For, like the visual dynamic punctuating the boulevards, the languages and imagery crystallised in official policy fed into the formation of that peculiar social dialogue with nature which we are going to explore.

The planning and policing of Paris

Official ideologies

In 1828, under pressure from struggling entrepreneurs, the Prefecture of the Seine initiated a statistical inquiry into current problems afflicting the building industry.[87] The official report by Louis Daubanton, general inspector of highways, asked why, when both population and accommodation had increased, there appeared to be a housing shortage *and* a savage building slump. Daubanton's detailed investigation demonstrated conclusively, area by area, that the recent spate of building activity had been located in those *arrondissements* furthest removed from the populous and impoverished centre which had witnessed most population growth. His specific brief led to an analysis of the poorest quarters in the centre and on the left bank, in comparison with and in contrast to the newly-emergent city of broad streets and technological progress. Of the old fourth *arrondissement*, between Les Halles and the Louvre, he wrote:

> Here there is no space at all, no public promenades. There is a maze of streets but they are practically all narrow, winding and filthy; and yet the need for open and well-aired communication is all the more imperative given the proximity to establishments such as the Great Market and the corn market.[88]

The population had far outstripped available accommodation, with the result that while in 1817 'the average was only twenty-three inhabitants per block; but what appalling blocks for the most part!', now the inhabitants were 'even more meanly accommodated'. Evidence from the Académie Royale de Médecine on infant mortality was brought to bear on the relationship between death and insalubrious housing. Lack of sanitation was linked to a range of environmental factors:

> the harvest of death is far greater in those narrow quarters than in areas where the air circulates easily and which benefit from the nourishing rays of the sun ... [but] poverty, the privations which it causes, the absence of personal hygiene and the immorality of a part of the lower classes, the stubborn prejudice against the benefits of vaccine, these are also real causes of high mortality.[89]

Daubanton's survey vividly delineated an image of poor Paris which was to haunt the official imagination for the next forty years. Remember Luchet, writing at the same moment. His radical republican perspective identified the working classes in terms of those populous and hard-working districts – the Rue Saint-Denis, the Rue Saint-Martin and the politically literate workers of the Faubourg Saint-Antoine.[90] The function of his polemic was to draw out the difference between those who laboured productively and those who lived parasitically off the labour of others. Fixing the poor in particular areas of the city was aligned with positive references to their trades and culture. The state inquiry, on the other hand, specified poor Paris in a series of negative terms set against the dynamic metropolis. What was produced was a menacing rhetoric around the decaying core of the city and a working-class constituency referenced through a continually sliding scale of urban vice. This ran from insanitary living conditions, high child mortality and general ill health, through immorality and fecklessness, to riot and political sedition. As familiar to official perceptions of contemporary Manchester and London as to the topography of Paris, here were representations of the labouring poor that were to marginalise any more positive appraisals of 'heroic artisans' within the confines of metropolitan culture.[91]

The inspector's report is useful in that it drew together three differentiated forms of knowledge which structured the official conception of the city. First, the use of statistics to assess the capital as a whole by means of quantifiable data. Then, second, there was the question of the planning measures taken by the state to regulate urban development. Third, and most important, built into the logic of Daubanton's argument were expansive definitions of healthy and unhealthy space deriving from a powerful medical discourse on the environment. Taken together, these urban programmes delivered a strategy for 'policing' the population in the broadest sense.

Daubanton's findings were published in the 1829 edition of the *Mémoires statistiques de la ville de Paris* – a periodical statistical survey initiated in 1821 by the Comte de Chabrol, the energetic Prefect of the Seine during the Restoration years.[92] Statistical research was by no means new.

Surveys had formed a major element in the abortive departmental investigations at the beginning of the century. But they became especially prominent from the 1820s to the 1850s.[93] This was due both to a clarification of methodology – foregrounding the role of arithmetical quantification – and to their perceived application to social and political issues. Following Napoleonic precedent, Chabrol's surveys were premised on the coherence and governability of Paris as a socio-geographic entity. The publication of these figures had the positive effect of unifying the different areas of the capital under the eye of quantitative science. The distinction between one *arrondissement* and the next, when converted into the uniform language of figures, became one of degree rather than of kind. As the internal discourse of statistics developed, there emerged a particular emphasis on the 'vital statistics' of life and death, morality and immorality. From the rapid explosion of the population, through diseases such as the cholera epidemic, to questions of prostitution and crime, these issues tended to produce the metropolis in terms of problems. Further, such figures were given wide circulation beyond their official contexts by the press and best-selling novelists like Honoré de Balzac and Eugène Sue.[94] Here, the appeal was as much to do with the drama of the figures themselves – their huge size and vivid contrasts – as with the picaresque subjects of urban squalor and crime.

Where planning was concerned, the state oscillated between intervention and cautious *laissez-faire*, under pressure from conflicting economic and professional interests. The main input came from engineers and highways officers concerned with street management – cleansing, lighting, traffic clearance. As Prefect of the Seine between 1833 and 1848, Charles Rambuteau built on and expanded the initiatives of his predecessor. Pavements were laid, lighting extended, the water and sewerage system improved.[95] Moreover, in the light of the arguments laid out in the Daubanton report, he obtained sufficient funds both to open up a number of new streets which penetrated the 'noisome' quarters of the centre (notably the Rue Rambuteau), and to ameliorate the appearance and ventilation of prestigious public spaces and monuments such as the Place de la Concorde and the Hôtel de Ville. As always with such environmental projects, material improvement went hand-in-hand with social intervention designed to promote the governability of Paris – and specifically of the urban poor. Yet the Prefect resisted all attempts at more ambitious programmes, proudly claiming to have left the books balanced at the end of his administration.[96] In this respect, Rambuteau was a figure typical of Orleanist government. The appearance of a do-nothing approach is misleading. His priority of 'good' administration lay in piecemeal social engineering rather than initiating major changes, a process of pragmatic mediation between competing sectional interests.

Pressure for intervention of a different kind came from the municipal council, from 1834 an elected body strongly marked by the political advance of new bourgeois industrialists and professionals.[97] The council was at the forefront of debate on disturbing shifts in the city's population and on the relocation of the central markets, Les Halles.[98] Particularly active on commissions of inquiry appointed to examine these questions in the 1840s was the wholesale wine merchant Jacques Lanquetin. Though originally a provincial from the Franche-Comté, Lanquetin's long-standing identification with the capital extended from economic self-interest to a much broader social vision.[99]

It was Lanquetin who argued most forcibly that there had been a radical 'displacement' of the Parisian population from the centre to the north-west. He published a series of papers dense with statistical material to back up his case, and these were widely reported in the press.[100] His answer was to produce a coherent plan for the development of the *whole* city, and specifically to transplant Les Halles to the left bank where they would rejuvenate land values and general prosperity. The concerns and the analysis were above all economic. Lanquetin's thinking here echoed a wider statistical insistence on concentration of population as a key to economic progress and puissance.[101] But what was particularly interesting about the structure of his argument was the way it reproduced the cultural categories of decaying and dynamic Paris. In the 1840 report, for instance, he pinpointed the states of different *arrondissements*. The second was 'well constructed, the streets broad, satisfactory in terms of sanitation. Occupied by a considerable number of prosperous households and inhabited mainly by financial *notables*'. The Ile de Cité, on the other hand, was full of 'fetid roads and passages, the lairs of the majority of the freed convicts who come in such quantities to Paris'.[102]

It is clear that, as in the Daubanton inquiry, the inadequacies of the old city were forced into visibility by comparison with the dynamic metropolis. Though Lanquetin's own business was located on the Ile Saint-Louis, it was to the new quarters that he looked for the standard of evaluation. Moreover, crucial to the operation of that comparison was a set of linked environmental perceptions and images: choked communication, insanitary housing and a vicious population set against broad streets, circulating air and wealthy inhabitants. These were more than striking observations on the 'real' state of filth, poverty and vice existing within the city. They were discursive constructions which shaped and structured the dominant image of Paris's social problems in the first half of the century.

The debates about population movement and the siting of Les Halles rumbled on through the 1840s. Different schemes were reviewed by the council, publicised in the press, and throttled by cautious administrators and *laissez-faire* economists. Yet the failure to achieve effective action belies the importance of the issue. If this was in part to set some of the conditions for Haussmann's grandiose plan in the quite different political climate of the

1850s, it was also to circulate an environmental common sense as the official reading of the city and its problems. Economists, planners and architects, though offering different and often competing views, all accepted the authority of the environmentalist logic in prescribing the terms of debate. But what were the intellectual underpinnings of this discourse which became the ideological cement of so many areas of official policy? The question directs us to the role of medical hygienics in the policing of Paris, and its implications for metropolitan culture.

2 From cholera to crime – environmentalism personified

> I remember the day when it struck its first blow; the sky was sapphire blue, the sun full of warmth, all nature blossomed forth in her fine green garb with the colours of youth and health on her cheeks.
>
> The Tuileries were studded with ladies like a lawn covered with flowers; the riots had some time since quietened, permitting audiences to venture out to the theatres once more.
>
> Suddenly, this terrible cry rang out, uttered by one of those voices of which the Bible speaks, that echo through the air raining down curses from heaven to earth:
>
> — Cholera has arrived!
>
> Someone added:
>
> — A man has just died in the Rue Chauchat; he has been literally struck down.
>
> It seemed that at that very instant a veil stretched between the blue sky, the sun so pure, and Paris.
>
> People fled through the streets, hurrying to get home; people shouted Cholera! Cholera! as seventeen years before they had shouted: the Cossacks!
>
> But however tight doors and windows were shut, the dreadful Asiatic demon slid in through the cracks in the blinds, the keyholes in the doors . . .
>
> The corpse was *visible*, the assassin was *not*.[103]

As one might expect from Dumas *père* – one of the contemporary 'masters' of popular melodrama – the cholera narrative was taut with theatrical *frisson*. But, though fictional reconstruction, it graphically encapsulated the arrival of the calamitous epidemic of 1832. Cholera stole in, like the proverbial thief in the night, unseen yet all too visible in its deadly effects. It glided through the streets, infiltrated its way into the sanctuary of the home and cast a shadow over the sky, blighting the sunlight, like the Egyptian plagues of the Old Testament. Note, too, that Paris in this scenario of doom figured neither as modern metropolis nor crumbling medieval nightmare, but a natural landscape – full of health-giving sunlight and blossoming spring flowers – suddenly transformed by the incursion of this noxious ether. Vivid imagery which turned the event into spectacle, part, almost, of the city's panorama of 'shows'. But the metaphors also highlighted a certain visual dynamic within environmentalism itself, a way in which the correlatives of dirt and disease were carried in perceptions of urban spatial topography. Here was another occasion where the visual entered into discourse as an important element in the shaping of Parisian identity. First, though, to understand cholera we need to chart the rise of medical expertise and its position within the state. For it was a specific domain of medical discourse which glossed Paris in environmental terms.

While official recognition of the profession as a whole was limited until mid-century, medical authority in specific areas achieved notable successes.[104] The prestige of the Académie de Médecine, the major honorary body tied to the state, emerged triumphant from its battles with the government under the Restoration, which had been implacably opposed to the expansion of professional power. There were also distinctive gains elsewhere. For example, the 1838 law on alienism authorised the setting-up of asylums throughout the country, increasing the jurisdiction of the medical specialist over certification of the insane.[105] In the field of hygienics, doctors and researchers advanced their claims to social relevance – in Paris at least – through the *conseil de salubrité*, situated within the police department. The latter was as much concerned with sanitary regulation and the hygienic upkeep of the city as with policing in any more narrow sense. Though the Prefecture of the Seine had overall control of urban planning, much of the day-to-day administration came under the rubric of the equally powerful police department. Policing in France always had an extensive brief, with a totalising conception of social and political regulation.[106]

The Parisian *conseil de salubrité* had been set up as early as 1802, and was then rigorously reformed in the 1830s. Other towns were slow to follow the capital's example until such councils were made compulsory under the Second Republic.[107] One leading member between 1825 and 1835 characterised the council's aims and achievements – Alexandre Parent-Duchâtelet, author of the authoritative survey into prostitution.[108] Duchâtelet embodied the stern high-mindedness of the new cadre of environmental professionals. He was said to have taken his public responsibilities with the seriousness of a judge who had to be worthy of public esteem. The monumental *De la prostitution dans la ville de Paris*, published posthumously in 1836, was an influential exercise in statistically-based social inquiry and furnished a model both in France and abroad for decades. Much of the evidence was drawn from the files of the *bureau des moeurs* (responsible for moral regulation) in the police department. The results were intended as a direct contribution to social policy. Along with a number of colleagues, Duchâtelet was responsible for starting the periodical *Annales d'Hygiène publique et de la médecine légale* in

1829.[109] Here, theoretical research sat easily with practical projects relating to many of the pressing sanitary issues of the day, from food contamination to industrial accidents, from madness to epidemics.

It was hygienics which from the late eighteenth century had advanced the pre-eminence of environmental equations in conceptualising the public health – material and social – of Paris. While other domains of medical discourse were shifting towards a physiological or anatomical focus on organic pathology, the two key areas of *social* medicine – psychiatry and hygienics – stood somewhat apart.[110] With regard to infectious diseases, the dominant (and politically liberal) wing of the Académie de Médecine was firmly anti-contagionist from the 1820s, claiming that disease was a product of environmental rather than physiological factors. Dr Chervin, elected as an expert in yellow fever in 1832, argued forcibly against the extension of quarantine on the grounds that growth of infection was 'due in every case to the particular conditions of the locality', and that such sanitary establishments were an unnecessary drain on the public purse.[111] Thus, doctors were preoccupied with the material conditions that stimulated illness, often privileging the circulation of air and sunlight as critical preservatives.

This was no less evident at the popular level of medical tracts and handbooks than it was among the doyens of the medical establishment. Take the case of Dr Dagoumer, a humble officer of health, anxious about the mortal effects of damp. In a brochure published in 1825, he told of a family who moved for business reasons from the spacious and well-aired outskirts to the 'sombre, humid and wretched' Rue Saint-Merri in the Les Halles area.[112] There, fetid water polluted the gutter and the sun could only penetrate through reflection. The three daughters – 'fresh as roses' – rapidly fell into a decline; but only when the youngest had died did the father recognise his error and send the other two out to *pension* on the healthy heights of suburban Belleville. Though framed in more scientific vocabulary, what the *conseil de salubrité* came up with was much the same. One report of 1839 reworked Daubanton's contrasts between two classic loci of decay and modernity.[113] The figures indicated, so it argued, that the squalid quarter of the Hôtel de Ville – with a jumble of cheap and insanitary lodging-houses, a shifting and overcrowded population of immigrant labour and (consequently) an innate tendency to disease – was responsible for numerous pauper deaths in hospital, in contrast to the well-spaced and salubrious Chaussée-d'Antin.

Most immediately obvious in the layout of this discursive argument is the broad and infinitely expansive rubric. The focus on the environment was fluid – what actually constituted an environmental factor? – opening a passage from the physical to the moral, the material to the social. The interlocking problems of the city, as revealed by statistical research, were condensed in and through the concept of the environment. Thus, Daubanton invoked poverty, ignorance and immorality to explain the high mortality figures of the Ile de Cité. Similarly, *dirt* was a pivotal image in Duchâtelet's repertoire, linking the sewers where he had begun his studies to prostitution where he ended up! This much is familiar. Commentators on early nineteenth-century France and England have frequently noted the fusion of moral and physical concerns in the work of social reformers and state ideologues.[114] But what also needs to be foregrounded for our argument is the active role ascribed to the senses. Recently, Alain Corbin has persuasively shown how in the late eighteenth century scent and smell became vital indices of putrefaction and corruption.[115] For the early nineteenth century, equally important were visual images and perceptions. Medical discourse made tangible the spatial topographies of the capital in peculiarly visual terms. Warming sunlight and dank shade, fresh moving air and stagnant cluttered alleys, open light and dark closure – these descriptions were written into official perceptions. Urban space was shot through with vivid contrasts of form and tone that projected a dense network of moral and social warnings.

At moments of relative social stability, the unhealthiness of Paris could be physically distanced, allocated to the decrepit old quarters of the centre and south bank – so ripe for infection – and their 'vicious' inhabitants. It could be seen as part of a separate, indeed alien, city; a city of gothic architecture, stinking piles of filth and roaming vagabonds. In the the 1832 cholera epidemic – a seminal event, fixing some of the conceptual parameters for the next twenty years – such areas were blamed as the breeding-grounds for pestilence. Yet recurrent moments of crisis like cholera dislocated that order. As the ravages of the disease demonstrated, the problem was that so-called healthy quarters of the capital were by no means immune from danger. If environmentalism could predict that infection would usually erupt within the ghettos of the poor, it was completely at a loss in the face of the epidemic's spillage on to the well-paved streets of the modern quarters. This discursive inability to explain events, to hold cholera or crime topographically at bay, was what made 'problem' Paris so immediate, so close to the boulevard *flâneur*.

When the unstoppable haemorrhaging of disease was run together with the volatility of political unrest or 'mob' violence, the notion of invasion became even more pressing. In 1832, riots broke out following a rumour that cholera was a right-wing plot and caused by poison in the water supply.[116] The violence quickly escalated. With voyeuristic fascination, the leading Orleanist politician the Duc de Broglie catalogued individual acts of 'barbarism' that fanned out from poor to respectable streets and even to the élite haunts of the aristocracy:

One man chased into the Place de Grève, took refuge on the bridge of the Hôtel de Ville, was dragged off, and ripped open, his entrails left for the dogs . . . Other murders equally horrible were executed in the Faubourg Saint-Antoine, the Place de Bastille, in the Faubourg Saint-Germain, on the Boulevard Saint-Denis and in the quarter of Les Halles. It was as if an epidemic of murderous violence had, for several days, grafted itself on to the disease.[117]

Violence, here, was conceptualised in natural rather than social terms – as a plague infecting the capital. In the turbulent revolutionary clashes of June 1848, Hugo was to summon up a similar rhetoric when he railed against the 'insurrectional virus' oozing from the 'entrails of the city'.[118] In both cases, political unrest was pathologised through the use of medical imagery. More to the point, written into the metaphors was the importance for metropolitan commentators of *visual* emblems in reading for the intrusion of danger and menace. Like the Vicomte de Launay with her warnings about rose thorns and night assassins, it seemed necessary to be eternally vigilant, to watch out for tell-tale signs of encroaching ill-health, immorality or anarchy, to catch at the half-seen presence of crime and prostitution in their midst.

The condensation of epidemic disease and spreading working-class violence came to a head in the climate of near-continual political crisis punctuating the late 1820s and early 1830s. In the capital, at least, the legitimacy of the new Orleanist regime was far from secure. Sporadic uprisings in protest against the hollow compromise of the July constitution brought together popular Bonapartists, Jacobin revolutionaries and militant artisan groupings.[119] Uprisings at this period were as much a distinctive icon of modern city life as Café Tortoni or gaslight. And even if the barricades were thrown up in the traditional strongholds of labour, the implications of violence were not to be neatly structured out of metropolitan consciousness. At a ball held by the Rothschilds in 1831, the Austrian attaché noted: 'Between every dance dreadful reports, each more terrifying than the last, kept arriving from all sides . . . Mme Rothschild was almost frightened to death at the thought of her house being ransacked: despite that, the dancing continued apace'. And again two weeks later: 'Dancing in the salons, fighting in the streets, we are in the midst of a revolution; everything seems to crumble, we sit on top of a volcano, it growls, it threatens to erupt, the new monarchy is shaken to its roots'.[120]

By the early 1840s the emphasis had shifted. Less overtly troubling to the political health of Paris, the urban poor were now dissected as as *latent* menace. Under the eye of scientific research, the tendency was increasingly towards the isolation of specific recalcitrant groups and their problems within working-class Paris. The major study was by Honoré Fregier, chief clerk at the Prefecture of the Seine. *Des classes dangereuses de la population et des moyens de les rendre meilleurs* won a prize from the Académie des Sciences

Morals et Politiques in 1840.[121] Fregier cleverly mobilised statistical data to show that the capital held around 63,000 dangerous individuals. The categories ranged from those who did not work to those who would not work, from the inebriate to the depraved and criminal. Harping on the usual environmentalist equations – laziness and drunkenness bred in conditions of overcrowding and squalor – it was hardly surprising that the author pinpointed the old decaying quarters as the habitat of vice. But – and here the implications became more worrying for the metropolitan audience – the underclass was also the enemy within. Pickpockets, cheats, gamblers and prostitutes were ever intermingling with the respectable on the pavements of the healthy city. This was the register so eloquently orchestrated in the popular rhetoric of Delphine Gay. Fregier went even further. He located two elements among the so-called educated classes which could also be identified as both depraved and corrupting: courtesans and plagiarists (those commercial hack writers who worked for or under a famous assumed name).[122] The paradox was, of course, that these groups carried particularly strong connotations of Parisian modernity. Yet now they were seen to stand in a continuum with the viciousness of the dangerous classes, as part of the latent undercurrent eroding the strength and vitality of the city as a whole. In other words, as with cholera, official investigations such as this identified representations of danger right at the heart of the new metropolis. Such imagery was always pressing hard at the edges of visibility, ready to taint the boulevard and penetrate the glamour of public space.

Fregier's stands as one of the most comprehensive of official analyses of urban problems and their solutions. What needs drawing out, though, is the impact of his kind of environmental discourse beyond official circles and professional debate. For popularised versions of environmentalism were part of common-sense thinking about the city, whether in serialised novels or anecdotal journalism, crime reports or caricature. A sophisticated visual language was projected within that rhetoric. This did not simply offer a series of *images*; it produced distinctive ways of seeing, ways of deciphering Parisian topography. In such a process, the press was instrumental. Moreover, for readers both within the city and across France it effectively married the perceptions of urban danger with the celebration of dynamic modernity, all under the rubric of information, leisure and entertainment.

The eye of journalism

1   The rise of the popular press

In any account of early nineteenth-century Paris press expansion needs to be
taken as a key constituent. It was innovatory both in harnessing new
technology and work routines – unusual by the standards of contemporary
production in the capital – and in proliferating cultural forms. Taking off
during the Restoration, the industry boomed in the 1830s and 1840s. Political
dailies, commercial advertisers, professional journals, artistic and literary
reviews, fashion magazines, educative material aimed at the lower classes and
children – all flourished.[123] Development was stimulated by large-scale capital
investment, enabling the application of new technology alongside reorganisa-
tion of the labour process. The introduction of the steam press multiplied the
speed of printing and the quantity of copies produced, and was often
accompanied by the rationalisation of different aspects of production – from
writing and editing to printing and distribution – under the control of an
entrepreneurial owner-publisher.

But there were other conditions apart from the economic. Also vital was
the function of the press as an instrument of political opposition after 1815.
Politicians right across the spectrum wrote for or edited papers.[124] Under the
Bourbons, rigorous forms of censorship and repression stimulated an imaginative repertoire of strategies for putting across an oppositional political
viewpoint in an acceptable guise, from satire to literary reviews and art
criticism. Though partially relaxed during the constitutional monarchy,
censorship continued to encourage heterogeneous approaches to political
debate. After 1835, direct attacks on king or constitution, and any whiff of
republicanism, could land the writer in prison.[125]

Economic and political factors opened up possibilities for new kinds of newspaper which carried a specific cultural repertoire. These papers were self-consciously popular, with a new emphasis on apolitical content. They were keen to forge connections between news, information and entertainment. It was Emile de Girardin, with *La Presse*, and Armand Dutacq, with *Le Siècle*, who pioneered the cheaper and more mass-circulation paper in 1836.[126] If recent innovations in steam technology were exploited to extend production, equally a reduction in price was financed through the heightened use of advertising. At this time, Girardin was less interested in pushing a political line than in promoting newspaper-reading as leisure, both informative and pleasurable.

In the context of these transformations, a diversity of genres and types of writing made their mark: the serialised novel (*roman-feuilleton*), an explosion of literary and art criticism, and the gossip column. Take the serialised novel. This pooled the talents of well-known writers and beginners, from Sand and Dumas to Balzac and Sue.[127] The regular appearance of instalments hot from the writer's pen established continuity, along with the pleasures of suspense and textual variety within each edition. It was, too, a useful mechanism for publicising the paper, through adverts for future dramatic episodes or soon-to-be-published attractions. In a famous satire on contemporary society, Louis Reybaud's *Jérome Paturot à la recherche d'une position sociale* (itself serialised in *Le National* in 1842), the hero, currently an aspiring popular novelist, learnt from a newspaper editor of the ideal way to end an episode. This involved the mysterious appearance of a severed head, for 'out of two million readers', he enthused, 'there won't be one who isn't dying to find out whose is the head so boldly suspended between two issues'.[128] Now it was possible for thrilling fiction to rub shoulders with the classic repertoire of news-reporting on crime and assassinations, mortality statistics and railway disasters, as well as the standard political commentaries. In the mix, many of the official problems of the metropolis were inflected with titillating connotations.

But it was Sue's contemporary tale of the rotting Parisian underbelly, *Les Mystères de Paris* (published in the *Journal des Débats* in 1843), which most vividly caught readers' imaginations. Drawing extensively on official sources, and set, naturally, on the Ile de Cité, the narrative offered a heady mixture of prostitution, violent criminality and the heroic actions of the secret police agent Rodolphe (an English aristocrat). So powerful was the evocation of that other Paris as an alien yet all-too-familiar scenario that the book was republished endlessly and inspired numerous spin-offs, ranging from literary sequels and stage adaptations to decorative bric-à-brac.[129] In 1844, the luxury dealer Susse Brothers even advertised a series of statuettes after Sue's characters at six francs apiece. Representations of poor Paris were becoming arrive parfois qu'un chaland sérieux, après avoir acheté la chaîne de sûreté, ne trouve plus se montre dans son gousset. Preuve irréfragable de l'utilité de la chaîne.

Mais le soir vient, et les trois compères vont déposer leur fonds de commerce chez un marchand de vin. Ils font sur une table vineuse l'inventaire de leurs opérations: il se trouve souvent que le vendeur a vendu soixante chaînes, bien qu'il n'en ait que vingt-cinq dans sa boutique, et qu'en dernier résultat ces vingt-cinq lui restent intégralement pour servir à la vente du lendemain. Ce problème, qui embarrasserait peut-être les syndics les plus experts du tribunal de commerce, s'explique et se résout par un mot: — les soixante chaînes vendues par l'associé vendeur ont été achetées par l'associé *allumeur*.

Le mystère est expliqué. Cependant, comme trois associés ne vivent pas en s'achetant réciproquement des chaînes de sûreté, nos industriels laissent leur boutique au cabaret et

(Ramoneur.)

vont se livrer, à la clarté du gaz, à un autre commerce plus lucratif: ils deviennent marchands de contre-marques; si le trafic ne donne pas assez pour occuper les trois intéressés, l'un d'eux, l'*allumeur*, endosse une blouse et devient *ouvreur de fiacres* à la porte des théâtres et des concerts; il place un petit tapis ou son mouchoir sur la roue pour garantir contre

(Joueur de serinette.)

la souillure de la boue la robe de la bourgeoise ou le tweed du bourgeois; ce bon office lui rapporte quelques doubles décimes qu'il verse fidèlement dans la caisse sociale.

Non loin de la fameuse échoppe où se fabrique et se dé-

(Marchand de peaux de lapins.)

bite la galette du Gymnase, n'avez-vous pas remarqué encore une petite industrie en plein vent? C'est là, sur le bitume du boulevard Bonne-Nouvelle, qu'un modeste et savant astro-

(Étameur et fondeur de cuillers.)

nome vient chaque soir demander à l'industrie les profits que la science seule ne donne pas. Cet estimable Galilée moderne, coiffé d'un bonnet grec et revêtu d'une redingote à la propriétaire dont la coupe surannée témoigne de la part

de celui qu'elle couvre un profond mépris pour les futilités de la mode, établit, à l'heure où le gaz s'enflamme dans les

(Marchand de chaînes de sûreté.)

lanternes, un magnifique télescope sur le trottoir du boulevard.

Moyennant la faible rétribution de dix centimes vous pou-

(Astronome en plein vent.)

vez vous donner l'utile récréation de voir des *montagnes* dans la lune, ou de découvrir une comète et sa queue non prévues par les savants de l'Observatoire.

(Marchand d'ombrelles pour les enfants.)

Urban street traders, from *L'Illustration*, 1843.

[*facing, at head*] *L'Illustration*'s view of its own editorial team, 1844.
[*at foot*] The subscription office of *L'Illustration* suggesting great public enthusiasm, from *L'Illustration*, 1844.

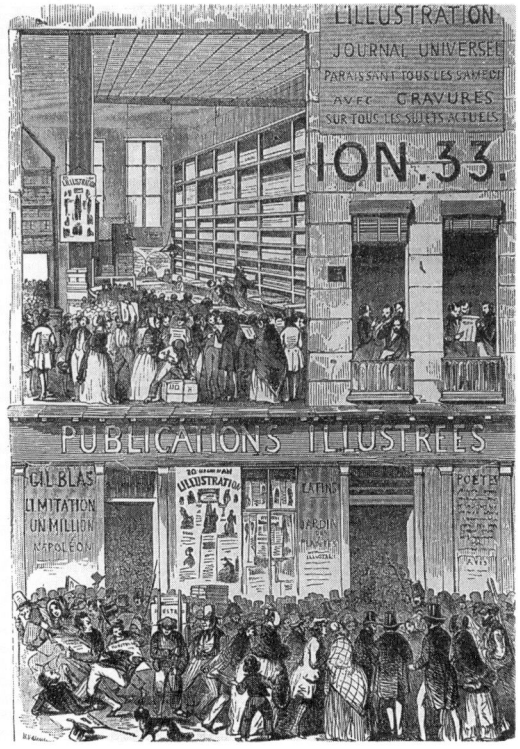

1839 587

Mme EMILE DE GIRARDIN,

Née Delphine Gay.

Delphine Gay/Mme Emile de Girardin/Vicomte Charles de Launay,
from *Galerie du Voleur*, 1839.

part of the cultural exchange of the modern city.

If popular, the *roman-feuilleton* was also viciously attacked.[130] Dumas, especially, was denounced for plagiarism, opportunism and the ruthless exploitation of his protégés. More generally, the genre came under fire from conservatives for disseminating immoral and pernicious doctrines. In 1850, the new right-wing (and anti-metropolitan) majority in the Chamber of Deputies seized their opportunity and put an end to the practice by taxing the publication of novels in newspaper form. This effectively terminated the first moment of popular-press expansion. The conservative analysis came close to that of the bureaucrat Fregier. Here, imagery of creeping moral corruption was displaced from the rotten core on to a dynamic and enterprising fraction of the modern city.

The regular chronicle of Parisian daily affairs and social gossip was another component of the new journalism. Again, right-wing social critics condemned its popularity, making a link with all the flotsam and jetsam of contemporary society. News trivia, they wailed, encouraged the lower orders to slump around in cafés drinking absinthe and dreaming of social utopias.[131] Gay's *Lettres parisiennes* had opened the space for a perpetual light-hearted peroration on city habits and foibles. Hers was an accomplished juggling act. Beyond the formal assertion of the political and cultural status quo, it balanced the pervasive celebration of the boulevards with the discreet threat from 'below' – all laced with her own brand of ironic humour. Further, to an audience outside Paris, columns like this acted as a metaphorical eye through which to view the city, as a chaperone who taught the 'uninitiated' how to look and how to decipher urban space.

2   The provincial audience

The *Lettres parisiennes* presented the provincial as buffoon, butt of many a joke, foil to urban sophistication. From afar, the provincial admired everything, even down to the follies of the capital. 'If Paris', chortled Gay, 'is thrown into a terrible panic, the provinces want to get in on the act; if Paris starts criticising an honest man, the provinces only want to become its accomplice and then share its remorse'.[132] On arrival in the city, their wonder at the ostentatious parade turned them into 'open-mouthed boobies'. But very soon they had adjusted:

> dressed up like our most elegant young dandies . . . they walk like everyone else without gazing up in the air, nothing stops or surprises them, they are up-to-date with everything . . . and frankly speaking so perfect is their learning that they become quite unbearable; they humiliate us at every instant with the diversity of their knowledge.[133]

In other words, because they tried too hard, their dissimilarity to 'natural' Parisians rapidly became apparent.

If Gay's irony was razor-sharp, behind her approach stood a welter of similar accounts. In 1829, the *chevalier* Jacob-Kolb published his observations on Paris, inspired by the satire of the Chaussée-d'Antin's Hermit.[134] The author adopted the persona of a successful businessman from Bourges, Monsieur Lefranc, who, on the insistence of his wife, had come to live close by the opening of the Boulevard des Italiens. Much amusement was had at the expense of visiting relatives marvelling at city sights: 'My provincial opened his eyes wide before Paris, overwhelmed me with questions, and stopped before every boutique he came across on the boulevards'.[135] Coming from a quite different political direction, Louis Montigny, the ex-soldier and friend of radical poet Béranger, took up a related pose in his *Le Provincial à Paris* (1825). This was a comprehensive three-volume almanac, full of the sort of official statistics on population, policing and hospitals that would allow provincials to impress their Parisian hosts.

In all these texts the same device was at work. Provincials were framed as comic outsiders whose distance from Parisian etiquette was matched only by their desire to simulate it. Yet, despite the ridicule, the narratives also seemed to be directly addressed to them as avid consumers of Parisian news and street-life. By the mid 1840s, *La Presse* and *Le Siècle* were turning out average daily runs of approximately 22,000 and 33,000 copies respectively.[136]

In provincial *cercles* or clubs, the availability of the Parisian press was indicative of contact with the latest developments – artistic and scientific as well as political.[137] 'In every town I have visited,' wrote a correspondent to the editor of the liberal *Courrier Français*, Léon Faucher, in 1841, 'in all the reading rooms, cafés, *cercles* I have frequented, your paper was the one most prized. I have had sometimes to wait an hour or two before being able to get my hands on it'.[138] While for the young Haussmann, sent out as a sub-prefect to the remote Garonne region in the mid-1830s, devouring 'literary, scientific and artistic reviews, bulletins on jurisprudence [and even] new sensational works' was his only means of keeping in touch with Parisian ideas and events.[139]

Among these provincial constituencies, writing on Paris may well have been savoured less for its literary charms or narrative excitement than as a fertile imaginative experience. For those who were interpellated – and, as we shall see, there were plenty who fiercely resisted the magnetism of the capital – the writer's persona became an authoritative eye or lens, conjuring up scenarios and focusing attention on specific icons of city life. This worked to stimulate desire for Paris, but it also supplied the mental furniture for a fictional participation in metropolitan culture. Along with the fashion plate and the crime report, it taught the 'uninitiated' how to find their bearings, helped them to locate a position for themselves within social space – in the provinces as much as in Paris.

> She bought a guide to Paris and traced her way about the capital with the tip of her finger, walking up the boulevards, stopping at every turning along the lines of the street . . . Eventually she closed her tired eyes, and then in the darkness she saw gas jets flickering in the wind, carriage-steps being let down with a great clatter at theatre entrances.
>
> She started taking the womens' papers *Work-basket* and *Sylph of the Salon*, devouring in their entirety all the accounts of first nights, race-meetings and parties, and becoming interested in a singer making her début or a shop that was being opened . . .
>
> So Paris swam before her eyes, like a shifting ocean glimmering through a rose-coloured haze.[140]

For the fictional world of Emma Bovary, Gustave Flaubert drew precisely on the pictorial codes and structures linking Paris and provinces that we have been charting.

3   Metropolitan eyes: two case studies

So far, much of the analysis has been pitched at the level of structure and representation, concerning itself with the way constructions of the capital implicated certain constituencies in structures of looking and feeling. Let us now close in briefly on the careers and life-styles of one familiar pair of cultural producers working at the heart of the modern city – Delphine Gay and her husband, Emile de Girardin. In many ways they encapsulated the social alliances, political fluctuations and cultural authority welded together by the Parisian framework. Yet their case histories also reveal some of the contradictions between the discursive map of urban culture and the ways in which that culture was lived out.

Emile, born on 1806, typified the self-made entrepreneur.[141] Bastard son of a distinguished aristocratic line, he gained establishment education and allegiances but without economic backing or guaranteed social acceptability. The combination proved explosive, motivating a public career that ran from fashion sheets in the early 1830s to the innovative *La Presse* and, finally, after several abortive attempts, election to the Chamber of Deputies.[142] Coming from this skewed social position, partly outside the power bloc, Girardin rough-shouldered his way forward, deploying every tactic available, from contacts to duels, from takeover bids to libel cases.

Girardin could be said to represent the most adventurous and unscrupulous type of metropolitan. What emerges of a self-image matches those activities. The debonair man of the world who enjoyed a public round of boulevard cafés and casual mistresses, he was nonetheless seen as taciturn and unapproachable. Even close admirers and friends like the writer Daniel Stern (Marie d'Agoult) viewed him as a modern Machiavelli, eager to wreak revenge on his enemies, followed by spies, threatened by assassination whenever he went out.[143] It was a persona of theatrical proportions which kaleidoscoped some of the most extreme facets of city culture – dynamism fused with menace – in what was almost a real-life, though more imposing, personification of Robert Macaire. Yet, busy with his multiple projects, busy with motivating others to write and produce, Girardin seemed supremely uninterested in reflecting on his own life and times. It was as if to be so active involved a lack of self-consciousness about what he was doing and why. Rather, it was Delphine Gay, positioned by her gender in a more ambiguous relation to Paris, who became the observer and commentator *par excellence*.

Born in 1804, Gay had been set up as a child prodigy.[144] Circulated in the traditional aristocratic salons of the Faubourg Saint-Germain as the 'muse of the fatherland' and a 'child Corinne', observers reported that her success lay in the spirited rendition of her own patriotic verse. Pushed by an ambitious and literary mother, she was presented to the king, Charles X, and, so the rumour ran, could have become a contemporary Madame de Maintenon. All this would have meant a sanctioned route into legitimist culture. Instead, to the disdain of her aristocratic acquaintances, she took up with Girardin.

The alliance made good practical sense. Both had a tenuous grip on establishment power. Their modernity lay in recognising that success attached less to the fickle patronage of an older social class than to the adaptation of aristocratic codes of conduct to the priorities of the changing city. For Gay, this came to fruition in her prose writing of the next decades – novels, plays and, especially, the *Lettres parisiennes* – and in a powerful reputation as a salon hostess in her own right. Based in the Rue Saint-Georges in the 1830s, at the very epicentre of the new quarters, she presided over a rival establishment to that of Mme Dosne.[145] Though traditional in format, these salons, like other aspects of aristocratic society, were appropriated for another language, pulled into the service of a different ethic, twinning conspicuous display with the lionisation of talent. As Véron remarked:

> With the July monarchy a new world opened up. The salons of the previous regime continued but nostalgically, with spiteful and bad-tempered side-glances at the new government . . . Then one saw appearing young ladies who aspired to the frivolous and transient glory of fashion, young ladies who were undoubtedly charming and always elegant, but with an elegance more deliberately rich and *recherché* . . . They took pleasure in displaying wealth, whether in their expensive costumes and jewellery or through luxurious furnishings including art and antiques.[146]

Unlike the Faubourg Saint-Germain, Delphine Gay's salon juggled politicians of quite different colours, as long as they had the public eye. Both Guizot and Thiers frequented it at one time, rubbing shoulders with legitimists and constitutional radicals like Odilon Barrot. Gay herself, let it be said, declared late in life that the real political divide lay between those who washed their hands and those who did not.[147] The emphasis of her quip was less on polarities between cleanliness and dirt – the poor as the great unwashed – than on the cultural volition and rituals implied in the *act* of washing; a terse reminder of the etiquette of metropolitan social relations.

Unlike the Faubourg Saint-Germain, Delphine Gay's salon welcomed littérateurs – Balzac, Lamartine, Sue – not as exotic entertainment but as publishing/business associates and equals. The extensive participation of literary and artistic types, with their self-conscious stress on transgressive behaviour and appearance, also distanced the salon, at least partially, from establishment moral codes. It was Gay, for instance, who reintroduced into Parisian society the notorious Marie d'Agoult, soon to be known under the pseudonym of the writer Daniel Stern. As a legitimist aristocrat's wife who had embarked on a tempestuous and very public affair with the musician Franz Liszt, d'Agoult had forfeited all claims to her own class.[148] Re-entry into Paris some five years later was a kind of symbolic rebirth via the very different structures and social circles of the modern city. There was a piquant irony here which Gay would presumably have savoured, since in earlier days the Comtesse d'Agoult had been one of those haughty aristocratic hostesses who had called on the young poetess to perform her act. In *her* salon, Delphine Gay made quite sure she stayed – spatially and socially – in control. As her girth spread and her blond beauty faded in the 1840s, she took care to dress in a flattering black and had the walls of the salon hung in sea-green damask where, as one visitor hinted maliciously, 'stray brunettes looked yellow as quinces or illuminated like fairy lights'.[149]

The salon also fed Gay an endless stream of fresh information and anecdotes for the weekly column in *La Presse*. But there was an inherent paradox. Where her *mondain* husband could move freely from salon to café to boulevard stroll, Gay was far more restricted. Her active engagement with metropolitan culture was circumscribed by the changing relations of women to public and private space; emergent definitions of the domestic sphere complementing the perception of public space as potentially dangerous for women. Thus Gay had only partial access to the streets. To overstep the line demarcating feminine space, to take up an imaginary position on the boulevards as the Vicomte de Launay, meant to live vicariously in a terrain where she, as much as many in her audience, was a partial stranger. It seems, then, that Gay's double persona as both witty but very feminine hostess *and* aristocratic *flâneur* pressed at the limits of gender identity being carved out within urban space. The initiation into 'Parisianness' that she provided for provincials as well as city-dwellers was one in which she too was produced as a different kind of subject. Perhaps that insider/outsider quality was precisely what spoke so eloquently to a broad reading public.

Conclusion

Let us pause a moment for reflection. How, in conclusion, to characterise our analysis of early nineteenth-century Paris? This account has not followed standard histories of the capital. Indeed, at certain points it has departed radically from them. For instance, it has not dealt in that pack of medievalising images from Notre-Dame to Châtelet which present a picaresque, unreformed, pre-industrial city. Nor, on the other hand, has it explained contemporary urban transformations in terms of the underlying logic of industrialisation. In fact, we have discovered a different ordering of events. While always underpinned by material conditions, the formation of a self-consciously modern and urban culture in Paris *preceded* the generalised take-off of large-scale industrial capitalism. Our quarrel here has been with those functionalisms and reductionisms which always see cultural formations following economic imperatives. But it is important to reiterate the purpose of all this, which has been to show how the conditions for a new and distinctive appropriation of nature lay in the structures of the modern city. And the wealth of available evidence for this urban phenomenon prompts the reflection: just how and why is it that major historical developments can vanish into the interstices of accepted historical approaches? What we are dealing with is a city which has been squeezed between the revolutionary tradition and Haussmann's grand plan.

Two aspects of this formation have preoccupied us: the emergence of a modern culture of consumption steeped in new urban developments; and official versions of the dangerous and threatening city which followed the logic of environmentalism. The latter functioned as a counterpoint, a low but incessant ground bass to the celebrations of the former. Metropolitan constituencies were being produced along the lines of these cultural markers.

That is to say, the social limits of identity were fixed through identification with the forms of the modern city *combined with* perceived distance from the representations of dirt and danger equally permeating urban space.

The reader may still be wondering, though, where precisely is the link between city and country, Paris and nature. And isn't this going to boil down in the end to a rerun of those familiar oppositions – the social versus the natural, civilisation versus primitivism? The answer is no. As we shall find, where city crossed with country was in those specifically urban forms of perception and consumption that shaped spatial relations as social relations. In other words, there was a *continuum* between the ways the city was consumed and the countryside inhabited.

In both domains, modes of looking were critical. On the one hand there were those ritual looks and glances operating on the boulevards and in the new quarters, looks which took their cue from the layout and style of recent building and planning as much as the glossy accoutrements of new wealth. Here was a *consuming* gaze; a pleasuring look produced through the desire for consumption, the confirmation of being an initiate, of looking and being looked at.

The *environmentalist* eye, on the other hand, visualised the city in both more official and more explicitly anxious terms. Projected through categories of dark and light, closed and open, Paris was seen as a map where moral and social meanings were read into the contrasting quarters of the capital. Yet, despite the efforts of hygienists and planners, these spaces were never kept wholly apart. In the minds of metropolitans, diseased and dangerous Paris was always threatening to invade *their* habitat, to infiltrate *their* field of vision. What we shall now move on to explore is the way the working-together of these distinct visual registers – consumerism and environmentalism – lay at the heart of the urban dialogue with nature.

PART TWO

Natura naturans: the formation
of an urban vision

Introduction

Looking back from the 1890s, Jules Simon, moderate republican politician and educationalist, reminisced on the events of his long life. He recalled student leisure hours of the 1840s spent not in the fashionable crush of the Tuileries but away from the crowd in the solitude of the Luxembourg's *jardin anglais*. Here, he mused,

> in certain corners you could almost believe yourself in the countryside. There was nothing more delicious, after a wearying day, than to find yourself hidden among these great trees, to forget Paris in the centre of Paris, to smell the invigorating scents of earth and vegetation . . .[1]

Simon's vision – an old man's nostalgic dream – was of course coloured by the glass of memory. In retrospect, the savour of nature's sensations was immobilised and eternalised like gold-dust in quartz. Yet the selective distillations of the past, filtered through the fine gauze of his personal experience, also provide illuminating insight into the dominant formation of early nineteenth-century nature.

For a start, the Luxembourg was one of Paris's few public gardens in the first half of the century to sport a picturesque landscape park in the so-called English style. This dated back to the 1790s, though it was considerably enlarged and replanted around 1801.[2] And there is evidence to suggest that it soon gained a particular reputation for meditative students (like Simon), poets and lovers.[3] Though, as the blind poet the Marquis d'Avèze thrilled in 1818, all types and classes – aristocrat, banker and artisan – mingled easily here, for 'in the Luxembourg it is just like in the countryside'.[4]

It is just like in the countryside! What are the resonances written into that assertion? Something may be gleaned from Simon's choice of images. For him, too, the garden was to be read as if it *really were* the countryside. The displacement was engineered through hiding, finding seclusion among the trees; getting close, physically, sensually, to the sights, sounds and smells of the undergrowth. Thus cocooned, Simon could cast off the weary cares of the city; he was invigorated and refreshed. And yet equally central to the structure was a self-consciousness about the illusory, even artificial, quality of the experience; some recognition that pleasure was generated by forgetting Paris *in the centre of Paris*. There was, it seems, a slippage between being inside and outside the frame.

The interleaving of artifice and naturalness, illusion and reality, was to be an overriding priority in the later state-planned parks of Haussmann's administration from the 1850s and 1860s. Under the auspices of the engineer Adolphe Alphand, gardens like the Bois de Boulogne, Vincennes and the Buttes Chaumont were laid out to *re*-present nature.[5] Cement was cunningly piled up in dramatic rock configurations. Water, trees and carefully modulated slopes were combined in a series of pictorial vistas, both intimate and grandiose. But, as with so many aspects of metropolitan ideology, this was no sudden inspiration of Napoleonic centralism. Nor, as garden historians have argued, can it be put down to the late adoption of the eighteenth-century and aristocratic *jardin anglais*. Rather, the way to understand this creation is as official legitimation of the wholesale *reinvention* of nature which had been distinctively articulated in and around the Paris of the 1830s and 1840s. As one utopian planner, Hippolyte Meynadier, was already insisting in 1843, what the capital required was an open space the size of London's Hyde Park; what it *needed* was a 'real countryside in the town'.[6]

That is one beginning to our nature story. Another would be to listen to a young man whose talents, hopes and fears were invested in the metropolis of the 1830s and 1840s, a man young enough and new enough to the capital to be simultaneously sincere and disingenuous in his invocation of this type of nature. Here is Théophile Thoré writing to his mother in 1837:

> I will ask of you only a bed in the countryside and some provisions. For the rest I will make my arrangements to live with the peasants, particularly as I want to work among them.
>   Our Parisian life is utterly abnormal. We have given over too much energy to developing intellectual life and none to *natural* life, so to speak. All equilibrium is broken, that is one of the reasons we suffer so. Thus it is my resolve to try out, for a time, a life that is simple, restful and primitive . . .[7]

Scurrying between political projects, a popular dictionary of phrenology and art journalism, Thoré was a typical aspirant metropolitan.[8] While pathologising Paris as abnormal and out of joint, his attitude to the city bristled with excitement and self-congratulation. It was, for this ex-provincial, *our* Parisian life that was so sick. There was a deliciousness to the suffering he felt. Consequently, his projected return to nature did not simply mean going home to relations in the provinces. It was altogether more exotic and literary – more constructed. As with Simon, the fantasy was of a complete but temporary immersion which would restore the mental and spiritual equilibrium ruptured by the city's frenzy. Yet that very desire for natural well-being depended on a massive investment in the spectacle of the modern city.

In Thoré's journalism of the next ten years, those private equations were worked into a more public rhetoric. Take his open letter of 1844 to the landscape artist Théodore Rousseau. There he conjured up intimate shared memories, like the tree in the Rothschilds' garden viewed from an attic window, or long hikes out from the centre to the woods of Meudon and Saint-Cloud, south of the Seine.[9] Potent icons, these, of a natural breathing-space within the metropolis. And in 1847, musing before landscape paintings by Narcisse de la Peña at the annual art exhibition, he came up with the following powerful, if carefully contrived, formula:

> We all have quite enough worries in our political and private lives to forgive the arts for reminding us of natural nature, *natura naturans* as the ancients called it, that nature eternally fecund and luxuriant which contrasts so cruelly with our artificial ways and all the grievous inventions of a topsy-turvy world.[10]

Once again, the pictorial is a constant theme. But for metropolitans, pictures and prints were not just reminders of a nature already visited and enjoyed. Like urban gardens and walks in the country, they made present a structured space through which the Parisian viewer could live out, briefly, *natura naturans*. Here, I am shamelessly appropriating Thoré's phrase, dusting it off and reworking it (as he himself had) to evoke the ideological relations which were shaping his own experience.

Of course, the above quotation can be read in quite another way – as a coded political attack on the decaying Louis-Philippe regime, gripped in the clammy conservatism of Guizot. Art criticism, as many art historians have insisted recently, furnished one means of representation, if a minor one, for oppositional political views in the period. No one could mistake the pointed references to a world that was cruel and artificial as well as turned upside-down. But the sorts of relations posed here around nature were no more a product of republican politics than they were given by Thoré's personal life. They were set by that overall balance of forces – as much social and cultural as political – played out in the Paris of the first half of the century.

All these introductory narratives give some flavour of the objects, themes, relations and processes from which the distinctive discourse on nature as the countryside was put together in early nineteenth-century France. One obvious hallmark is the constancy of Paris as a major point of reference. As we look more closely, what will come into focus is the way in which the experience of nature was moulded by those structures of looking that were peculiar to the contemporary city – by a fusion of consumerism with environmental awareness. Here is the link between what we have already explored as metropolitan ideology and *natura naturans*. Nature in this sense was produced not merely as a set of objects to be admired and enjoyed, nor even a repertoire of social values. Rather, it described a structured mode of apprehension, both of the world and of oneself. Communing with nature could occur in an urban garden – as with Simon in the picturesque Luxembourg – as well as in the wilds; it might involve a metaphorical excursion into the heart of a painting as much as a trip out into the countryside. And though private, even solitary, this was a profoundly *social* relationship, organised and regulated through ideologies of looking which placed the spectator in relation to the social dynamics of metropolitan class and gender. That dialogue between the *placing* achieved by structures of perception and forms of cultural power will be one of the themes to concern us later.

What this section explores is the emergence of *natura naturans* from the 1820s to the 1840s. Three dimensions of that process are charted. First, there are the shifting connotations of open space around Paris as the environment was reworked through changing patterns of health and leisure. Then we turn to the projection of nature imagery – from diorama spectacles to picturesque prints and Salon paintings – as a distinctive mode of urban consumption. These were images and events integral to the metropolitan parade. Finally, some account must be given of the professional ideologies and kinds of expertise informing the producers of nature imagery. If the most obvious ideologues were painters and print-makers, by implication some of the same codes underpinned the injunctions of guide-writers and tourist entrepreneurs. Separating out the strands is a deliberate analytical device. It is, after all, the force of the argument to suggest that nature was forged at their intersection – that healthy pleasures were appropriated through Parisian modes of consumption, that looking at nature images was coloured by environmental values. So, in the attempt to unravel the story of this formation, these apparently distinct themes need to be understood as synchronic and historically interwoven.

Shaping the environment

1   The urban garden: from dancing to hygienics

In the 1820s, Paris was shot through with overlapping and sometimes competing images of the natural world. It figured, for instance, in Chabrol's official statistics under the following headings: a meteorological table, records of water levels on the Seine and of river traffic, regional flora.[11] Such categories – to be jettisoned by the 1830s – referenced multiple concerns, from eighteenth-century natural history to economic profit and even elemental threat. For this was a moment when winter weather still made roads impassable, cutting off one quarter from another, and when deer from the forest of Vincennes were rumoured to stray across the *barrière* and on to the outer boulevards.[12] Divisions between the urban and the non-urban were by no means as fully crystallised as we like to think. Hardly surprising, then, that the significations of the natural were still double-edged; as much invasive nuisance or threat as something to be celebrated.

    There were parks and gardens to be found within the city, though none quite like the Luxembourg. The Tuileries, then as now, offered a formal layout of dusty avenues and squat, lopped trees – a parade ground for the wealthy, a backdrop for the display of children and fashionable costumes. The blind bard d'Avèze, in his 1818 invocation of Paris's gardens, sneered at the extravagance of attire, the richness of childrens' toys and the stilted theatricality of behaviour which characterised this spatial extension of 'polite', if not aristocratic, society.[13] At the other extreme were commercial gardens like Tivoli and Beaujon, north-west of the centre. These were entrepreneurial initiatives that flourished during the Empire and still resonated with the *frisson* of social mobility generated by the First Revolution. In a vaudeville play, *Tivoli, ou Le Jardin à la mode*, performed in the fifth year of the Republic, the garden was celebrated as a place to flirt, to eat ice-cream and, most important, to dance.[14] In the play, the pleasure-seekers drawn by its charms ranged from respectable artisans to ladies and gentlemen as well as those unscrupulous ex-servants and lackeys who made fortunes out of turbulent times. Dancing figured as the medium that could disguise, distance, even defuse hierarchies of class.

Some thirty years later, an anonymous brochure bewailed the passing of the old Tivoli, fallen victim, like Beaujon, to the boom in land and building speculation.[15] Happily (for this was its *raison d'être*), the same brochure was able to publicise a new Tivoli, bigger and better, which was opening up further west. While dancing was still to the fore, this scene of enchantments was far more diversified, including among its flowery bowers: fireworks and jugglers, mime artists and rope-walkers, a marionette theatre, a gothic chapel, a launch-pad for hot-air balloons, and a hall of optical illusions! Most extravagant of all the spectacles were the *aeoliennes* or *montagnes russes*, supposedly introduced by the Cossacks in 1815.[16] These were enormous contraptions, between a big-dipper and a ski-run and apparently stimulating an exhilaration equivalent to both. Unlike the formal Tuileries, Tivoli was a popular fairground catering for a broad, cross-class clientele. The move towards a somewhat manic diversification of attractions suggests that it was struggling to retain its market. By the early 1840s, Tivoli had gone for good. The dance-halls or *bals* flourishing in that decade tended to be socially segregated through price of entry, indicating an increasing polarisation of social pleasures with the hardening of metropolitan culture.[17]

On the other hand, Tivoli, old and new, did resemble the Tuileries in one respect. Both used nature as the backdrop for a variety of urban entertainments and rituals. In a rococo fantasy, the 1827 publicity brochure hymned the return of spring, when 'vast and lovely *Tivoli*, decked out in all her seasonal dress, summoned to the shade of her groves the hurrying crowd of amorous couples from the great metropolis'. The arrangement of the new Tivoli included an area where 'it is the English taste that has traced the paths, shaped the borders, disposed the ornaments, according to the manner of the day and modern ideas which are not to be scorned'.[18] Picturesque sinuosities were marketed like the hall of distorting mirrors as the latest fashion or craze – a modish curiosity. Yet, paradoxically, this was to turn out to be an old-fashioned and anachronistic way of imagining nature. The new consumerism, by contrast, was to stress the naturalness of nature.

Such were the existing gardens of the 1820s, gardens largely moulded by earlier historical conditions and carrying the imprint of different class-cultural relations. But already in this decade, the environmentalist arguments prominent within the medical profession and state policy were advancing the formula that linked air and sunlight to good health. Chabrol's statistical reports explicitly twinned the hygienist rhetoric with the perceived disappearance of open space from the urban topography:

> The fields and gardens which used to exist within the vast enclosure of the capital are being transformed into streets. Soon we shall have no other well-aired open spaces apart from the public places which have long existed and the squares planted with trees which are being laid out in some new quarters. *Thus, what we need to create are other gardens, new promenades.*[19]

One gets the suspicion that Chabrol's sober schemes were conceived as much in antithesis to Tivoli's boisterous vulgarities as to recent building campaigns. The stress was on carefully-planned and healthy spaces provided by the state, as against the anarchic turmoil of private ventures. A similar emphasis on 'wholesomeness' pervaded the approach of the *conseil de salubrité*. A report of the late 1820s argued that the city's vitality depended on spacious places,

> planted with trees and surrounded by a rail, where the children of all classes could, without fear or surveillance on the part of their parents, enjoy the games and exercises appropriate to their age, and where the inhabitants of all ages could feel the benefit of the sun and breathe air far fresher than in their houses.[20]

Open space, fresh air and sunlight: these were familiar correlatives of a healthy environment. In the hands of some medics, they were entirely functional properties to be bottled up for prescription on demand. One Dr Cotterel praised Tivoli's *montagnes russes* in 1821 for their sanitary benefits.[21] The climb to the top, he claimed, and the sudden downwards rush, exercised the lungs and deeply refreshed the whole bodily system. This was hygienics transformed through the language of popular medicine into sanitary leisure. More generally, as we have seen, environmentalist discourse projected urban space as a topography whose potentially healthy features, like air, light and running water, were to be maximised against incursions of disease and decay. This was clearly the logic underpinning Rambuteau's own improvement of the sewerage system, provision of drinking-fountains and embellishment of public places – all policies dramatically expanded under Haussmann. Implicit, however, in the imagery of the *conseil de salubrité* was a slightly different proposition; the imagining of gardens as concentrated enclosures of wholesomeness, moral as well as physical, as breathing-holes punctuating the dense skin of metropolitan space. These were to be sites, according to the health council's apparently radical and egalitarian formula, where all classes and ages of the population could enjoy themselves *appropriately*; where, *secure*, they could immerse themselves in the goodness of air and light and restorative exercise.

The expansive repertoire of environmentalist discourse provides the key to the kind of healthy nature referenced by Simon or Thoré. In dealing with city pollutants, medics and their allies were quick to elide different forms of filthiness, moral and physical, forging transparent equations between insanitary conditions, criminality and popular unrest. In like manner, the language of good health was elastic, stretched well beyond the mechanistic requirements of air and light for physical well-being to include mental, moral and spiritual qualities like peace, quiet and equilibrium. Paradoxically, though, the urban *malaise* against which the spiritual health of nature was posed by polemicists like Thoré was less that of the decaying cesspit of the old central quarters than the dynamism, the never-ending bustle, the scrambling for position and fortune endemic to *modern* Paris. In other words, all the things that made Paris so exciting – the flickering collage of rich and decorated surfaces, the consumerist spectacle – could, when viewed *environmentally*, become threatening, claustrophobic, unhealthy. In a picturesque guide to Montmorency of 1846, the Marquis de Salvo provided a graphic, if conservative, slant when he spoke of the capital as

> tumult, a mass of objects which every day reproduce the sensations of the day before: the sight of beautiful shops, richly-decorated cafés, elegant carriages, lovely costumes, lovely women . . . and all this kaleidoscope which changes, stirs, bemuses . . .[22]

In this frenzied phantasmagoria, the moral faculties were frequently poisoned. De Salvo declared that as soon as the weather permitted 'one hastens to escape to the countryside like a sick man who yearns to leave his bedchamber and breathe the pure air of which he has been deprived'.[23]

How close was the rhetoric to Luchet's republican evaluation of the Boulevard des Italiens some fifteen years before! Both were caught oscillating between the delights of the consuming gaze and the fear of an all too heady miasma. There exists, of course, a long tradition linking the rejection of city tumult with praise for nature's simplicity.[24] The point is that we are dealing not with an evolutionary history of ideas, but with a materially-situated ideology whose specific organisation does not simply translate from one period to another. In that sense, the particular working together of environmentalist priorities with Parisian modernity produced a nature not antithetical but *integral* to the living-out of metropolitan culture.

Teasing out this argument has pulled us a long way from the cautious prescriptions of the *conseil de salubrité*. Moreover, little was officially implemented in the way of parks and gardens. As with other areas of sanitary policy, Rambuteau's tight grip on the exchequer and administrative caution put paid to any such grandiose schemes as Meynadier's vision of a Hyde Park north of the Champs-Elysées. So what was the alternative to intensive enclosures of healthiness provided by the state within the city? What other possibilities of healthy leisure and mental refreshment were being countenanced by metropolitans? Along with so many contemporaries, Meynadier himself moved outwards, to the picturesque delights of the suburbs and beyond. That move involved two complementary factors. It insinuated a new recognition – not a natural or inevitable one by any means – of the city's edges, its ideological as much as its material boundaries. And it pointed to the beginning of a long invasion; the invasion of surrounding regions by and for the Parisian spectator.

2   *Carnaval* time at the tax barrier

In the most immediate sense, the suburbs began at the *barrière* erected during the 1780s to raise taxes on goods and produce brought into the capital.[25] Until the construction of fortifications in the 1840s, this was the only line of administrative and economic demarcation between Paris and non-Paris. If we compare the historically changing map of Paris with, say, London, it is clear that both *barrière* and later fortifications have been used to represent the city as a compact organic unity (the 'heart' of France), swelling outwards in concentric circles. But such neat descriptions bear little relation to the heterodox patterns of economic development and cultural use actually in play at the city's edges. In other words, some sections of the surburban fringe were more flourishing than isolated corners of the left bank, while others were untouched by the city but for the prevalence of market gardening.

Homing in on this zone as it was in the early nineteenth century brings a number of quite contradictory pictures into focus. The first point to make is that emergent environmentalist conceptions of healthy space had to negotiate competing and well-established traditions, often with predefined class articulations. The construction of a refreshing nature outside the capital had to contest, and was resisted by, quite other class-based forms of leisure and entertainment.

Let us begin with the plethora of working-class bars and dance-halls, the *guinguettes* or *goguettes* which clustered round the *barrière* on routes leading to the commercial and industrial centre of the city. In his 1829 account of Paris, Luchet painted a warm and colourful description of the Sunday excursions by artisans of the Rue Saint-Martin and Rue de Temple.[26] They would promenade *en famille* along the faubourgs to the well-known restaurants of Menilmontant, La Courtille and Belleville, just outside the tax limit. On the way there and back would be frequent halts, perhaps for another drink, perhaps for some of the acts at one of the popular theatres. The bars of the Belleville area dated back to the middle of the eighteenth century. From the Restoration, their pleasures took on a distinctly political tone with the formation of popular singing societies that improvised a wide repertoire of oppositional tunes.[27] For migrant workers, too, the *barrière* was a privileged site for relaxation. Speaking of his youth in the 1830s, the self-educated Limousin mason Martin Nadaud (later to be a moderate republican deputy) recalled the blend of leisure, group autonomy and male cameraderie. By his account, heavy drinking would lead to friendly brawls among rival regional gangs or to casual sexual encounters with Parisian women – both forms of behaviour asserting an aggressively masculine as well as provincial identity.[28]

For all these social groups, the attractions of the near suburbs were clearly not just cheaper food and drink outside the tax limit. Nor were they necessarily political in any formal sense. They were as much to do with the production of a certain regime of pleasure through interrelated rituals of eating, drinking, dancing, popular spectacle and singing. Yet Jacques Rancière has shown us how such activities – from anarchic representations of drunkenness and violence through to the aspirant dreams and visions worked up in poems and songs – were potentially subversive of the hierarchies of dominant economic and social relations.[29]

At one point in the year, all the most subversive facets of *guinguette* culture collaborated in a monstrous celebration: *Carnaval*. During the week of Lent, Belleville invaded Paris. Of course, the festival was played out with more or less decorum right across the city, from the élite Opéra and select gatherings of the aristocracy to the 'vulgar' offerings of vaudeville shows on the grand boulevards. But it was the 'descent from La Courtille', near Belleville, that represented the apotheosis of *Carnaval* in the 1830s and 1840s. This was the last, exuberant fling of a pre-industrial theatre of excess which cut hard against the nascent ideologies of the metropolitan city.[30] Popular reversals and transgressions rooted in the symbolic order of an older peasant culture – over-eating, over-drinking, vomiting, farting, shitting, lewd sexual displays, cross-dressing, insulting the respectable – rubbed up against newer social tensions and dislocations in the rapidly-changing capital.

To visualise *Carnaval* solely in terms of working-class or popular festivity would, however, be to miss something of its contemporary com-plexity. According to police statistics, the night of *mardi gras*, 1836, saw 182 public and 814 private balls, while one moralist calculated that half the Parisian population were out dancing.[31] The celebrations not only traversed class; they disengaged class behaviours from their habitual frame of reference. For a moment, they violently shook those spatial closures so carefully, so anxiously, measured by Delphine Gay and Rambuteau alike; mingling, jumbling, packing different social constituencies cheek-by-jowl into the same spatial continuum. As at the failing fun-fair of Tivoli, in the riot of dancing and the anonymity of masked disguise laundry girls could 'neck' with 'nobs' at the Opéra, while 'aristos' threw drunken punches in the taverns of La Courtille.

Listen to the eloquent testimony of one such aristocratic witness, the Count Apponyi.[32] Accompanied by three friends and disguised as a clown with an outsize nose, whiskers and moustache, he plunged into the *Carnaval* of 1835. Moving off from a discreet masked ball in the Rue Saint-Honoré, the companions worked steadily eastwards across town via the Variétés to the *barrière* and Belleville. Even at the first port of call, events concluded with a comically voluptuous quadrille danced *à la Saint-Simonienne*, the participants constantly swapping partners in a parody of the free-love doctrines of utopian socialism.[33] Then the departing couples disintegrated into a braying, shrieking, swearing mass of sweat and flesh. At the vaudeville theatre 'the people', exclaimed Apponyi, 'reigned supreme', demanding that everyone should adopt their clothes and manners. The crowd applauded only what was vulgar and brutal, 'the most basely ignoble and vilely trivial' of jokes, acts, gestures. By the time they got near Belleville, around five in the morning, the frenzy was at its zenith. In one eating-house, Apponyi looks on with fascinated disgust at the carnage left by two days' saturnalia: tables dripping with grease, sauce and broken bottles, men and women sleeping dead-drunk, children playing in the filth with shards of plates and glasses. At another stop, the Ile d'Amour, a fight breaks out. Stones are thrown and windows smashed, followed by a hail of carafes, plates and furniture. On one side the 'enraged populace', on the other the notorious Lord Seymour and his troupe.

Lord Seymour was the personification of aristocratic involvement in the *Carnaval*. A genuine English noble (uncle of the art collector Sir Richard Wallace) and first president of the boisterous but exclusive Jockey Club, he adopted the nickname Milord Arsouille, which translates roughly as crook, hooligan, debauchee.[34] His costumes, *bons mots* and adventurous exploits were widely circulated in the 1830s and 1840s and took on the aura of popular fantasy. He was mythicised as the 'people's hero', the model for Sue's dashing protagonist, Rodolphe, in the *Mystères de Paris*. Viewed historically in relation to the wider mores of aristocratic culture, Milord Arsouille's behaviour was far from untypical. It can be compared with the debauched soirées or relishes held by young bloods in London clubs, as observed by Flora Tristan at around the same period.[35] There, according to the stern critique of this early socialist feminist, wallowing in filth and degradation was the ultimate mark both of aristocratic licentiousness and abuse of power. In both cases, what is hinted at is an earlier, amoral and almost Sadeian construction of masculine ruling-class pleasure built around intense sensual intoxication and excess. Suitably, Apponyi's *mardi gras* episode concluded with the traditional procession down into the city from La Courtille – Lord Seymour and retinue well to the fore, flinging sweets, flowers and filthy remarks into an appreciative crowd.

What can be unpicked from this account, remembering Apponyi's noble and foreign perspective, is how very specific was the social reordering generated by *Carnaval*. Drink, dancing and disguise may have *seemed* great class levellers. And it is certainly possible that 'nicely costumed' working girls gained access to 'quality' gatherings, especially if accompanied by upper-class gallants. But it was aristocratic men, or men who identified with an older aristocratic repertoire, who had most purchase on such cultural confusions. Confusions around gender were equally specific, though working in reverse. Alongside exaggerated sexual burlesque, there was a certain amount of cross-dressing, throwing normal sexual readings into abeyance. But, with the exception of the odd clown, it was mainly women who 'changed sex'.[36] Especially favoured was the docker or stevedore (*débardeur*) look: bandana round the head or flat cap, loose open-necked shirt, cut-away jacket, baggy trousers and pumps. It was a look frequently depicted by the caricaturist Gavarni in his many illustrations of *travesties*, usually with an eye to exotic voyeurism.[37] For women, though, freedom from corseting and extraneous decoration could provide an opportunity to dance and revel with the best. Given that men often dressed in the same *débardeur* costume, women were able to disappear into a kind of Saint-Simonian androgyny.

There is a wider point to be made here. The precise form of these promiscuous mixings and reversals – the irresponsibility of aristocrats, the sudden transgressions around femininity – was deeply threatening to the world-view of metropolitanism. It wasn't only police chiefs who were up in arms.[38] Our guide to social etiquette, Gay, raised her voice in 1839, as wittily as ever, against disenchanted young legitimists who threw all their energy into a delirium of sensual pleasures.[39] Most eloquently, an anonymous brochure of 1840 scrutinised *Carnaval* with a keen eye for environmental danger.[40] Public balls were shameless places where one thing led to another – dancing to illicit intimacy, drink to debauch. The first comer, if properly attired, could take a young lady by the waist, chat to her, dance with her; yet who knew who he was, where he had been? Perhaps he carried with him the stain of some vulgar dance-hall or, worse, orgy. The contagion was spreading. Every year the whirlwind reached out and seized new victims. Paris would end up with a population of exhausted women drooping on day-beds, pallid young people strangely decrepit even at twenty, and stunted, sickly children hardly fit to survive, let alone to reproduce!

Written into such an apocalyptic vision of degeneration were fears newly crystallised by and within metropolitan culture. *Carnaval* too rudely mocked the careful modulations between spectacle and urban menace staked out across the city. In making gestures, looks and appearances both more explicit and more explicitly counterfeit, in mixing them pell-mell as if no ill would come of the brew, it called the bluff of the Boulevard des Italiens, the Chaussée-d'Antin and the Rue Notre-Dame-de-Lorette. With the authoritarian repression of the early Second Empire and the extension of the city's limits at the end of the 1850s, *Carnaval* was to go into a steep decline.

Telling this story in such detail alerts us to the main issue for our argument, the contradictory 'nature' of suburban space between the 1820s and 1840s. A dense skein of meanings, grounded in long-established activities and often with strong class articulations, was already in place. There was, therefore, to be no smooth appropriation of the 'outside' of Paris for an urban fantasy of healthy refreshment. *Natura naturans* had to undercut and displace both more popular and more aristocratic cultures in order to gain legitimacy. Far from conflict-free, this formation was already beginning to be caught up in the shifting class relations of early nineteenth-century French society.

To chart that process, let us examine the changing profiles of two particular cultural practices associated with the healthy suburbs: the excursion trip out from the city – what might be termed the beginnings of nature tourism – and the proliferation of the *maison de campagne* (the house in the country). These patterns of leisure and recreation were sharpened in the early 1840s by a condensation of material factors – industrialisation, fortifications, railways – which sealed that blend of difference yet nearness characterising metropolitan nature.

3   Take a trip out from Paris

The very activity of travelling out from the city, whether for the day or the week, whether by foot, coach or train, was to become constitutive of the environmental experience of the countryside. It twinned the representation of difference – marked, however fleetingly, by the passage of time and space – with that of transience, the temporary immersion in something else. Thoré remembered his walks out to Meudon and Saint-Cloud with the artist Rousseau (modest though they were, on fifty centimes between them) as occasions of immense excitement, as if they were setting out on a trip around the world. Much later, the literary critic Jules Levallois recalled his youthful excursions from centre to periphery during the 1840s in similar terms.[41] For both, the journeys were set up as pilgrimages sanctified by the precious stigmata of bruised feet and broken shoes.

At a more popular level, Jules Janin's light-hearted guide for tourists, *The American in Paris, or Heath's Picturesque Annual for 1843*, made much of the annual Parisian jaunt to spots like the valley of Montmorency, rich with ancient groves, limpid waters and poetical remembrances.[42] On Sundays the crowds would arrive by hackney coach, carriage or even cart. Hardly had their feet touched the ground when cries of delight rang through the air: 'The grand young men, the best behaved and most unaffected girls are at once seized with this sweet folly, which consists in shouting, running, climbing, lying upon the grass, mounting on horseback and galloping through the hilly and venerable forest.'[43] The image of different classes of Parisian released into a child-like freedom by the plunge into nature echoes the medics' vision of the urban garden where children could play and exercise in safety.

Of course nothing written by a Janin is to be taken quite at face value, given the nature of the journalist's discourse, which was to be as piquant as it was documentary. Yet similar observations recur across many contemporary commentaries.[44] The caricaturist Honoré Daumier often returned to the theme in his series on modern manners, usually highlighting the incongruities of urban behaviour in the countryside.[45] In one print from *Les Bons Bourgeois*, a respectable though modest-looking couple are sitting on the grass watching a butterfly. The punch line runs: 'Don't frighten him Eudoxie . . . he's going to land . . . he thinks my nose is a rose!'[46] If the joke ridiculed *other* people's unselfconsciousness, it also worked with structures of recognition, nudging the audience's own sense of familiarity with getting-away-from-it-all in the outskirts of Paris.

But to say all this is not to stake out a grandiose claim for the modernity of the activity in itself. What, if anything, was new about this appropriation of the countryside? Many historians have claimed a much earlier genesis among rationalising *philosophes* and landscape gardeners. As early as the beginning of the twentieth century, Daniel Mornet marshalled an armoury of evidence to demonstrate that Parisians had been making rural excursions from the 1760s – and not just aristocrats visiting their estates.[47] The point, then, needs to be more subtly articulated. It concerns a qualitative shift in the construction of such trips, in what you went to see and in how the experience was structured.

As an illustration, let us travel out to some of the earliest sites of nature tourism in the northern neighbourhood of Paris: Enghien, Montmorency and Ermenonville. Common to all these places was the legacy of Jean-Jacques Rousseau, so renowned within literary culture for his philosphical-cum-moral reveries on nature. From the 1780s were published descriptions of and guides to Rousseau's retreat, the Hermitage; to the Montmorency forest, where books such as *Emile* and *La Nouvelle Héloise* were conceived; and to the Marquis de Gerardin's landscaped estate at Ermenonville, where the great man died.[48] Often posing as educational or philosophical reflections in the manner of Rousseau, such guides conflated the interest of the places with the life of the writer, his literary creations and his friends. Try, for example, the *Lettres à Sophie* (1813) by Monsieur Le Normand. This took the form of a series of illuminating letters to a young girl (mimicking the format of *La*

Nouvelle Héloise), mixing poetry and prose in what the author called an 'inconsequential literary trifle' (*bluette de littérature . . . sans conséquence*).[49] Extracts from Rousseau and reminiscences of his life and circle alternated with fragments of verse by the author to produce nature as the medium for poetic/pictorial contemplation, for the education of a refined sensibility. The feminised epistolary format might suggest the special link between women and nature that was already being established. But, as in Rousseau, the implied 'philosophic' reader was more likely to be male.

There was a quite particular vocabulary for dealing with the projection of nature here. He was enchanted, wrote Le Normand, with his little rented maisonette 'which seems purpose-built for a painter or poet', while the Hermitage's garden was described as small but 'greatly pleasing on account of its variety and romantic air'.[50] The terminology of enchantment, pleasing variety and romantic airs gestured to states of mind and the values of a simple, ordered life offered by nature. In other words, as in contemporary treatises on landscape gardening, equations, often explicitly Rousseauesque equations, were being set up between the nature rendered by poetic or pictorial codes and a human nature of moral virtues.[51] This puts the ritual denunciations of city life in a rather different light from their nineteenth-century equivalents. For Arsène Thiébaut in *Voyage à l'île des Peupliers* (1798), wealth, luxury and voluptuous pleasures caused the urban man to 'become insensible and *he dies without having lived*', while the moral state of the man attuned to nature was steeped in 'the two great principles of *resignation* and *recognition*'.[52] Symbolic oppositions between town and country were rooted in a rationalist cosmology that worked with a static, classificatory approach to the moral order.

The literary and moral ethos embedded in this kind of excursion was reinforced by the *objects* to be visited, which tended to be the estates and gardens of the famous – Rousseau and the like – rather than the countryside as such. A passing view, composed with all the art of a picture, or a dramatic sunset may have seized the attention of the guide, but these were peripheral phenomena. The aim was to peruse the charms of nature as ordered by human hands, to enjoy a picture in three dimensions. Nature, for such guides, meant the landscape garden! Implicit was some recognition of social exclusivity, a coded compact between proprietor and visitor. You need not ask the permission of the owner, an early itinerary to Gerardin's estate informs us; just send up your card to the house. If you are sufficiently celebrated, the Marquis himself will be keen to take you round.[53] The confident presumption was that no one socially unsuitable would so much as think of sullying the Marquis's doorstep.

Visiting estates and gardens was a structure that persisted well into the nineteenth century, as did the stress within guides on well-known literary or historical characters. An 1826 *Manuel du voyageur* referenced villages near Paris in terms of the many attractive *maisons de campagne* worth seeing.[54] And even as late as 1846, de Salvo's tour of Montmorency retained a central focus of private gardens.[55] There was no clear-cut historical division between one cultural moment and the next, between the late eighteenth and the early nineteenth centuries. But, despite these older continuities, newer resonances were transforming the underlying priorities.

One anonymous itinerary to Chantilly and Ermenonville brought out in 1828 signalled the new mood.[56] Why was it that existing guides seemed suitable for the library rather than for travelling? They were more concerned to tell you about Jean-Jacques Rousseau's last moments than about monuments and places to see. This author's intentions, to the contrary, was to provide a clear guide for the city-dweller who wanted to make an *extended promenade*. To that end he included a description of sites, of the quickest and most agreeable routes and the best inns, information on coaches and maps of the area. It was a brochure that twinned awareness of the nascent economic infrastructure of nature tourism as a form of consumption with the shift to environmental pleasures.

Some twenty years later, Julien Lemer's *La Vallée de Montmorency* (1847) offered a more sophisticated version of the argument. Existing publications have, he claimed, been too obsessed by 'literary preoccupations' and 'have forgotten nature, the landscape, everything except to dream about Rousseau and to be carried away on a tide of memories'.[57] Though his own book did include literary vignettes and philosophical digressions, its central theme was an extended promenade through nature as a succession of views, spaces and experiences. What Lemer loved was

> solitude and walking through the woods and fields; I love especially the spectacle of nature's changing apparel in spring, the tender green of young shoots in the first days of May, and the wonderfully sweet scents exuded by the early blossoms.[58]

As with Simon's souvenir of the picturesque Luxembourg, the pleasure of this trip was steeped in a sensual response to sights, textures, smells. Nature was staked out as an environment – implicitly a healthy one – of colours and forms as well as tactile and aural sensations. To experience it was to step inside that individualising structure of perception, a structure that seemed made for and by you alone. And bound in now with the environmental rubric was a heightened sense of the transformative act of travelling out of Paris. Where for the eighteenth-century excursionist travelling was largely an unpleasantness, an unavoidable pause in the business of living, now it became a sign of transposition from one kind of environment to another. The anonymous guide of 1828 had celebrated a sudden liberation on crossing the tax barrier; so too Lemer praised the railway – that wonder of 'human genius' – which brought him so swiftly and so magically from Paris.[59] The power of the train, as railway companies were quick to realise, lay not merely in covering massive distances fast but in kaleidoscoping the gap in time and space between quite different places. This was to have important consequences for the Parisian's enjoyment of the suburbs. It introduces the issues both of the spread of *maisons de campagne*, and of the changing physical and social geography traversed by the trains taking metropolitans to their countryside.

4   *Maisons de campagne*

Like the rural trip, the country house or *maison de campagne* is a major factor in our understanding of nineteenth-century nature. For it radically reworked the shape of the suburbs in terms of both material layout and ideological implications. Most important, the social meanings accruing to this cultural practice registered the changing class appropriations of the countryside. During the 1840s, country retreats were being advertised everywhere around Paris, from Passy and Belleville on the doorstep of the city to the distant Loire, from the heights of the Seine or the 'primitive' Fontainebleau forest to remote agricultural villages. But what is meant by the *maison de campagne*? Who used it and how? And in what sense was it specifically bound up with definitions of nature forged in the nineteenth century?

If the excursion carried an earlier history, so too did the house in the country. But continual expansion marked a qualitative as well as a quantitative shift. Compare two months from 1750, when the legal and property magazine *Affiches de Paris* listed thirty-four such properties for sale or rent, with the situation ninety years later: the figure had now risen to eighty.[60] A more problematic issue for historical interpretation is that there is little obvious similarity among the buildings marketed as *maisons de campagne*. One of the specialist agents in the field, Boutillier-Démontières, offered in January 1840 to sell or exchange a complete range running in price from 3,500 to 350,000 francs – a huge spectrum which not only reflected the plethora of building types available but also the very different financial means and cultural investments of the consumers addressed.[61]

At the higher end of the scale, we find large and elegant properties which enshrined the earlier taste for Rousseauesque meditation and landscape gardening, usually allied to productive agriculture. Drawings by the architect Charles Krafft of late eighteenth-century rural residences in the Parisian region illustrate a number of classic types.[62] The architecture was usually Palladian in style, combining a sober feel for harmonious proportion with more idiosyncratic decorative touches in the detail. Bizarre and extravagant garden ornaments, together with elaborately-winding garden designs, often projected a theatrical sense of leisure and pleasure. These were villas and parks belonging to the aristocracy and to a select cadre of financial entrepreneurs which themselves began to be the object of picturesque visits during the early nineteenth century.

At the other end of the scale flourished modest properties, mostly close to the *barrière* and owned or rented by successful Parisian shopkeepers, traders, clerks and professionals.[63] Take the case of the republican historian Jules Michelet, in the 1820s a modest teacher who inhabited the area near Père Lachaise cemetery. Looking back from the 1880s, Athénaïs-Mialaret Michelet, his second wife, invoked the charms of 'gardens among which were dotted attractive bourgeois houses. Nowhere could the fences surrounding these enclosures be seen. They disappeared under the ivy and wild falling tresses of clematis clinging to the virgin vine.'[64] The picture of flowery seclusion took on particular pertinence in contrast to the dense industrial jumble of the eastern periphery confronting Mme Michelet towards the end of the century. But her account was not untypical. According to a popular gardening encyclopaedia of 1834, such a layout, the *potager pittoresque*, constituted a subsection of that class of garden which mixed the useful with the agreeable. Common only in the environs of Paris and easily recognisable by the bowers of lilac or vine, the trellises and clematis, it 'accompanies suburban country houses and usually belongs to the retired man of business'.[65]

The attractions of this kind of retreat were numerous. They ranged from the cheapness of living or retiring outside the tax limit, through the traditional investment of accumulated capital in land or the reclaiming of older provincial roots, to the newer insistences on environmental health. As one light-hearted essay put it in 1844, the heights of Belleville were the 'haven of the *rentier*, the breeding-ground of the employee who finds the cost of living economical ... It is the retreat of the poet, the garden of convalescence of small property interests who come to take the air, being unable to go as far as the spas.'[66] *Rentiers*, small property investors, economical employees husbanding their resources – these referenced social constituencies whose economic circumstances and cultural patterns were far removed from the codes of taste and 'refined sensibility' invested in the Palladian-style villas of the aristocracy.

That social gap was exposed as early as 1812 by the cynical Hermit. There was nothing more ridiculous, he sneered, than the current mania for a rustic property which extended right down the social order: 'The meanest draper of the Rue Quincampoix [close by Les Halles], the most junior clerk in a minor branch of administration, wants to be able to say: *my countryside* [*ma campagne*]'.[67] What he meant by that, of course, was not an attractive residence on the Seine or Marne, nor a good estate in the forests of Saint-Germain or Fontainebleau, nor even a cottage in the woods of Meudon or Montmorency. No; what he meant was a little bit of marshland on the Allée de Veuves or, more usually, a rented second-storey room on the Rue de Chaillot (both close by the Champs-Elysées).[68] Mocking the post-Revolutionary pretensions of rising echelons of metropolitans – tradespeople, clerks and minor professionals – was a recurrent obsession of this hard-bitten conservative satirist.[69] However, it is worth taking issue with his argument because it contains a mode of cultural analysis frequently to be found in modern histories dealing with the bourgeoisie.[70] The assumption is of a homology between the *maisons de campagne* of the gentry on the one hand and of bank clerks on the other, whereby the latter are seen to be patterned (though badly) on the former and rooted in some essential principle of upward mobility. Based on a view of class as social stratification, it works with an osmotic or filtering-down approach to cultural class formation. The problem for us is that it pays scant regard to the conflicting resonances which the same cultural practice could have for different constituencies. As with the historically-differentiated forms of the family and morality, so, here too, a term like *ma campagne* was actively struggled over. As at the *Carnaval*, alternative meanings rubbed up against one another – a social friction that confirmed class identities.

So, there was no single, unified rationale underpinning the development of the early nineteenth-century country house. Having said that, it needs to be argued that the years from the 1820s to the 1840s marked a critical moment. For these decades saw the ascendancy of a dominant image of the *maison de campagne* grounded in the emerging Parisian feel for the countryside.[71] That process did not simply mean that the world-view of rising sections of the middle class won out over an older gentry culture. Rather, the urban vision of nature, taking its cue from ideological modes of seeing peculiar to the city, was able to pull into its symbolic orbit the aspirations of Orleanist aristocrats, financial notables and big entrepreneurs quite as much as professionals, small traders and bureaucrats. This magnetic force began to shape the way people experienced space, though what different social groups actually *did* in the country was quite another matter.

Our specific narrative throws into relief some of the more general themes concerning changing class relations in early nineteenth-century France. In what sense was the *maison de campagne* or rural excursion characteristic of broader transformations? This takes us to the core of the argument about the city, culture and class. Metropolitan ideology worked by forging social languages and identities that cut across economic categories. In other words, the striking novelty of this formation was that it addressed widely-differing class fractions. Historians ignore the urban question at their peril. For it made a key input into the dominant power relations of the period. While not a 'bourgeois' formation in any straightforward sense, it had specific and material effects on the make-up of French society.

Let us return to the more local argument about the *maison de campagne* by showing how the language of marketing in the 1840s registered these newer emphases. Advertisements and publicity announcements spoke to the largely Parisian audience at the point of their desire for consumption, marketing the investment in nature as a luxury commodity. In the vocabulary of notaries and advertisers, even the title *maison de campagne* was endowed with specific connotations. It was differentiated both from established property, like château, territory (*terre*) and ancestral estate, and from productive property – farm ground (*terrain*), premises. What was implicitly foregrounded was the use or enjoyment of the countryside *for and in itself*.

On its own, though, the term does not take us very far. Other facets of the notaries' specifications fill out the picture. First, the central focus was on *accessibility* to Paris. Even as early as 1840, adverts were promoting rail links, mostly potential rather than actual, as an advantageous feature. This could be used for the near-at-hand: '. . . very lovely rural residence, twelve hectares of *jardins anglais*, cover and grounds, magnificent view over the Seine, ten minutes from Paris by railway . . .'; as well as the far-away: '. . . house with ornamental and kitchen gardens . . . three hours' travel by rail via Corbeil'.[72] Another advertisement for a 'capacious rural residence' suitable for renting to a large family played up the theme for all it was worth. Communications, it trumpeted, were practicable whether by 'coach, steamboat or the railway from Paris to Corbeil'.[73] Access to Paris was the major selling point. That only made good sense if the audience were Paris-based or Paris-orientated and, moreover, if the user's priority was to be able to move between city and country quickly and regularly. In other words, the imagery held out the possibility of being in two quite different environments at almost the same time, of being able to dip into that other, restful space while holding hard to Paris.

Second, internal aspects of the property – number of rooms, interior decoration, and so on – were given short shrift in comparison with the considerable attention devoted to the overall *site*. This took two separate, though related, forms. On the one hand, there was the play on the healthy enclosure within: the *jardin anglais* or more modest *potager*, the lake or fountain, the well-filled fishpond, the comforting frame of gates and walls. These were features to conjure up an intimate and private world. They promised *safety*, especially for women and children, and they implied *immersion* in your own sensations and experiences – here you could circulate unseen! Yet, on the other hand, if the privacy of nature meant being invisible to others, your own powers to *see* were paramount. The house as eye on to the countryside was constantly reiterated. To take some samples:

> . . . small country house . . . garden and very attractive view . . . the view is magnificent and offers the most beautiful panorama of all the outskirts of Paris . . . its raised situation above the Seine gives it one of the best viewpoints in the area . . . charming position half-way up a hill by the side of the Seine . . .[74]

The accent on situation delivered helpful information on the purely physical, health-giving properties of the place: the presence of breeze, sunlight, moving water. But there was more to the equation between house and surroundings than that. The language of views and panoramas prescribed a certain visual structure to the *nature* experience. The healthiness of the site was condensed with the actual process of looking at it, of absorbing it and moving round it with your eyes. Environmental values were here articulated in relation to visual modes of consumption that enabled the visitor simultaneously to look at 'the picture' and plunge into sensation.

Paradoxically, though, the exponential growth of *maisons de campagne* proved contradictory in itself. For some observers it sharpened perceptions of what the countryside was *not*. According to Meynadier in 1843, apart from the woods of Vincennes and Boulogne,

> The vast belt of districts linked to the walls of Paris generally present a picture of highly-cultivated ground subdivided into thousands of tiny plots where multitudes of small maisonettes, buildings quite without character, offer us an extremely monotonous ensemble of the woeful taste of the suburban bourgeois . . .[75]

On Sundays, he expostulated, the great mass of hard-working Parisians were forced to seek their leisure in this 'oasis of plaster, shaded by the walls of all these vulgar "villarettes", [and to] trample through the alfalfa and beetroot'.[76] Now, Parisians with sufficient money and a 'decided taste for the pleasures of the countryside' were travelling further out. Following the logic of his own thesis, he worried that the devastation was still spreading. It was no longer possible 'to find within a radius of about four leagues . . . the picturesque variety which could be found even thirty years ago'.[77]

Our utopian planner was speaking from a very specific perspective. Along with other republican intellectuals, he had a strong investment in the availability of nature for 'the people'. Note, however, the double-edged character of his democratic indignation. While berating the surburban burgher for rural devastation and blight, he paraded a classic Parisian assessment of the pleasures that the labouring classes ought to be enjoying in a truly 'picturesque' nature. Monotonous alfalfa plots and vulgar maisonettes would not do at all, despite what 'the people' themselves might think! More generally, there was an implicit notion that country-house development (significantly, that of the 'vulgar' suburban dweller) destroyed that which it sought, driving the 'real' countryside ever further from Paris. Suburban house-building helped clarify the idea of nature as 'unspoilt' while imbuing it with increased rarity value. Lurking, too, in Meynadier's anxieties was a tension running right the way through this ideological formation – the sense in which, as a personal engagement with a private environment, it repeatedly foundered on its own popularity. This conundrum will figure most graphically in the clash between landscape artists and the 'hordes' of day trippers unleashed by cheap excursion trains at the end of the 1840s.

5   The impact of steam and cement

Guidebooks and excursions, country houses and their advertising; all were active components in the changing landscape of the Parisian suburbs. They reinforced Parisian insistences on health to reveal nature as a kind of environmental balm, a plunge into sensual refreshment, an air-bubble opened up in the claustrophobic vacuum of city life. In the early 1840s, that structure was pulled into sharp focus by a cluster of material factors affecting the outskirts – fortifications, factory growth, the railway network. The relation of these infrastructural changes to the culture of metropolitanism was complex. Undoubtedly, the rather uneven pattern of economic growth was a major condition underpinning the direction and pace of such developments. But in the 1840s, at any rate, there was little sense in which industrialisation alone dictated the course of events. In fact, what is striking is how often economic imperatives were overdetermined by the political and cultural priorities of the capital.

Perhaps the most powerful agent transforming the relationship between city and suburbs was the fortifications erected between 1841 and 1845. It is strange how this massive defensive monument has dropped out of the history and geography of Paris. How many readers are aware that Haussmann's new city boundary of 1860, setting the administrative limits of the city down to the present, and the notorious ring-road, the *périphérique*, follow the line of the 1840s walls? It seems as if the fortifications, which failed to keep the Prussians out in 1870 and were the site of the most bitter civil war at the end of the Commune, have left only sour memories. As a result the most extensive programme of public works, arguably the boldest state intervention of the decade, with widespread economic and cultural ramifications, goes largely unnoticed.

The idea of fortifications had been canvassed since the early 1830s. Strong military and financial objections were only swept aside, however, in 1840, on the high tide of anti-British feeling engineered by Thier's aggressive foreign policy.[78] The scheme tried for the best of both worlds by twinning two alternative military strategies – a series of huge fortified camps *and* a continuous defensive wall. All of which added up to thirty-nine kilometres of wall, ninety-four bastions, eighteen forts and nine outworks, seventeen gates for main roads and twenty-three barrier gates for secondary roads.[79] Popular with sections of Paris's labouring and artisanal classes (both for patriotic reasons and as an important source of work), the walls were loudly condemned across a spectrum of élite metropolitan opinion. The subject was an obsession in memoirs and salon talk.[80] On the republican left, deputies like the leading astronomer François Arago and Laffitte feared (not unreasonably) that military forts would furnish a permanent garrison watching the city, ready to repress working-class militancy.[81] The historian Michelet's view was that it was a fruitless attempt to contain the inevitable expansion of the capital, while Gay, claiming that nearly all 'men of intelligence' were against the project, reiterated the elegant phrase of her friend Lamartine: 'Other towns are commercial, political and industrial centres; Paris is the only one which thinks. Paris is a philosopher; do not let us turn it into a soldier.'[82] Interestingly, Thiers, chief protagonist of the fortifications, adopted the same argument in reverse. Paris was the 'thinking head of all France', therefore it needed special protection. Strike Paris and the body of France would fall – a view grounded in the experience of both foreign invasion in 1814 and revolution in 1830.[83]

The common chord in all these positions was the naturally-assumed pre-eminence allotted to Paris as an entity representative of yet separable from the rest of France. The debate around the separateness of Paris, together with the actual building of the walls, worked physically and metaphorically to confirm the specialness of being a metropolitan. Equally reinforced were notions of difference and otherness when Parisians travelled out of their city, for the fortifications drastically cut into those more casual, everyday and unremarkable contacts between centre and periphery still usual till that point. As Apponyi noted with some foresight in 1841:

> Even the Parisian *petit bourgeois* has found that this measure interferes with one of his more cherished habits: that of passing his Sundays beyond the *barrière*; for him the whole area outside that enclosure possessed all the values and pleasures of a trip to the countryside . . . the suburbs he considers today as his countryside are to be locked in between the old wall of Paris and the line of fortifications.[84]

In a more light-hearted vein, the journalist Maurice Alhoy compared Romainville, just beyond Belleville, as it was under the Restoration with the Romainville of the present, 1844. Then, it combined the '*rendez-vous* of the carefree artisans from Parisian workshops' with 'countless villas where the bourgeois from the Rue Saint-Denis and the Marais could take up rural residence and evade service in the National Guard behind his rustic trellis'.

Now, the place has become a fort: 'Turrets crown the trees where before there were crows' nests; you search for a nightingale in the foliage and come face to face with a sentry!'[85]

As a major construction project, the fortifications impinged heavily on the economic geography of the suburbs. Sucking in successive waves of migrant building workers, they also stimulated a multitude of secondary and service industries. This coincided with tentative moves towards larger-scale industrial production that exploited cheaper land and plant outside the existing tax zone. This was where industrial capital began to make its most obvious impact on the city. Take the southern suburbs. The area had remained relatively neglected owing to its distance from Paris's commercial centre, regular flooding between the Seine and Marne, and generally poor communications.[86] The 1840s saw the beginnings of industrial take-off with the move to factory operations: two chemical plants, ceramics and metallurgical installations at Ivry; rubber, cloth-printing and tile works at Choisy; and the expansion of chalk quarries at Vitry. The scale and pace of development was hesitant in comparison with the economic boom of the next twenty years. But it marked a very distinct break from what had gone before. This worked, for instance, in terms of shifting class relations. Together with migrant building workers, the concentration of poor factory-hands contributed to the first stirrings of an industrial proletariat, what the political commentator Alexis de Tocqueville was to signal as one of the sources of the 1848 revolution.[87] More pertinent for our analysis, though, were the adverse effects on the resonance of suburban space for Parisian excursionists.

Many factories concentrated on the processing of raw materials, chemicals, rubber, gas; 'dirty' industries producing a good deal of waste matter. Alongside rubbish dumps and abattoirs situated on the city's edges, the proliferation of industrial filth and smells intensified the separation, the break between the city and a space that could be experienced as naturally healthy. Inevitably, this meant that refreshing countryside was now pushed well beyond the suburbs. A popular train guide to Fontainebleau in 1853 made the point plain:

> One of the great charms of the trip to Fontainebleau is that you find the countryside, the real countryside, immediately you leave Paris. Certainly, the outskirts of Paris are charming on all sides, but generally you cannot reach their charms all at once: usually it is necessary to cross a tedious plain scattered with factories, without shade, without greenery, where the flowery hedgerows are replaced by plaster walls of a pinky-grey colour and tainted by all kinds of unhealthy effluvia and noxious smells.[88]

By the end of the 1840s, the near suburbs were ceasing to be a Parisian playground, the taken-for-granted extension of urban terrain and activities.

Fortifications, a nascent industrial hinterland, even the growth of the *maisons de campagne* observed by Meynadier, had worked a drastic change. Increasingly, the suburbs functioned as a transitional *rite de passage* into nature, dramatising the symbolic distance of natural regeneration.

Looking through the train window, the Fontainebleau travel guide observed a succession of landscapes flickering by. Implicitly, these evoked and confirmed the voyager's passage from one state to another. If material developments in the suburbs forced the contrast into bold relief, it was the availability of train travel which crystallised the movement between different spaces and made it available to a broader social audience. Of course, as Meynadier pointed out, the wealthy had always availed themselves of existing means of transport, from the coach system to steamboats along the Seine and Marne. However, what the opening-up of the railway system engendered was not simply a quantitative but a qualitative transformation in communications.

The rapid expansion of railway companies and routes dates from the mid-1840s, establishing Paris as the focal point of the whole network.[89] Before that moment, in a pattern typical of early French industrialisation, activity had been sluggish and piecemeal. By itself, French capital was unwilling to invest in the infrastructure and technology where British companies and engineers had already built up a leading position. On the other hand, central and local state were reluctant to embark on what was at best an uncertain financial gamble. Conservative deputies, and some republicans, worried about the possibilities for financial *and* moral corruption, while powerful vested interests at the local level, especially innkeepers, argued loudly for road improvements.[90]

Eventually, it was the state rather than private capital which took the decisive step. Following guidelines laid down in a path-breaking commission of 1840, the law of 1842 espoused the principle of a *national* rail system. Paris was to be at its heart, with major lines radiating out to the northern borders, Strasbourg, Lyon and the Mediterranean. Under further legislation in 1845, the state assumed responsibility for the expropriation of land for railway construction. Only at this point did banking interests move in, backing the formation of a plethora of competing companies. Speculation in railway shares – an 'epidemic' so characteristic of Parisian modernity – escalated steeply, challenging land as the primary investment option even for small city savers like clerks, cooks and footmen.[91]

At stake in this early statist *putsch* into economic planning was less the linking of production with distribution and markets than an ideological commitment to the pivotal position of Paris. Grand schemes like the Paris–Lyon or Paris–Strasbourg routes articulated the unequal relationship between the provinces and the centre – that thinking head of all France. Yet, in the practical business of mapping out the precise contours of rail routes and the towns to be served along the way, something else transpired. A host of more local and nearer-to-hand pressure groups came into play. Towns in the regions close to Paris were pulled into a taut relation with the capital, able to taste the delights of metropolitan consumption but also to push their own goods and services to city consumers. And one of the commodities that stood to gain from a train station was the place itself. Such areas could now be marketed as an accessible unsullied nature, distanced from urban turmoil and suburban squalor. As will become only too obvious later, the regions were not simply the passive receptacle of urban ideologies. They took their revenge by extracting maximum profit from Parisian excursionists. Already in 1841, one travel guide to Fontainebleau promoted the line from Paris to Corbeil, even though it took the visitor only half-way there![92] By the beginning of the next decade, train brochures for tourist attractions such as Fontainebleau, Chantilly, Versailles and Saint-Germain-en-Laye were commonplace, produced as often as not in association with the new and cheaper excursion trains.[93] At three francs fifty (roughly equivalent to a skilled labourer's daily wage) for a third-class return ticket to Fontainebleau, the trip could not be said to have been cheap, but it was now within reach of a wide section of small business people, respectable traders and clerks.[94]

In much of the modern literature on tourism written from a sociological or business-management standpoint, *travel* – its development, accoutrements and associated services – is the central motif.[95] Tourism (and such accounts are concerned with air-based mass tourism) is defined principally as 'going places'. But in the case of 1840s nature tourism, there exists an equally significant complementary dimension: the facility of train travel to bridge or close up distances, to synchronise the unsullied nature out there with the presence of city existence. Just as important as the move out across the suburbs through physical and geographical space is the possibility of remaining within the same *temporal* continuum. In the morning you are gambling on the stock exchange or seated at Tortoni; by the afternoon you are walking solitary among woods and fields, watching the sun set behind the trees. It is precisely that counterpoint between moving (physically) away from the city and yet remaining in touch with it which gives a distinctive shape to the urban experience of nature.

A related dualism between distance and immediacy, being simultaneously inside and outside nature, characterises those more symbolic equivalents to the tourist excursion such as the diorama spectacle or the prints and pictures displayed in the Salon and dealer galleries. When Thoré luxuriated in landscape before the paintings of Diaz or Rousseau, his immediate reading of the artifice of the painted image was played off against an imaginary (though nonetheless effective) voyage into a different cosmos – 'that nature fecund and luxuriant', so far removed from the artifice and inventions of Parisian civilisation.

Across a range of texts, images and practices dealing with nature, we find similar dynamics linking immersion with transience, distance with immediacy. But surely, comes the common-sense rejoinder, a picture is a very different kind of thing from a tourist excursion by train or the monthly retreat in a rented country house? Art historians, in particular, have tended to concentrate on the specificity of the picture within its frame as a mode of representation separate from other systems of visualisation. That specialist stance has contributed to the pigeon-holing of visual analysis and the lack of emphasis on the visual as an important component in broader-based histories of social relations. Here, in contrast to art-historical method, I want to hold at bay some of the divisions between pictures and practices and to suggest that their (con)fusion was integral to the Parisian investment in nature in the early to mid-nineteenth century.

There are two dimensions to be explored in tackling the slippages between the picture and the 'reality' of nature. First, though taking its cue from the environmental equations of the city, the trip to the countryside was never solely that. It was never simply dictated by the pressures of moral and physical health. Whether in the form of the tourist guide, the *maison de campagne* or even a railway ticket, it was always simultaneously projected as a leisure commodity on offer to the urban consumer. By which I do not just mean that to be experienced satisfactorily nature had now to be bought, that it was only available to those with sufficient economic resources to lavish on rustic leisure and pleasure, but that its intrinsic appeal was built on *being* a visual commodity. It fed off and into the range of pictures and entertainments marketing a visual spectacle of nature within the city. Here was where the cultural slippages took place, where the *maison de campagne* at Corbeil collided with the lithograph of the Fontainebleau forest on sale in Susse or Giroux. In that sense, being in the country and viewing images of nature in paint and print were equally set up as a *pictorial* treat, to be pleasurably consumed with the eyes.

Second, country-house advertisements, as we have already noted, conveyed the charms of the scene through a language of views and panoramas. What was so significant was that this was a rhetoric culled from the technology of *picture-making* rooted in art. The codes of landscape art which were fixed at the beginning of the century furnished the grammar and syntax put to work across the whole spectrum of picturesque nature commodities on offer in the capital. The way these codes defined perception facilitated the move into *natura naturans* by means of the picture hanging on the wall of your home, or the pages of an illustrated book. Turning to nature as leisur ecommodity in nineteenth-century Paris and then to the legacy of art discourse takes us into the next stages of our argument.

Consuming the picturesque

1   Definitions

The concept of the picturesque in France has been and is applied to three distinct phenomena. First, to those élite private gardens accompanying grand *maisons de campagne*, which from the 1750s were modelled according to 'Chinese' and 'English' principles to achieve a more natural landscape effect.[96] Then, it has been used to describe the vogue for exploring France after 1815; for rediscovering the wealth of historical monuments and sites, the richness and variety of local customs, as revealed by a multitude of travel publications.[97] On a quite different plane, the picturesque has also been employed from the eighteenth century onwards to classify landscapes which in some sense looked like pictures. This usage could vary from a generalised and abstract invocation of pictorialism – composition, balance, and so on – to a detailed package of rules and prescriptions.[98]

All these definitions play some part in this account. But our intention is less to explore the picturesque as an idea or style than in terms of its circulation as a set of commodities – produced, marketed, consumed. The starting-point is therefore as much the material sites where social and cultural interchange took place as images to be decoded. From that angle, the first and most striking observation is just how *much* nature imagery was being made and sold within Paris at the period. Landscape, it seems, was a spectacle which slotted easily into the consuming rhetoric of the city. Visiting entertainments on the boulevards, taking a closer look at the prints and pictures in dealer shop-windows, scanning the newspaper columns; these three instances will show how the process of consumption inflected *natura naturans*.

2   The magic of the diorama

Imagine you are a visitor to Paris in the 1840s. Janin's guide *The American in Paris* in hand, you stroll around the quarters of the Bourse, Notre-Dame-de-Lorette and the Chaussée-d'Antin, excited by the complicit interchange of looks and glances between people and costumes, shop-windows and mirror reflections, café interiors and street spaces. After a drink and a perusal of *La Presse* at the Café Tortoni, you walk east in search of amusement. Your luck is in! On the Boulevard Bonne-Nouvelle the diorama has just opened its latest show.

Passing through a gloomy antechamber into a darkened circular hall, spectators settle on benches facing what appears to be an open window. Revealed is a view of Mount Etna by night – a calm night, this – with, in the foreground, the ruins of the theatre of Taormina lit by the moon. Day breaks. Gradually, the whole landscape comes to life under the powerful influence of the mediterranean sun and the volcano's white peak is boldly etched against the deep azure of the sky. Then, with the lengthening of the shadows, night returns once more – though not as before. Now, there is a rumbling, there are jagged flashes of light, and suddenly flaming Etna spews out molten lava and boulders. In the mid-distance, liquid fire engulfs the beautiful bay. Abruptly, the vision fades, leaving you shocked and amazed, titillated by the drama, the immediacy of it all, delighted by the ingenuity of such illusionistic effects.

Such was the diorama, an invention credited to Louis Daguerre, also of photographic fame, which was operating in Paris between the early 1820s and the 1850s.[99] It was one of a number of competing mechanical contrivances – the panorama, the néorama, the diaphanorama, the cosmorama! – which flourished in the post-Revolutionary city, twinning technical novelty with entrepreneurial skill. Basically, the diorama was a framed picture lit from behind by natural or gas light passing through coloured filters to induce successive changes in the image. In this way an impression could be given of clouds moving across a valley, of water falling over rocks, of shadows deepening in the recesses of a medieval church. Further technical developments in the early 1830s made possible both more powerful and more subtle effects. With the canvas now painted on both sides and variously lit from back and front, the scene itself could be radically transformed as well as the light effects. An empty cathedral could be filled with worshippers or a green and smiling valley reduced to barren desolation by earthquake.

Offering two or three alternating scenarios, the whole performance lasted only about half an hour – a relatively expensive entertainment at three francs a go![100] Yet the essential character of the diorama could hardly be said to have been exclusive. True, the represented scenes (Canterbury Cathedral, the valley of Sarnen in Switzerland, the Alps near Chamonix, Mount Etna) were authentic depictions. Wealthy and educated patrons who knew their Europe had the pleasure of judging the pictures' accuracy by the litmus test of their own experience. But that was not really what the fun was about. At the heart of the entertainment lay sensations that owed little to education or establishment social rituals. In fact, they had as much in common with the hot-air balloons and exhilarating *montagnes russes* of Tivoli gardens. All these things registered the fluidity of urban cultures in the first decades of the nineteenth century, before any clear polarisation between bourgeois and working-class culture had been stamped across the face of the city.

Pictures of nature were well to the fore in the diorama: landscapes made immediate by the impression of moving shadows, running water; and landscapes made sensational by the drama of the elements – storms, fires, earthquakes. In the instant changeability of nature lay both the credibility and the magic of the performance. Throughout contemporary reviews these two themes predominated. 'Never has any representation of nature struck me so vividly', marvelled *Le Miroir des Spectacles*, while an English magazine commented in 1824 that

> The representation of a stream of water flowing down a small and slight declivity is so perfectly natural as to impress every observer with the conviction that the artist has contrived, by some ingenious mechanism, to let real water issue from an aperture made in that part of the canvas.[101]

The illusion of reality was forcefully conveyed through the actual presence of contrasts, change, movement – techniques which, as we shall see later, drew on the codes of landscape art training. Yet there was more to it than that, as the following exchange recorded by the German writer and actor August Lewald made clear. He was invited to a sumptuous extravaganza in 1832. This juxtaposed a panorama of the Swiss Alps with the actual serving-up of an authentic Swiss breakfast. An English girl in the party exclaimed: 'Here is an extraordinary mixture of art and nature producing the most astonishing effect, so that one cannot decide where nature ceases and art begins.' At that moment Daguerre himself joined the group:

> 'It is just for this mixture of nature and art that many art critics blame me: they say that my live goat, my chalet and my real fir tree are illegitimate aids for the painter! My only aim was to provide the most complete illusion: I wanted to rob nature, and therefore had to become a thief . . .'
> 'But the singers, the breakfast?'
> 'We are in Paris, Mademoiselle. Dancers, singers, costumes, breakfasts of all nations and countries are supplied on our boulevards.'
> 'Incomparable! Yes, only Paris can offer such surprises.'[102]

If illusionism here was seen to depend upon the slippage between the projection of nature and the presence of real natural objects, its power was intensified by the specific context and site within which it was consumed. For this was a truly *Parisian* phenomenon – yes, only Paris could offer such surprises – and not just in its ability to display the cosmopolitan cultures present on the boulevards. The diorama also worked as an entertainment which played on artifice, novelty, the never-before-seen. Reviews were full of terms such as *magical* and *marvellous*.[103] Such sensations were enhanced by the very brevity of the performance and by the spatial set-up, with the mysterious entrance via a darkened passage. In other words, the diorama twinned illusionism with artifice, the experience of reality with the recognition of the clever counterfeit. That structure projected nature both as the 'real' and as the material for cunning transformations, scintillating surprises. Switching easily between registers was, of course, a sign of the urban initiate.

3   The dealer boom in landscape pictures and travel prints

Out into the daylight from the gloom of the diorama and into the sleek aisles of the arcades. There, in the window of one of our dealer shops, rubbing up against bronze statuettes, paperweights and dolls, are pictures of nature – masses of them. Topographical views, spectacular mountain scenery from Italy or the Pyrenees, cosy farmyard scenes with thatched cottages and cheery peasant girls, mysterious gothic ruins lit by moonlight; all these and more are regular items in any dealer's stock. At Giroux's 1830 auction of art stock, out of one hundred and twenty-five pieces fifty-six can be classified by title as landscapes, sixteen as architectural views and several more as marines.[104]

Already by the late 1820s, it was a standing joke that every little bit of painted nature would fetch a fine profit on the Parisian market. Witness the comic tale of the woodcutter and the artist told in the professional magazine *Journal des Artistes* in 1828:

> The woodcutter: Monsieur, what are you doing there?
> The painter: As you see, I am lost in admiration.
> — Eh! And at what, if you please?
> — This enchanting site.
> — Do you mean my hut?
> — Why yes . . . and this charming composition of foliage that crowns it.
> — Well yes, there I'll agree with you; that burns all right . . . but to be brief what is it you find so admirable there, and what is the point of *paintificating* it as you seem to be doing? If you like it so much, I'll let you have the lot for fifty guineas. At least that'll bring you something.
> — Thank you, but no. In my view, this will bring me double the price, without need of buying it.

On that the woodcutter burst out laughing, yet our young painter at the end of three hours carried off a pretty little picture, almost complete, and on his return to Paris he showed it to M. Schrott [Schroth] who begged him on the spot to sell it to him for a hundred guineas.[105]

With sardonic wit, the story played on the confrontation and miscommunication between two opposing cultures. Nature as a tenuous source of material livelihood was counterposed to nature as a pretty little bauble. The meaning of money and labour, too, shifted across mutually exclusive poles. If from the peasant's viewpoint fifty guineas represented a goodly sum for a miserable, back-breaking plot, double that amount was a mere trifle on the Parisian market for luxury consumption – though it might have been regarded as ample return on a bare three hours' sketching time! Given the journal's clear-cut art-political stance (a stern defence of neo-classical values and hierarchies), it is possible to infer here an implicit critique of the landscapist's easy money. Unlike 'true' art, where thought and labour combined in a carefully worked-up composition, such nature commodities required all too little effort and imagination to be successful. That kind of interpretation played a role in fixing the ambiguous position of landscape imagery in the 1820s and 1830s, confirming its status as pleasant souvenir, object of reverie, novelty item, but rarely art.

The quantitative build-up of nature material within dealer stock obviously intersects with the whole rise of interest in the countryside as healthy refreshment. But there are other, more local histories to be charted here which underpin the presence and popularity of *pictures* of landscape. We need to gesture to the outlines of these to discover to what degree they set the terms of validation for the urban consumption of nature. One internal factor, for example, concerns shifts in art practices, specifically the connections between dealing and the speculative collecting of Dutch seventeenth-century domestic landscapes.[106] From early in the nineteenth century, Netherlandish art was taken up by big collectors as a secure financial investment.[107] Dealers like Giroux, together with their painter-copier protégés, were instrumental in stoking the market by refurbishing originals and supplying copies and look-alikes.[108] By the 1830s, the financial and critical success of the Dutch tradition was a powerful stimulus for painters fired with the ambition to become landscapists.[109] But *contemporary* paintings of an unidealised nature rarely garnered the same kind of aesthetic cachet as their Dutch models. Still placed near the bottom of the official hierarchy of artistic value, there was little interest in them, at least before the end of the 1840s, as potential investment material.[110] To the contrary, such landscape imagery was manufactured and consumed in mass quantities. Ultimately, the demands of broad-based leisure consumption overdetermined any more artistic or aesthetic considerations.

Far more important as a condition for the circulation of nature imagery within the city – though equally contradictory in their implications and effects – were the travel prints and publications, the *voyages pittoresques*, also widely available in dealer galleries and art exhibitions.[111] Books primarily on France, they used topographical and architectural images to document the diversity and wealth of the nation. In material terms, it was the 1820s boom in publishing that paved the way for the phenomenon. Exploiting the flexible technique of the new print medium, lithography, printer-publishers were instrumental in taking the initiative, commissioning artists and writers to investigate remote regions and bring back material first-hand.[112] Throughout the decade, the *Journal des Artistes* overflowed with advertisements for such choice gems as *Promenades de Chailly*, *Voyages dans les Pyrénées françaises* and the more mundane *Département de Loiret*.[113] The most ambitious project was the *Voyages pittoresques et romantiques dans l'ancienne France*, a collaborative venture published over four decades.[114] Among the earliest volumes were those on provinces rich in traditional folklore: Normandy, Brittany and the Auvergne. The written accounts waxed lyrical in descriptions of the scenery, architecture and traditions, interspersed with poetic invocations of the characters and episodes bequeathed by a colourful national past.

It should come as no surprise to find that the majority of illustrations were commissioned from landscapists. Work of this kind opened up an expanded employment field for the whole spectrum of makers of nature imagery, from the highly-qualified artist, winner of state-sponsored prizes, through to humble artisanal print-makers. Further, many of the paintings displayed in dealer windows or the Salon were oil equivalents to the picturesque travel print, identical in format, choice of location and title. By the early 1830s, the visibility of topographical and 'naturalistic' themes was sufficient to lead to exaggerated critical claims for a new school of French painting.[115]

Explaining the appeal of the *voyages pittoresques* is somewhat problematic. In terms of our argument, they do not fit neatly into the pattern of urban consumption. Indeed, contemporary evidence suggests that in the 1820s some of the most potent ideological responses were generated outside the orbit of metropolitanism. What commerce-led ventures and high-art-trained entrepreneurs tapped into was a deep and widespread involvement in *exploring France*. In fact, it was less any notion of nature as physical and spiritual refreshment which predominated at that moment than a cluster of ideological resonances around the nation precipitated by the fall of the Empire and national crisis. Only gradually, and with the magnetic pull of Paris steadily gaining in force, did picturesque travel become re-articulated in terms of the metropolis and nature.

To trace these themes and developments in slightly more detail. One early and 'educated' response was framed by historical conservation, if not antiquarianism. In a review of the many views of France gracing the Salon of 1827, the *Journal des Artistes*, not an avid partisan of the genre, remarked:

> It is with a certain pride that France can still be seen to offer, in this class, the largest number of models to her native artists, who every day exploit with increasing success her picturesque and historic sites, her ruined monuments on the point of disappearing. By these works, as by engravings and lithography, their appearance will be handed down to the future.[116]

The tone was stern, the purpose of the imagery functional. Preserving a record of France's historic past for future generations defined the task in hand. That process of conservation implicitly involved the rediscovery of regional customs and the density of history embedded in places and names, a process which at times carried a more overt political resonance. In the 1820s, it made good sense to the traditional forces of the right. For legitimist nobles, many of whom had spent long years in exile, the Restoration seemed a moment when it was still possible to rebuild a power base through the stable hierarchy of social relations rooted in the regions. Imagery which identified with their estates and chateaux, which in celebrating France's past glories privileged their history, helped shore up that ideology.[117]

Competing with antiquarianism and its potential nostalgia for the *ancien régime* was a nationalism of a very different colour. Listen to the account in *Le Magasin Pittoresque* (1834) of the painting *Vue de la vallée de Grasivaudan*:

> One of the most remarkable valleys of France is that of Grasivaudan in the Dauphiné; the traveller rarely finds a more varied perspective, a richer or more fertile nature . . . The viewpoint is taken from alongside Sassasue, a little village whose cheese is much praised; several of the inhabitants can be seen scattered among some fine clumps of nut trees; there are workshops powered by the Furon, a small torrent which rushes off to join the Isère; we can follow the course of the river by allowing our eyes to promenade across an immense plain, which extends right to the foot of the Alps at the horizon.[118]

Here was a description which explored every corner of the image, leading the viewer in and through deep space. But it did not do so in the interests of immersion in nature, of *natura naturans*. No; for this popular education magazine what mattered was the richness and variety of *useful information* embedded in the topography. The view was projected in such a way as to spell out geographical diversity and economic wealth, from the streams and rivers connecting mountains and plains to the cheese, nuts and workshops signifying local productivity.

That wealth of information, moulded by an encyclopaedic tradition, sat snugly with the educational aims of benevolent republicans like the editor

Edouard Charton, keen to instil codes of self-improvement in the artisan and labouring classes.[119] (Though it was also appropriated for more radical purposes by working-class intellectuals.)[120] At the same time, the context of post-Napoleonic defeat sounded a sharper and more narrowly political note. In the detailed enumeration of regional products and appearances was an echo of the official statistical surveys into French departments initiated in 1801 but never completed. They, too, had integrated data on the local economy with descriptions of scenery, natural curiosities and antiquities – a comprehensive catalogue of the nation's resources.[121] For former Bonapartists, whether from the lower ranks of the army or the higher echelons of the administration, the knowledge buried in the lie of the land could articulate an ideology of France's essential greatness, only temporarily blunted by imperial failure.

Clearly, in floating competing definitions of national heritage, picturesque topographies simultaneously meant quite different things to different audiences. Common to the interpretations singled out was the symbolic rupture signified by 1815 and attempts to recuperate, reconstruct. Whether of the left or right, gentry or artisans, the move was towards an ideological construction of the nation centred on the land, the regions. At a time when France had little sense of social or even geographical unity, here was a nascent rhetoric of nationalism which was to find full political and cultural expression only under the very different conjuncture of the early Third Republic.[122] From the 1830s, with the reshaping of political constituencies and vocabularies, there was a decline in this type of nationalist imagining. The retrenchment of legitimists was matched by the splintering of the Napoleonic tradition. As professionals and the military rallied to the Orleanist call, easing into comfortable positions within the state bureaucracy, popular Bonapartists, quickly disenchanted with the chimera of reform, shifted towards a new, more specifically working-class brand of republicanism.[123]

The point to recognise here is that the initial impact of picturesque travel prints cut against the grain of metropolitanism. While speaking to many constituencies within the city, they addressed them less as Parisians than as political/national subjects. Yet, pulled into a dialogue with urban thinking and priorities, they were now set up as the 'raw' material, the exploratory field on which Parisians' pictorial conception of nature was modelled. By the early 1840s landscape was still burgeoning, but topographies and travel imagery were on the slide. That is to say, while many landscapists continued

[facing, at head] 'When it's thirty degrees in the shade, happy is the bourgeois when he goes to sleep in the forest of Saint Germain, in the company of his wife and several lizards', lithograph by Honoré Daumier, words by Charles Philippon, 'Les Bons Bourgeois' from Le Charivari, 1847.

[at foot] Parisian contemplating the beauties of nature, by Daumier and Philippon, from 'Les Plaisirs de la Villégiature', Le Charivari, 1858.

Te souvient-il de cette amie,
Tendre compagne de ma vie ?
Dans les bois en cueillant la fleur
Julie.
Hélène appuyait sur mon cœur
Son cœur.

Oh ! qui me rendra mon Hélène
Et ma montagne, et le grand chêne ?
Leur souvenir fait tous les jours
Ma peine ;
Mon pays sera mes amours
Toujours !

producing virtually the same kind of scene, they stopped bothering to label their pictures and prints with specific topographical titles. Instead they switched to generalities like *Landscape, Cows by a Pool, Sunset behind the Trees, Autumn*, which made appeal less to particular places than to the audience's involvement with *natura naturans*.[124]

If some part of the explanation for that development may be given by the reordering of political discourse, the other part, of course, has to do with the steadily-increasing weight of metropolitan culture. It was Paris, as we know, where the vast majority of print publications were produced and circulated. Within the context of urban consumerism, the representation of travel gained a new meaning. Remember how handbooks to the capital and newspaper gossip columns depicted provincials as comic outsiders. The trajectory of the voyage of discovery now slotted into the same pattern. Where, after all, did writer and artist set out from and finish up if not the centre, Paris? The regions 'out there' were set up as quaint and exotic for 'our' eyes. Whether it was the much-prized local cheese, the decaying ruin of a celtic shrine, or the curious angle of a thatched roof, all these particulars produced the provinces as charming in their variety and yet homogeneous in their unchanging life-style, in contrast to a Paris that was turbulent and ever changing.

At precisely the same moment, picturesque nature was also being reworked by forms of urban literary leisure. The collaboration of littérateurs was central to the *voyages pittoresques*, introducing some of the protocols of literary discourse. From the beginning of the century, if not before, writers had exploited the image of nature as a privileged site for personal and poetic reflection.[125] What was quite new to the 1830s was an analysis that situated the experience as 'romantic', modern *and* decisively urban.

It was journalist-cum-critics like Charles Augustin Sainte-Beuve, along with the dynamic publishers Hetzel and Curmer, who pushed for the concept of a self-conscious tradition of romantic literature in which nature played an integral part.[126] The 'rediscovery' of Senancour's *Obermann* in 1833 and the lavish republication of Bernardin de Saint-Pierre's classic *Paul et Virginie* in 1838 were major milestones. The argument laid out a distinctive sequence of authors culminating with best-sellers like Sand and Lamartine. This was the *modern* tradition. Further, an individualised response to the external world, especially the non-social or primitive world of nature, was one of the central,

[*facing, at head*] 'Combien j'ai douce souvenance' in *Chants et chansons populaires de la France,* lithograph by Charles Daubigny – landscape as popular literary reverie!

[*at foot*] *The Castle of Pesteil at Polminhac, in the Cantal (Auvergne),* lithograph by Charles Delaberge for the *Voyages Pittoresques et romantiques dans l'ancienne France*, ed. de Cailleux, Nodier and Taylor.

unifying threads to recognise romanticism by. But the credibility of such definitions of romantic literature depended on a shift in literature's social role and locus of consumption. Alongside a continuing powerful official presence in the Académie Française, the literary industry had its sights set on new markets opened up by expanding technology and literacy. If on the one hand it was looking to emergent modes of private consumption (like the middle-class woman novel-reader in the sanctity of the home), on the other it was aware of the possibilities for popular public consumption via the columns of the metropolitan press.

If there was one site where these new forms of popular literary leisure closely intersected with pictorial readings of landscape, it was in the art reviews of newspapers and periodicals. Here was a didactic discourse spanning public and private which graphically encapsulated the new emphases on a Parisian response to the countryside. For newspaper-readers in the provinces as well as in the capital, here was a form of writing which laid down the law about how nature was to be consumed.

4   Critical guides to landscape

Let us begin by stating the obvious paradox. 'Naturalistic' or imitative landscape paintings had little value as collectable or aesthetic items. Yet in the Salon exhibition they were prolifically displayed and widely discussed by critics. This raises questions about whether we are dealing with categories of art or the aesthetic, as they have come to be understood, or with images and texts that were much more fluid artefacts, ambiguously placed via consump-tion between high and low culture. These ambiguities are highlighted in reviewers' responses to landscape in the 1830s and 1840s.

Salon criticism moved centre-stage from the 1820s as one of the key elements defining art.[127] Criticism helped direct public attention away from the academic system and on to the very visible form of the annual or biennial Salon exhibition. Then there was the political dimension. The covert politicisation of newspaper articles in response to ongoing censorship led to a lively cultural politics, especially in the early 1830s.[128] Radical art critics implicitly challenged the failure of the Orleanist regime to introduce real reforms by attacking the authoritarian and undemocratic Academy and Salon jury. In a complementary move, they heroicised certain artists rejected by the jury – Delacroix, Préault and Théodore Rousseau, for example – as martyrs to an antiquated and partisan system. Critical scandals had contradictory effects. While often fuelling official intransigence, they made quite sure that readers would not forget the name of a Delacroix or Rousseau, projecting the hagiography of an unjustly spurned outsider. In this way, artists were made visible as much through notoriety as official acclaim or success. The device was analogous to that familiar range of characters produced as newspaper exotica, from titillating tales of the great *demi-mondaines* to the rise and fall of bankers or the extravagant adventures of romantic poets.

This introduces a way of placing and reading art journalism rather different from conventional treatments; that is, less as a discrete subdomain of art than as another mode of urban consumption which, in its own terms, generated and transmitted visual spectacle. Salon reviews formed part of the literary repertoire across the gamut of the media – through political dailies, women's fashion sheets and the caricature press to specialist professional journals.[129] Recall how the miscellany column and serialised novels coloured newspapers with a new stress on entertainment and gossip. Page layoutlocated arts reviews in precisely the same spot. In other words, the material setting offered up such columns as equivalent forms of literary leisure. There were also connections with the mode of address used by gossip writers like Gay. In criticism, too, the relationship with the audience was disingenuous. While posing as a *boulevardier* speaking to 'his' peers, the critic participated in an active process of initiation. Not only did reviews circulate the names, reputations and images of Salon favourites (and 'martyrs'); more fundamentally, they furnished a vocabulary of description, evaluation and enjoyment. No less widely disseminated outside than inside Paris, these formulas drew in far more than a traditional clientele of élite patrons and connoisseurs. They brought Paris-style sophistication to a broad, literate audience whose only experience of the art concerned might well have been through reading or prints. In such a scenario, the critic functioned like the gossip columnist as a *pair of eyes*. It was he (for the persona was usually male) who directed readers' attention in selected directions, who conjured imagery into visibility by the power of prose. These were mechanisms through which the small shopkeeper or the provincial doctor's daughter could imaginatively inhabit metropolitan culture.

That said, how did the popular literature of art cricitism talk about pictures of nature? Immediately apparent were divisions marked out between high and low art forms. Taking their cue from official art discourse, the majority of reviews paid their dues to the so-called hierarchy of genres, which meant that pride of place was devoted to large and imposing history paintings – all the paraphernalia of Roman togas, noble temples and patrician gestures.[130] Next came religious works, pious portraits of eminent personages and their wives, and emotionally-charged genre scenes – the round of births, deaths, marriages and seductions. The section on landscape tended to be well down the list, run together with the flotsam and jetsam of marines, flower painting and still life. Within nature painting itself, a similar pecking order was observed. While landscapes with antique content were given special pleading as a branch of history painting (judged by traditional criteria of intellectual conception and noble style), pictures without learned references were lumped together as imitative, picturesque or naturalistic, whatever they actually looked like. They were positioned as inferior precisely because of their difference, and hence distance, from *high* art. And all this despite the fact that from the early 1830s most reviewers savaged history landscapes and welcomed the proliferation of picturesque nature with open arms.[131] Nonetheless, their critical language was still caught up in existing categories. Instead of style and intellect, what was at issue were the accuracy of technical reproduction – a question of *craft* – and the charms of the scene depicted – a question of *experience*.

Take the response to the youthful Théodore Rousseau, one of the martyrs to be lionised in the press in the later 1830s. A review of 1833 in the new and self-consciously radical arts magazine *L'Artiste* assessed his performance as follows:

> In the foreground, a little rise covered with moss and stunted ferns, a lush green meadow and a pool of water mirroring a woman and her pasturing cow. Further off, a curtain of vegetation behind which you can divine rather than see some houses and the distant horizon. Here is nature raw and alive. The whole foreground is painted with vigour and reality. Your eye pauses to contemplate the naturalness of the trees, the delicacy and shimmer of the leaves, you really get the feeling of an autumn morning with a sharp fresh breeze rustling through the foliage. Never has the slightly harsh physiognomy of our climate and vegetation been better comprehended. It remains for him to study the look of our sky more carefully; in a landscape that is so lively and striking in colouring, his is false both in form and colour . . .[132]

Add to this the appraisal of the same picture by the archaeologist and librarian Charles Lenormant, in his *Salon de 1833*:

> In its ensemble this picture is even better than that of M. Delaberge; there is more suppleness, but also more moderation in its handling; the horizon is transparent, the building through the trees harmonious and clear, the middle distance admirably luminous. What M. Rousseau lacks above all is study; his touch in the foreground is uneven and rough; one sees that the young landscapist was unable to sustain the quality of his picture.[133]

Perhaps our most immediate response to these texts is how boring and bland they seem! Reviewers were repetitively obsessed with the technical reproduction of reality as an indicator of success. How well was the sky painted? How luminous the horizon? How convincing the atmosphere? Attention was thrown on the material make-up of the object. Here was a focus on the workmanship of landscape as commodity, gesturing to the luxury artefact set among the paperweights, dolls and parasols of the dealer shop.

But if such a terminology insisted on the craft status of the work, its distance from high art, simultaneously it allowed the reviewer's descriptive powers full rein in evoking the actual scene – a delicious, and at times poetic, revelling in sights and sensations. That involved an active process of cultural production on the part of readers. They were invited to step inside the picture in their imaginations; to test the solidity of the ground, the luminosity of the horizon, the shimmer of the leaves, against the benchmark of their own experience. Listen to Janin on the pictures of Rousseau's friend Jules Dupré, exhibited in 1839:

> Approach full of confidence these beautiful landscapes so clear and so solid, do not be afraid that a breath will cause them to evaporate. You can sit down at the feet of the trees, the branches will not collapse on you; you can walk along these sandy paths, they will not sink beneath your step; you can plunge into the lake, the water is limpid and deep.[134]

This was prose that conjured up the very presence of the countryside, exploiting to the full the function of criticism as literary leisure. It was a literary discourse which initiated a series of pleasurable identifications between image and audience. But the effective production of pleasure depended on a crucial third term: the audience's experience and enjoyment of such things as ponds and trees, luxuriant vegetation and autumnal sunsets. It relied upon the common sense of walks beyond the *barrière* into the flowery suburbs, an organised trip out to the forest of Montmorency or, later, Fontainebleau. It tickled the thirst for environmental immersion generated by tourist guides and the advertising codes for *maisons de campagne*. In other words, the spectacle of nature visualised by criticism closed the gap between image and environment. Like the diorama's cunning combination of illusion and artifice, it used the literary persona to oscillate between the glossy surface of the well-crafted commodity and the move into natural space. Or, to put it slightly differently, criticism activated a popular illusionistic rhetoric which plugged landscape-as-luxury-consumption into the pleasure of getting out into the countryside.

Throughout this account we have been concerned to pin down the social location of nature imagery in the cycle of Parisian leisure and pleasure. By the 1840s, readings of landscape, while often remaining framed by literary and artistic codes, were increasingly overdetermined by forms of metropolitan consumption. With art criticism, just as much as with the diorama, there were specific modes of perception at work; a constant modulation between the crafted quality of the commodity or entertainment and an immersion in the nature it represented, between being outside and being inside the picture. It was in and through these forms of consuming that the Parisian identification of looking at pictures with being in *natura naturans* was secured. We should say at once that if this was realism it was not realism in any abstract sense but an equation between these two cultural forms that was underpinned by specific historical conditions. In trumpeting the advantages of view or panorama, advertisements for country houses twinned the projection of healthy refreshment with a sense of pictorial looking. Equally, Julien Lemer's guide to the seclusion of Montmorency was typical of many in the painterly evocation of rural delights – the vivid colours of sky and foliage, the subtle variety of effects as the sun changed position, the continuous sequence of natural pictures.[135] The eyes of the guide reduplicated those of the Salon reviewer, painting the scene for us to admire and step inside. Of course, what was also common to both tourist guides and metropolitan consumption was that third component – the heritage of art discourse. This heritage was both elusive and contradictory. For if art supplied the syntax of a pictorialising vocabulary, as in the case of art criticism it was rarely *as art* that its effects were felt. Far more important was its role as a technology of perception.

A technology of perception

1   The landscape expert

Cultural analysis often envisages its object as a cycle of production and
consumption, with the first awarded theoretical precedence over the second.
This is true of widely differing perspectives, from élite accounts of high art
forms to radical readings of popular culture. The whole cast of our argument
has been to dispute that sequence and to stress other moments in the circuit.
For in an analysis of early nineteenth-century Paris it is the sites of
consumption which seem so significant. Reading novelettes or looking in
shop-windows involved active processes of cultural work quite as strenuous as
that of the entrepreneur, the artist and the artisan.

That said, the ways in which Parisians read, looked, consumed, were
obviously affected by the professional ideologies of the cultural producers.
Here were codes grounded in the expertise and ambitions of the landscape
artist. Engaging with this material means something of a digression, both
historically, into a slightly earlier moment, and analytically, into the internal
logic of art theory. But the detour is useful for two reasons. First, because the
struggles around a professionalising landscape art laid down ground-rules for
the relation between perception and representation which were registered
across the spectrum of nature image-making from the 1820s to the 1850s.
And second, because, built on these foundations were the aspirations of a
whole generation of landscapists who were to become key ideologues for
nature: artists who not only painted trees and rocks and cows and forest
glades with obsessive repetition, but who went out and colonised the
countryside, subjecting it to their very metropolitan scheme of things.

To start with an overview. Economic and political upheavals following the 1789 Revolution gave a new edge to developments in art. Along with other fields like law and alienism, art aspired to new definitions of professional expertise.[136] One symptom was clarification of the legal status and rights of aesthetic products and producers enshrined in the law on artistic copyright of 1793.[137] Equally, the reformulation from 1795 of the art academy as a section of the Institut (an umbrella organisation bringing the arts and sciences more closely under the control of the state) helped promote the intellectual prestige of the visual arts.

Under these conditions of nascent professionalism the stylistic language of classicism, codified and promoted by Louis David and his followers and dominant in the state's education programme, contributed to art's shifting social position.[138] On the one hand, the style worked with a set of rational propositions concerning the relationship of artistic form to universal beauty, exemplified by the grand tradition from antiquity to Poussin. On the other, it required a complex and lengthy training process.[139] As we know from our earlier look at art journalism, not all were to gain from the new system. Internal to the discourse, indeed integral to the marking-out of the true artistic professional, was the precise hierarchisation of artistic production. At the point when art as a category was successfully making the bid for professional esteem, the genre of landscape was suddenly marginalised, declared low, mechanical and fit only for artisans. Here was demotion and de-skilling! It was in the attempts of landscapists to contest such a ranking system, to lay claim to status equal to the history painter's, that the rules governing the imitation of nature were expanded and systematised.

The major figure in the struggle for recognition was Pierre-Henri de Valenciennes. Born in 1750 and a member of the Academy since 1787, he participated in a variety of reforming initiatives after the Revolution.[140] His treatise *Elémens de perspective pratique à l'usage des artistes* (1800) was the most authoritative intervention into the debate about landscape's aesthetic calibre. The professionalising strategy was evident in two ways. First, in the absolute emphasis on the qualitative division between a rustic or imitative painter of nature and the idealising or imaginative painter.[141] The social distinctions were made brutally clear: the latter was the artist, the former only an artisan. To distance themselves from the connotations of subordinate labour, students were encouraged to master the science of composition as dictated by linear perspective *and* to soak up the aura of the classical past through travel and an intimate knowledge of the literary tradition.

The second central theme was the mapping-out of a detailed technology of perception. This was to demonstrate the specialist expertise of the landscapist. Though imitative or pastoral images were downgraded as an end in themselves, careful study in front of 'the motif' (that is, directly from nature) was not to be abandoned in favour of idealisation. Quite the reverse.

The true artist should have an encyclopaedic first-hand knowledge of all the components making up the natural world. The first injunction of J. B. Deperthes, one of Valenciennes's protégés, was 'to observe nature continually and to employ the greatest skill in seizing the extreme variety of its features'.[142]

The wide range of technical operations recommended by manuals to capture nature's extreme variety was symptomatic of the attempt to rival the academic training programme for figure painting. Paying close attention to linear perspective (the geometrical construction of space by means of outline drawing) was a primary requirement, but it was also essential to master the study of the variety of forms and motifs in various media: close-ups of rock shapes and the texture of foliage and bark in shaded chiaroscuro drawing, sunsets and misty panoramic horizons in quick, fluid oil studies.[143] Once learnt, the repertoire, like so many forms of knowledge, had to be continually practised and kept up to the mark – ever enriching the artist's copy-book of experience with an accumulation of motifs, groupings, effects. Perception, here, was structured in an immediate relation to representation. Hand and eye moved in tandem. Vision was splintered into a gamut of classified *operations*, codified according to different objects, functions and their relevant techniques. This was, it seems, a late product of the obsession in late eighteenth-century scientific thinking with systems of categorisation modelled on Linnaean natural history.[144]

2   From theory to practice

Such was the project initiated by Valenciennes, one that was highly successful in institutional terms. In 1816, the newly-renamed Académie des Beaux-Arts instituted a series of competitions leading to a *Grand Prix du paysage historique*.[145] To be awarded every four years, this was to confer status equivalent to the prestigious *Prix de Rome* for history painters. Winning the prize meant a spell of four years in Rome along with potential access to official honours and state commissions. It was with some justification that Deperthes could proclaim in 1817: 'Among the diverse genres which constitute the domain of painting, it is undoubtedly landscape that now takes first place immediately after history painting.'[146] Paradoxically, the radicalising professionalism of the early Empire was now being implemented as a form of Restoration cultural conservatism.

The organisation of the competitions put into effect the dual emphases of Valenciennes's injunctions. Preliminary stages were split into a painted compositional sketch and a tree competition. In 1821, the students were instructed in the first stage to represent a landscape of a noble type. You will indicate a Temple of Diana situated on the side of a hill, by the edge of a stream. In the distance a town will be visible, and in the foreground a group of young girls moving towards the Temple to offer the Goddess crowns and garlands of flowers. The scene is set at sunrise in the season of autumn.

And all this in the space of a single session! For the second stage:

The competitors will paint on a canvas of about three feet, a plane tree standing against a pure, blue sky, or one slightly ringed with clouds, beneath which a philosopher discourses with his disciples. The figures must not be more than four inches high and no more than six are to be included.[147]

It is all too easy to dismiss these as sterile academic exercises in idealisation, with their temples, garlands and discoursing philosophers. Yet equally intrinsic were the instructions concerning technical mastery over motifs, light effects and seasonal colours, which required comprehensive experience of study before nature. And note that the rubric for the second competition specified that it was the *tree* which should dominate and not the figures – history painters need not apply! Though the final, prize-winning stage was always explicitly mythical or religious in theme, throughout the early years directions to candidates also stipulated certain topographical details, regional climate, weather and time of day.[148]

However, the high-art pretensions of history landscape are hardly an important historical issue. Despite official recognition, the genre was not readily harnessed to the requirements of current state commissions. Where history paintings on themes like the death of Socrates or the coronation of Henri IV could still (just about!) be seen to embody generalised messages on political affiliations and moral behaviour, the death of Hyacinth under a horse-chestnut tree remained locked in the world of the literary élite. It lacked the accessible didacticism of facial expressions and bodily gestures, or the grandiose scale necessary for effective mural painting. Critical and commercial success, too, was limited and short-lived. Few prize-winners after the first, Achille-Etna Michallon, won more than passing acclaim; and, as we have seen, by the early 1830s history landscape was the regular butt of critical sarcasm. Where the project did have an immense impact, though, was on the aspirations of landscapists across the board, including painters of topographies and commercial illustrators. Furthermore, it furnished the pictorial common sense, the technology of imitation taken for granted as the stock-in-trade of picture-making.

Undoubtedly, the training and prize system fostered professional ambitions. During the first half of the century, rapidly-growing numbers of students embarked on a career as *landscapist*. Many enrolled in Parisian studios to prepare for official competitions, though few were to complete the arduous course. Typical was our acquaintance Rousseau, born in 1812.[149] After training briefly with Charles Rémond (the 1821 prize-winner), he moved to another studio in order to perfect his grasp of linear perspective. He only got as far with the official programme as entering and failing the compositional sketch stage in 1829, but that hardly mattered. Far more noteworthy was that Rousseau, along with so many of his peers, inhabited the sometimes contradictory structures laid down by the academic system. He took on board the soaring ambition to be a professional genius who could speak general truths through his art, while yet abandoning the sterile route of historical compositions for picturesque topographies in a variety of guises. As an unabashed polemicist for nature, his is a story we shall take up again shortly.

But the influence of landscape theory went far beyond moulding the aspirations of would-be prize-winners and professionals. Its major impact was on the codes of imitation governing all those 'non-art' or 'low art' commodities circulating in the city – so-called imitative landscape. Here is a good example of our broader cultural argument, a case in point where training and professional protocols crossed the divide between high and low forms. Twinning perception with the process of representation, the official model of imitation had worked to define what nature was through a series of pictorial types: the close-up, the panoramic view, the wide variety of weather and light effects. Yet these were also the codes underpinning the choices made by the producers of diorama scenes and picturesque prints and paintings. Remember, for instance, how the magic of the diorama relied so heavily on striking contrasts of light and weather or the picking-out of vivid motifs like a torrent of gushing water. It was through such devices that the sensation of 'popular' reality was put across. Or take the way the *voyages pittoresques* promoted authentic, first-hand impressions. Writers and illustrators were seen as investigative reporters, setting out from the epicentre, Paris, to map the unknown. The stress on authenticity dovetailed exactly with the academic practice of sending students off to study in the open air, to travel through different regions and become thoroughly acquainted with all kinds of flora and fauna. In both, the angle of vision shifted from close-up on cottage with mossy thatched roof to elegant vignette of cattle resting under a tree to glimpsed panorama or distant peaks and valleys.

In the many popular lithography manuals for amateurs churned out in the 1830s and 1840s, a simple technology of imitation was the message pressed home.[150] Start by practising the parts, they tell you: bark, leaves, the tilt of a roof. Then try a bit of perspective, some modelling, light effects and a few basic compositional groupings. Put them all together and – hey presto! – you have a perfect record of the countryside. As one instructor, J. P. Thénot, enthused:

Without aspiring to be an artist, you can have a talent capable of giving great satisfaction when you live or travel in the countryside; for in the sombre days of winter you will be enchanted to rediscover in your portfolio all those places which were so seductive in the summer season: a picturesque rock, a group of trees on the edge of a river, a cluster of rustic farm buildings in a delightful valley. If it is on the return from a voyage you will be proud to possess the copy of famous places once visited.[151]

Thénot did not harbour any illusions about teaching his public to be artistic. That was not the purpose of the enterprise. Rather, what he offered was a simple tool-box: tools of selection, focus, composition. Through applying these basic techniques of imitation, you, the public, could transport yourselves into the countryside and in the winter months preserve a bit of nature as a souvenir. Thus, though not determining how nature was read or consumed, the official version of imitation clearly circumscribed what bits and pieces got into even the most popular images in the first place.

3	Barbizon

From the late 1830s, landscapists became leading promoters of *natura naturans*. This is hardly surprising. After all, both as professionals and as *commerçants* they had a strong investment in the circulation of nature within the city, while the legacy of Valenciennes bestowed a self-conscious sense of their privileged access to imitation. As important, artists embodied all the wider expectations and imaginings of metropolitan culture. They were typical Parisians! To conclude, let us investigate one instance of the invasion of unsullied nature by the city. Which takes us to the painters' colony at Barbizon, on the edge of the forest of Fontainebleau.

The Fontainebleau forest, some fifty kilometres south-west of Paris, was something quite unique. Throughout the century it came to stand for everything the countryside was supposed to be about – visual delight, spiritual balm, the plunge into sensual refreshment. As an extended case study, Fontainebleau will loom large in our argument in the remainder of the book. Here, we are interested in the story of Barbizon as an example of Parisian colonisation. But later we shall turn to the culture of provincial resistance and negotiation which rode on the back of the tourist invasion.

In the early nineteenth century, Barbizon was a tiny hamlet of around three hundred inhabitants, mostly peasant landholders and field-workers.[152] The forest itself had received occasional visits from artists and excursionists since the eighteenth century, but it was only in the 1820s that such a practice became routine.[153] Here, the professionalisation of art training was a key factor. The demand for intensive study in front of a wide variety of natural motifs, found in the forest a suitable set of models – rocks, different species of tree, sandy wastes, and so on. Concurrently, commercial exploitation of prints and lithography brought cultural entrepreneurs in search of viable picturesque material. Both explained the presence of landscapists as early as 1821 at Chailly, a larger village than Barbizon and on the main coach route from Paris to Fontainebleau.[154] From the following year or thereabouts, one enterprising peasant, Ganne, opened up an inn at Barbizon to cater for the influx of art students.[155] At that point, villages round the forest began to operate as an extension of the Parisian studio or *atelier*. Instead of painting in the *atelier*, artists sought their models in the open air. Yet they brought with them all the baggage of rising urban professionals.[156] Some thirty years later, one new arrival, Georges Gassies, commented on the all-male camaraderie of the artistic population at play:

> This bottle [of wine from the picnic luncheon] rarely reappeared in the inn once it was empty, because, if several of the company found themselves in the same part of the forest, at work on neighbouring *motifs*, they got together for lunch, which was usually followed by exercises in dexterity, consisting of throwing their parasol staffs, javelin-style, at the unhappy bottle placed on a rock not too far off.[157]

This was the boisterous jollity not just of students but of urban pleasure-seekers delighting in an alfresco picnic of bread and wine along with competitive trials of strength and skill.

Towards the end of the 1840s, the village underwent a second transformation. If its first appropriation had been in terms of a professional and picturesque base, now the place itself was annexed as *natura naturans*, with the accompanying cluster of *maisons de campagne*. The sophisticated Diaz was probably the first metropolitan to rent a cottage, closely followed by Rousseau, who had already frequented Ganne's inn for long periods out of season.[158] Environmental definitions of healthy space were beginning to work their effects and to change the face of Barbizon. In 1849, the engraver Charles Jacque and painter Jean-François Millet arrived from Paris to set up permanent homes in the village.[159] The immediate cause of their flight from the capital was the cholera epidemic of that year, following hard on the 'disorders' of the revolution. Millet, for one, sought a healthy place in which to raise his numerous family cheaply. The peasant cottages they rented were small in scale and primitive in facilities, but by and large they functioned much like any other *maison de campagne*.

Again, Rousseau's move into Barbizon is illuminating. If the early 1830s had seen him travelling to typically picturesque provinces like the Auvergne and Normandy, by the end of the decade successive rejections from the Salon together with the impact of more literary or poetic conceptions of nature brought a sea change, noticeable in the choice of barren and lonely locations such as the Berry and the Fontainebleau forest out of season. He assumed the identity of the mysterious and oppressed outsider which had been cultivated by press notoriety, hiring a cottage in the village where he installed his *atelier* and his mistress.[160] Yet though his public persona became that of the bohemian primitive – a persona since written into popular biography *and* art history – Rousseau remained in every sense a metropolitan. Despite close identification with Barbizon, he always retained apartments and studios in Paris. It should come as no surprise to find that these were located in or close to the most modern areas of the city.[161] Here he could keep in touch with dealers, middlemen like his friend Alfred Sensier and the Hôtel Drouot auction house, of which he was a keen *habitué* when later he had money.[162]

By 1856, the local census register recorded six artists permanently resident at Barbizon and five at Chailly, while there were many more who habitually rented property or, like Diaz and Rousseau, had now bought their summer cottages.[163] Later still, in the 1860s, around twelve painters had establishments of one kind or another in the village, some of them swapping cottages from time to time.[164] Particularly enterprising was Jacque, who was also persuasive in getting others to settle in Barbizon. In fact, Jacque brought a dynamic business spirit to the village in more ways than one.[165] At different times he established a chicken farm for rare pedigree breeds and an innovative asparagus plantation on the sandy soil at the edge of the forest. The same talents were put to use in building and renting out houses to other artists and in the production and sale of his engravings of animals and peasants. As with so many areas outside Paris struck with an epidemic of *maisons de campagne*, the injunction to 'bury yourself in nature' was contradictory, resulting in a wholesale metamorphosis of the peasant village in terms of both its economy and its social relations. In that sense, the artistic invasion was paradigmatic of metropolitan colonisation more generally.

If the painters transformed what they perceived to be valuable in the village, they also set themselves up as staunch defenders of the primitivism of the forest against the depredations of commercial interests, whether tourist trippers or the planting of pines. Take, for the moment, the way men like Rousseau raged with all the weight of their professional standing against a forestry policy which cut against their own interests. Though state property, the upkeep and commercial exploitation of the forest was controlled for many years by the Boisd'hyver family, who were keen to increase profitability by planting pines in the barren and sandy wastes.[166] As early as 1839, this plan had been opposed by an article in *L'Artiste* which railed against the vulgar and uniform pine threatening Fontainebleau's vestiges of 'virgin forest'.[167] In the same way, in 1847 Thoré conducted an interview with Rousseau for *Le Constitutionnel*, organised around a long walk in the forest, where the tree-felling issue was to the fore.[168] The benefits of the natural primitivism of the forest were posed against the bankrupt values of commercial exploitation, in what was an explicitly political critique of the Louis-Philippe regime. Such articles stood at the beginning of a long campaign, spearheaded by artists, to get the social relevance of nature recognised by the state.[169]

Other associations between nature and the painters were forged in the third significant transformation of Barbizon, which began to take place around mid-century. This was the representation of the village and its inhabitants as part of an expanding tourist repertoire for the Parisian visitor. The artists themselves were now perceived to be integral to nature as well as visual guides to it. Trippers came to see *them* at work in the forest as much as the forest itself. The earliest guide books of the late 1830s had mentioned painters as regular visitors, using their presence to validate the picturesque attractions of the scenery.[170] (If artists were so keen to paint it, it must be worth a visit!) By the time of Bernard's train guide to Fontainebleau in 1853 (the line had been opened in 1849), the artistic colony had been turned into one of the leading sights of the tour. The itinerary carried a detailed description of the artists' daily routine and of Ganne's inn:

> Barbizon . . . does possess the inn of M. Ganne . . . Ganne's inn is a most hospitable place, where for the most modest rent of three francs a day, you can obtain: a bed that is somewhat less than luxurious, food in abundant quantities, and, so say the wits among the daubers [*rapins*], a select company. All the illustrators of modern landscape have inhabited the inn at Barbizon: the likes of Diaz, Rousseau, Flers, Daubigny, Cabat, Français, Corot, Troyon have all passed whole seasons there, and they have left behind the traces of their passage. The panels of the cupboards, the wall-divisions, are covered with studies and painted sketches which have turned this modest inn into a kind of museum, curious in more ways than one.[171]

The decorated panels – linking the primitivism of the village with artistic culture – also figured prominently in articles popularising Barbizon in the Parisian press of the early 1850s.[172] Such souvenirs of painters past and present were an obvious focus for tourist interest.

By the end of the next decade a second establishment, the Hôtel Siron, expanded along these lines of specialist interest, hosting annual exhibitions of Barbizon painters.[173] The local newspaper commented that the 'owners of neighbouring châteaux and foreigners of distinction passing through Fontainebleau hastened to pay a visit to this little village museum'.[174] In 1868, the exhibition even received a surprise visit from the Emperor and his retinue, keen to display their goodwill towards all that was dynamic and modern in artistic culture.[175] Ganne's inn had by this stage been taken over by his son-in-law. The latter used accumulated capital to acquire land nearer the edge of the forest (a more picturesque location) and to build the comfortable Hôtel des

Artistes, catering to writers and tourists rather than painters.[176] In such a guise the village – now well on the map of artistic tourism – became a familiar component of contemporary novels by Flaubert, Edmond and Jules de Goncourt and Hippolyte Taine.[177] As usual, the Parisian press and literary discourse advertised Barbizon through the exotica of primitive, uncivilised nature, focused now on the artists themselves. Though rooted in the rituals of the Parisian *atelier*, their bohemian habits – bawdy songs, heavy drinking and practical jokes – were pulled into continuity with the rough simplicity of peasant life. In their power to see, to imitate nature, they were, in a sense, metamorphosed into their own images. They became what they painted. In much of the literature since written on Barbizon, that transposition has been taken for granted.

Barbizon brings together many of the elements we have encountered in the putting together of nature for Parisians. Initially singled out for the picturesque and training possibilities of the forest, it quickly became the site for *maisons de campagne* and all the elements were soon in place for a burgeoning tourist industry. Artists were doubly accented as nature ideologues, though not as the real primitives celebrated by art history. Rather, their importance for us has been in twinning the production of picturesque commodities with the living-out of metropolitan priorities. Not only active in coining pictorial images of the countryside, as a dynamic fraction of urban professionals they were also leading lights in the colonisation of rural space. As with country-house advertisements, this was a colonisation that worked to affirm a sense of individuality. For *natura naturans* was not just about constructed images and representations; it also delineated structures of feeling and personal experience registered as much in the pleasures of pictorial viewing as in the sense of immersion in healthy sensations. We might be tempted, thinking more broadly, to see all this as part of an emerging code of ethics for personal life and individual morality. And we might speculate – once again – on the connections between city (and country) culture and forms of bourgeois class power. We shall have more to say on that shortly. What has by now become clear is that 'experience' was generated through highly-codified rituals and devices, and that the investment in nature had much to do with the materiality of space and those historically-defined ways of looking grounded in urban life.

[*facing*] Contrasting oil sketches by Théodore Rousseau:
Cottage in Normandy, 1831 (the close-up).
Panoramic landscape, 1834 (the distant view).

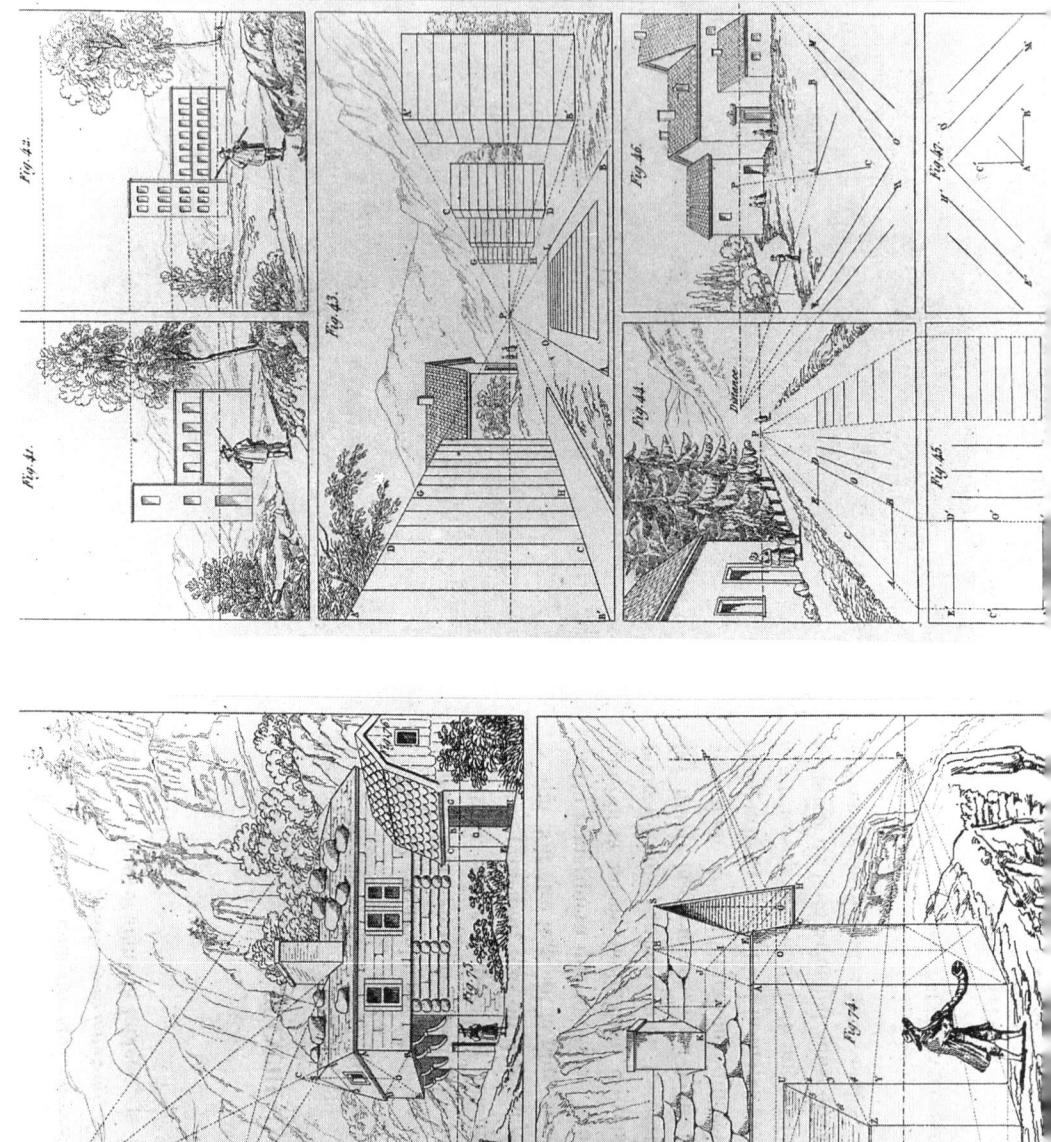

Fig. 42.

Fig. 41.

Fig. 43.

Fig. 44.

Fig. 46.

Fig. 47.

Fig. 45.

Fig. 73.

Fig. 74.

Fig. 75.

A la recherche d'une forêt en Champagne.

Looking for a forest in Champagne, by Daumier and Philippon,
from 'Les Artistes', in *Le Charivari*, 1848.

[*facing*] Instructions in landscape perspective from Thénot's *Cours complet de paysage*, 1834.

The Avenue of l'Isle Adam, by Théodore Rousseau, 1848/9.

[facing] Under the Beeches – the curé, by Théodore Rousseau, 1842/3.

Théodore Rousseau's intensely thought-out vision of nature draws on the focusing effects of popular ocular viewing machines as well as art perspective and strong contrasts of light and dark to propel the spectator into the landscape.

PART THREE

The subject in nature: experience and social power

[*facing*] Ganne's inn at Barbizon.

The problem of subjectivity

1   Introduction

It is no easy feat to square the circle between the delineation of a cultural form and the working-out of its power relations in concrete situations; or, to put it another way, to make the move from conditions and textual constructions to implementation and effects. So far, we have demonstrated that nature in early to mid-nineteenth-century France was framed by the contrasting dynamics of metropolitan culture, and more broadly, that it formed part of the cultural hegemony of metropolitanism. We know, too, that nature was set up as a sensual and rejuvenating experience which addressed the individual in individualising terms. But what did these sensations signify in a social context? What kinds of effect did they have? How did the dialogue with the countryside actively intervene in a broader field of social relationsips?

Unlike many ideological domains where we can point to materially-located institutions as the sites from which power is exercised, nature, it seems, hangs in a vacuum. Because it is to do with leisure time, because it is to do with personalised perceptions, it appears to lie outside or in the interstices of more obviously institutionalised power relations. In fact, the place where its effects can be most effectively measured is in the *personal experiences* and *identities* of participants. Subjective experience, it may be argued, forms its material locus of operation. The impact of *natura naturans*, then, depended on its capacity to carve out *personal* identities – albeit partial and fragmented ones – that extended and reinforced the *social* weight of metropolitanism. Teasing out the links between these types of identity and cultural power forms the substance of this section.

Unwrapping individual identity in an historically sensitive manner is in itself a problem. Much of the difficulty is conceptual. Perhaps with least to say to us are those individualising and biographical accounts which unselfconsciously place the individual at the centre of events. In tune with our overall approach, *experience* here is used to designate less the organic expression of inner feelings than a socially-produced category functioning through the construction of individuality. This, of course, draws on structuralist insights into the formation of 'the subject'. Yet a familiar criticism of structuralist analyses has been that they reduce subjects to passive bearers of ideology.[1] Where structuralism has offered a detailed account of subject formation – in the route via Freudian psychoanalysis – the solutions proposed tend towards the universalist and the transhistorical.[2] Neither a subjectless structuralism nor psychoanalytic mechanisms provide, in my view, the tools for thinking through a materialist approach to the subject *in history*.

It is the insights provided by Althusser and Foucault (both 'structuralists' in their different ways but both concerned with the mechanisms of subjectivity) which have been most illuminating for this account. Althusser, less for his general sketch of subject interpellation than for the potential elisions he invites between the subjects produced in and through specific ideological apparatuses and the more general formation of subjectivity.[3] That unresolved tension makes it possible to think the relation between mechanisms of interpellation and historically specific practices. It opens up a degree of relativism while holding on to some generalised strategies for theorising the subject. With Foucault, of course, the relativist stance is pushed much further; 'individuals' are nothing more or less than the subject positions produced in and through discourse.[4] In this methodology, the distinct cluster of individualities which concern us in relation to nature – experience, feeling, personal identity – would simply be read as positions within discourse.

It is within the rubric of this highly abstract debate, its problems as well as its strengths, that guidelines for our treatment of the subject in nature have emerged. To talk of subjectivity is not to appeal to some general or universal level of formation but to historically distinct modes of identity forged by ideologies and discourses. It is to see *subjectivities* as multiple and heterogeneous in form, in accordance with complex and changing historical conditions. But, at the same time, it is to argue for a certain mode of address, a certain interpellative mechanism that comes into play in the shaping of *personal* as of public indentities. Just that kind of culturally specific subjective dialogue can be located at the heart of *natura naturans*.

To demonstrate this hypothesis historically is rather a different matter. What follows is something of an experiment, moving from particular case studies to more general social and structural prescriptions about subjectivity and bourgeois class relations in mid-nineteenth-century France. By examining the private letters and memoirs of three individuals, I seek to distinguish the principles underpinning nature's mode of address and to pinpoint its forms of identity. Setting these experiences in a broader context, the aim is to construct synthetic 'biographies' which 'place' the dialogue with nature within the overall network of Parisian power relations. A word of caution, though, about how these experiments in biographical construction are to be read. Generally speaking, the biography carries deeply-ingrained codes and protocols which reinforce highly specific notions of coherent individual 'centredness'. Our trajectory is a different one, building a biographical picture of the *interrelationships* between private and public, personal identity and social relations.[5]

2   A sense of centred self

> I am writing to you here . . . in a delightful study between the bright day of the sunlit orchard with its green lawns and the deep greens of the great tree-lined alley which through the other window comes right up to me! No noise apart from the sounds of several insects and the birds singing . . . it is a luxuriant wilderness rich with fruit trees and vegetables. I am suspended, suckling at the breasts of nature.[6]

Listen to the historian Jules Michelet in 1852. After the *coup d'état* which deprived him of his Collège de France post, he had gone into voluntary exile, deep in the countryside near Nantes. The celebration of rustic retreats can be seen as a response to the intense trauma of recent political events. But we can profit from the accident of this occasion to probe some of the more general relations posed between nature and personal experience. For written into the familiar imagery of the countryside is a particular structure of feeling. And this sense of self is precipitated in and through the dialogue with nature: visual perceptions of sunlight on orchards, tactile sensations of the lush vegetation, the aural pleasures of bird-song and insects buzzing. The process has a double movement – the confirmation of self alongside the immersion of individuality in something larger. Visual mechanisms are central. On the one hand, nature is organised into tableaux: the atmospheric evocation of a bright sunlit day, the deep perspective of the green, tree-lined alley viewed through the open window. These are 'personal' – in spatial as much as emotional terms – to the onlooker. Michelet's correspondent is encouraged not just to share his vision but to stand in his spot, to occupy it in a perspectival relation. At the same time, the theme of personalised control is subsumed within or played off against the overall flux of sounds, smells and colours. Here, nature is envisaged as the all-encompassing environment – fertile, fecund, and indeed feminised. Michelet becomes the child suckling at the breast, vulnerable yet secure. These two ways of seeing and feeling work along distinct axes. Yet at their meeting-point they seem to be mutually reinforcing, producing a sense of *centred* subjectivity; the one through an ordering perspective, the other through being enveloped within the natural world. It is that double movement which is so characteristic of nature's mode of address.

Turn, for another example, to the correspondence of a man far less prolix than Michelet in his representations of the personal. Léon Faucher, economist and politician, quite clearly found the move into nature 'functional' for public life. Here are some extracts from letters he wrote (also in the early 1850s) while on recuperative holidays to the Pyrenees:

> Little work gets done on these trips. I drink the waters, I bathe, I walk in the mountains, my wife draws meadows and cascades, when she is not at her piano . . . I find nothing more charming than the sight of the snow on the peaks and the green at their feet. How all these grand aspects of nature refresh the imagination, when one has just passed a year contemplating the mud of Paris and the humiliations of politics . . . we are settled here in a very quiet cottage close to and in sight of the ocean. While you are choking in the autumn fog, we are enjoying the waves roaring loudly on the beach. Even at the end of summer the heat is with us, tempered morning and evening by the breeze. The horizon is vast, the sky brilliant and the sea blue. You never get tired of contemplating these great spectacles from the top of rocks beaten by the waves and covered with foam . . . [7]

At first sight, everything about Faucher's 'nature' – from the small spa at Eaux-Bonnes in the foothills of the Pyrenees to the Atlantic seascape near Biarritz – can be read as part of a quite traditional cultural pattern. The spa visit, as an established extension of upper-class leisure, had a rather different rationale from other metropolitan trips into the country; it was more a ritualised alternative to salon and estate than a solitary dialogue with nature. Though no aristocrat himself, our economist's excursions were functionally motivated. He came quite simply to cosset a delicate health, nervous as well as physical, that was badly buffeted by the rough-and-tumble of Parisian politics in the turbulent years of the Second Republic. Yet written into his rhetoric is a structure of feeling remarkably akin to Michelet's. Faucher's evocation of Eaux-Bonnes shows little awareness of or interest in the social dimensions of the spa town itself. For him, nature is essentially a private and indeed *domestic* affair, a representation of mutual conjugal bliss organised around a very 'modern' (for France) notion of complementarity. But the responses of wife and husband are clearly differentiated. Paradoxically, in nature it is she who is defined as *active* – sketching or playing the piano, herself part of the concert of his natural sensations – while he does nothing but bathe and walk, look and *be*. As with Michelet's emotive imagery of suckling at nature's breast, the consumption of nature works with gendered assumptions and definitions about what was to be done in the countryside and who was to perform it.

Most obviously, though, what comes across again and again from the letters is Faucher's profound sense of relief at escape from the mud as well as the anxieties and pressures of Paris, twinned with the simple refreshment gained from the generalised state of being – a suspension 'out of action'. This is the familiar repertoire of urban experience. Yet the process of being in nature is simultaneously projected in terms of the codes and pleasures of consumption carried through visual panoramas: the admiration of snowy mountain peaks, the contemplation of waves beating on the rocks as the sun sets over the sea. Though the images he draws on to dramatise his experience are a general stock-in-trade of the sublime, these were *his* pictures, conjured up personally for and by him. The viewing perspective is used to mark out a distinct sense of self. Rejuvenation in nature depends as much on the process of viewing – with its roots in urban consumption – as on the generalised passivity of doing nothing.

For the third account we will cheat a bit, selecting from a work published slightly later, Jules Levallois's *L'Année d'un ermite* (1870).[8] As an overtly autobiographical 'confession' of personal experience by an avowed polemicist for nature, this text represents a self-conscious attempt to theorise the ideology from the inside:

> As a young man [in the early 1850s] I lived right at the centre [of Paris] in a populous commercial and industrial area . . . [trips beyond the *barrière*,] which for most people were only an insignificant distraction and a health precaution, became for me an indispensable habit . . . a constitutive element of my life.[9]

The valley of Bressuire and the forest of Meudon are his 'great conquests' and 'earthly paradises', while the forest of Fontainebleau seems like the end of the world. Moving physically into nature is correlated with a series of stages that mark a psychological change of register. At first it takes time to become orientated; it is difficult to shed daily preoccupations and troubles. Then:

> in the midst of the country I heard nothing other than the buzzing of insects and the singing of birds . . . Never, in the lap of nature, have I felt my being diminish, weaken or dissolve. Rather, she has always, if I may put it thus, made me more present to myself . . . I have never walked through trees and under sky without returning all the more a man . . . for the social milieu diminishes and consumes, the natural milieu nourishes man and brings him back to life.[10]

For Levallois, this experience is no minor distraction, no simple leisure activity or investment in preventive medicine. It is a vital component in the way he negotiates social reality. And what he grasps is that the sense of self forged within nature both differs from *and* complements other, more obviously social and urban identities. He becomes, as it were, a different person in the countryside, but one who reinforces and reinvigorates his capacity for metropolitan living. Again, the process incorporates visual mechanisms, whereby his sense of a universal humanity is reflected back from the regard on nature. Such imagery formed the cultural corollary of Levallois's brand of liberal republicanism, with its ethical, even idealist, stress on human values.[11] Finally, given the linguistic ambiguities both of *la nature* and *l'homme* (humanity/*man*kind), the encounter seems inevitably underwritten by the forms of gender difference and complementarity that have consistently recurred in our other examples.

All three commentaries deal with experiences of the early 1850s, by which time *natura naturans* had a significant place in the ideology of metropolitanism. Clearly, these texts pick up on and rework themes and issues running through our account of the formation of nature. The same structure of feeling could be teased out by turning to other participants in the narrative, whether Thoré or Simon, Lemer or Meynadier. Yet, in the light of all that, perhaps the conclusions seem terribly obvious. Nature would appear to have endowed these men with a sense of personal strength and individuality. (We hardly needed detailed case studies, you may say, to tell us that!) My point, though, is a different one. It is that we are not dealing conceptually with the kind of monolithic individualism produced and celebrated by the humanist tradition as the gradual emergence of a self-conscious ego, but rather with materially-located personas, shaped by the historical conditions in play. In that sense, nature's was *one* subjectivity in an expanding and competitive field. At its kernel was the experience of a centred self. But that centring was projected by and through two perceptual mechanisms which carried quite distinct effects. If on the one hand the subject was subsumed in the organic wholeness of nature, on the other it was distanced, the eye behind the viewing aperture, pictorially ordering the visual field into a sequence of tableaux.

There is a related point that the subject in nature was dependent less on the actuality of the 'visit' to the countryside than on activating that particular structure of experience. The subject was forged in and through a dialogue that was *visually* organised. Thus its effects could be realised in an urban garden like the Luxembourg, before a diorama spectacular on the boulevard, or in the enjoyment of prints and pictures in Susse and Giroux. This was where a cultural form like landscape painting took on a potent social function quite removed from its artistic status. The complex perspectival codes of a landscapist such as Théodore Rousseau testify to this. In many ways the pictures seem simultaneously to propel the viewer into deep space *and* to hold them back on the edge of the perspectival frame.[12] They oscillate between a serious-minded 'realism' and a mode of consumption as tableaux or deluxe artifice. Take the *Allée de l'Isle-Adam*, an exhibition piece which heralded his return to the Salon in 1849.[13] Note how the exaggerated shadows of the foreground act as a barrier which frames and pictorialises the image. Yet at the same time the eye is gradually enticed inwards, encouraged to explore the hazy sunlit path by bright-colour touches that indicate the tawny colouring of a cow or the cap of a peasant girl. Pictures like this were polemics for nature in visual terms. For those initiates who could read the codes, they exploited perceptual mechanisms that made nature truly 'come alive' as a subjective experience.

3	Three biographies

So far, we have been concerned to identify the ideological mechanisms at work in nature through the isolation and analysis of certain texts. Now we turn to the question of how these mechanisms articulate with a wider field of social relations. If the materiality of nature was played out at the site of the subject, in the structuring of a private persona, then its social effects can be gauged only by locating such personas in the historically-produced 'biographies', public as well as private, of these men.

It is no surprise to find that all three – Michelet, Faucher and Levallois – were Parisians, by adoption if not by birth. Moreover, all came from outside the established Orleanist power bloc. Michelet, the only native Parisian, derived from an artisanal background. Born in 1798, son of an impoverished printer-publisher closed down by Napoleonic censorship, he built his successful career as historian and writer on a shrewd mix of establishment patronage, personal merit and secular politics.[14] From prize-winning pupil at the Collège Charlemagne to orthodox teaching posts and royal patronage, by the mid-1830s he held positions both at the Archives Nationales and the Sorbonne. The apogee of his career was reached in the 1840s, with courses on history and morality at the Collège de France that won notoriety for their flamboyant attacks on Jesuits and on priests in general. These lectures were elaborate performances played out in front of crowds of partisan students along with representatives from salon society.[15] They were as much part of the metropolitan parade as the soirées, spectacles and 'bohemian' circles he himself frequented.[16]

Neither Faucher nor Levallois was born in Paris, but their identification with the city was equally intense. The economist Léon Faucher, born in 1803, originally came from Limoges and a highly insecure bourgeois background.[17] Moving from one finance-house post to another, the Father finally abandoned his family, leaving them to survive on his wife's embroidery and needlework. Like Michelet, this *déclassé* provincial was a self-made professional who used the educational and publishing facilities of Paris to propel his career from academic and journalist (he edited several papers in the 1830s and 1840s) to director of a railway company and leading politician. Faucher carried the metropolitan's confidence in his own abilities, spectacularly represented after the 1848 revolution when this cautious liberal became Minister of the Interior and then Prime Minister, until opposition to Napoleon effectively brought his political career to an end.[18]

The critic and social commentator Jules Levallois belonged to the next generation. Born in 1829 in Rouen, his childhood, unlike Faucher's was rooted in the comfortable security of the professional middle classes.[19] A leading barrister in the town, his father was a member of a 'distinguished and cultivated circle', though one that deliberately turned its back on Paris.[20] As Levallois recalled, the only metropolitan newspaper allowed in the house was the comic *Charivari*. All political discussion was banished. To the well-to-do Rouennais of the 1830s and 1840s, 'parliamentary squabbles and Parisian riots seemed equally trivial', especially when compared with their enduring memories of the First Empire.[21] It was this kind of old-established professio-nalism combined with a dense provincial culture which was highly resistant to the centripetal pull of the capital. In personal terms, what propelled Levallois beyond this tight environment was the early death of his father, boarding-school, and his own intellectual aspirations.

Arriving in the capital in 1850, Levallois had, as it were, to begin again in class and cultural terms. A straitened apprenticeship on the edges of literary bohemia eventually stood him in good stead, opening the way to establish-ment circles as Sainte-Beuve's secretary and then collaboration on leading intellectual journals.[22] For Levallois, the early years in Paris must have contrasted unfavourably with the security of his provincial upbringing. Yet, unlike Normandy compatriots such as Barbey d'Aurévilly or Eugène Nöel, he never aligned himself with regionalism and its traditions. When in 1871 he returned briefly to Rouen, he contrasted the locals' opposition to the recent Franco-Prussian war with the attitude of 'us Parisians'.[23]

The careers of these three men indicate different social routes and differing degrees of success, but a number of common themes emerge. All of them belonged to the professions, or rather professionalising cadres. Further, they represented 'new blood'. Like the aggressive de Girardin, they gained entry to the power bloc, moving between reliance on old-fashioned vertical patronage and the more modern assertion of merit through education and self-promotion. Crucial to their social formation was the identification with Paris and Parisian culture, the mobilisation of chains of connections specific to the urban milieu (press, salons, boulevard society) *and* the playing the part of the Parisian initiate – dynamic, modern, but also neurasthenic and anxious.

Indeed, anxiety punctuated their private responses to the metropolis, conveyed in that urban language now familiar to us – environmentalism.

Writing to his wife from a railway inspection at Metz in the north-east of France in 1847, Faucher lamented:

> Decidely the year is cursed. Society is disintegrating like a rusty machine. The time has come to find it something great to do. Assassinations, suicides, we are never free from dismal stories; as for me who never reads the paper, I am terrified every time one falls into my hands.[24]

A society of assassinations and suicides, the disintegration of the social fabric; this imagery explicitly echoed the rhetoric of contemporary gossip columns – more evidence for the shaping of urban identity through popular journalism and reportage. Society, here, really signified the capital; and Faucher, despite his disclaimer about never reading the papers, was speaking from a perspective internal to Paris. With the troubled responsibilities of Second Republic government, his anxieties became even more acute. 'You will find us very sickly', he moaned to his English friend Henry Reeve in 1850: 'Mistrust, fear, lack of unity and blindness are wearing us down'.[25] The political infighting between competing fractions of the bourgeoisie was metamorphosed into the vocabulary of disease and condensed with his own state of health. At the same time, it is worth noting the assertive tone of the statement. This was very much the tone of a man who felt himself to be central to the political process and who believed he had the right to make general pronouncements on the progress of modern society.

The dual themes of health and the environment were a preoccupation with Michelet, too. His private journals were peppered with the usual range of comments on how best to avoid cholera or the inclement state of the weather.[26] But for the historian these perceptions seemed to feed a more general sense of unease about his personal identity. On Good Friday, 1843, he pondered the gap opened up between public and private:

> Bizarre contrast: a crowd at my courses and for my books (sales are honest and firm and show no signs of slipping), and back home solitude . . . The fact is that, on my own, I am no longer the man of my courses. When teaching I believe in the subject I am treating. Back here, the natural effect of great emotions, of moral fatigue, I am feeble and empty . . . [27]

It was not just that Michelet felt drained by the exertions of lecturing and publishing. There was more to his complaint than that. In fact, here was an implicit awareness of nascent divisions between public and private. The historian acknowledged that at home he was no longer the man of his classes. Yet with what to replace it? As an avowed secularist, he could not turn to prayers and confession – the standby of so many bourgeois women in the period. In other words, Michelet was casting around for the wherewithal to stock personal life. One language was to be the 'separate spheres' dualism which insisted on women's affective and complementary role to men. But in the early 1840s, ideologies of domesticity had yet to exert a dominant hold over definitions of the private. They were part of a gamut of discourses – among them nature – currently marking out the personal and the subjective.

The crux of the matter is that for these dynamic, self-made cultural producers and professionals, success in the city was accompanied by a feeling of unease and anxiety which was equally germane to urban living. It was within this framework that nature's clearly-centred ego, a subjectivity which reinforced our metropolitans' experience of control while easing their anxiety in the secure immersion in sensation, made so much sense. For all three, trips to the countryside were a regular occurrence. At the most traumatic moment of his career, from the late 1840s, Faucher not only made annual pilgrimages to the Pyrenees spa Eaux-Bonnes, but also took quick day trips beyond the walls of Paris 'to refresh my head in the countryside'.[28] Michelet, a frequent *habitué* of the Luxembourg garden in the 1830s when he lived on the left bank, made several momentous excursions to the Fontainebleau forest after 1841. On the first occasion, he was accompanied by his friend Mme Dumesnil and their respective children. Already sickening, and soon to die, she represented the kind of intellectual and emotional sympathy he had never shared with his first wife.[29] It was an intense and moving time. His journal recorded walks to popular tourist spots and look-out points. (These were almost certainly structured by the newly-expanded local tourist industry.)[30] Such occasions were rich with intimacy and meditation. But Michelet's commentary was revealing, revolving primarily around his own ego: 'My nerves, badly frayed by the visit to the château, calmed down in this freshness. Beeches mingled with Scandinavian pine dipped away towards the château with a charming lightness . . . .'[31] Mme Dumesnil, like the views of the forest, figured as the setting and complement to his own subjective experience.

As for Levallois, the hard grind of survival in the Paris of the early 1850s was sustained by summer jaunts to the leafy suburbs of Meudon, Fontenay-aux-Roses and Chatenay, where a modest picnic shared between friends would be supplemented by readings and recitations.[32] By the next decade he had settled at Sèvres, under the lea of the forest of Saint-Cloud. In effect, he was now a 'commuter' to Paris whose *maison de campagne* had become his permanent residence. The house gained a reputation among colleagues for the amusements the critic organised, a repertoire of singsongs, charades and practical jokes.[33] The 'house in the country' functioned as a place where sophisticated littérateurs, often of opposed political and cultural views, could mingle and relax, filling their leisure time with undemanding pleasures. What was most strongly projected for these male guests was the connection between nature and innocence; a temporary release from competition, career structures and urban power-mongering.

Natura naturans, then, was not just framed by metropolitan conditions;

it helped give shape and body to the *living out* of metropolitanism. This focused on the production of a private ego, an internalised sense of self that fed off and into modern urban life. Distanced from the individualities carved out on the streets of Paris, this persona was both active and passive – active in its pictorial ordering of nature, passive in the immersion in sensation. That double construction was both its strength and its limitation, the source of its rejuvenating force but also of its temporary and transient value. While clarifying and strengthening the sense of personal self, this was not a subject position that was ultimately to lead anywhere. For the Parisian, the trip to the country always presupposed a *return* to urban living. In a poignant novella of 1845, *La Recherche de la liberté*, Thoré came to the same conclusion.[34] His anti-hero, wrecked by Parisian decadence, sought a new start in the country, an innocent peasant girl his only companion. But nature was not, could not be, enough: and to push the message home, despair turned ultimately to suicide.

The nature of the bourgeoisie

1   Class relations

What broader insights into bourgeois class-cultural relations do these examples throw up? Here, we come to the nub of our argument about the articulation between nature and social power. First, at the risk of repetition, there was no simple tie-up between metropolitanism and the bourgeoisie defined in economic terms. The city–country couplet was ideologically played out in such a way as to preclude our reading it in terms of a problematic of 'class belonging'. Empirically speaking, it would seem as if the structure of address of metropolitan nature was most directly relevant to those cadres of new professionals and self-made entrepreneurs at the heart of the cultural promotion of Paris. But again we need to tread carefully. The nature of the evidence is itself part of the problem. Few accounts of the period, whether letters, memoirs or journals, have much to say about nature and the private. Memoirs of politicians and industrialists concentrated almost entirely on the worlds of work and politics, major events and public affairs.[35] By comparison, the new-enfranchised professional cadres spoke eloquently about leisure, the countryside and private life.

So far, so good. But how does the prominence of professionals in this domain relate to the class structures of Orleanist society? Gramscian concepts of the power bloc and hegemony can perhaps move the analysis further than a strictly discursive or ideological approach. Within that framework, professionals can be cast as one fraction in a wider alliance of forces within mid-nineteenth-century France. Intellectually, this cadre carried more weight than either its puny economic power or its political under-representation would warrant. Intellectually, in that they were instrumental in forging symbolic scripts about the progress of modern society within which metropolitan nature was an important component. However, for any ideological configuration to become hegemonic, it needs to move beyond its own orbit; it needs to win consent from other fractions and interest groups both within the power bloc and ultimately beyond it. This, metropolitan nature most certainly did. It put together a practical 'philosophy' of private life and behaviour which caught the imagination of many different social constituencies.

Of course, in class terms *natura naturans* was not successful in isolation. It competed with and cut against other experiences of city and country. We can demonstrate the specificity of metropolitanism by measuring its distance from conflicting class-cultural codes. Take the immigrant labour force constantly inflating the population of the capital, which often retained strong links with its place of origin. This was particularly true of the building workers who would return to their native Massif Central in the winter. The mason Martin Nadaud clung proudly to his Limousin identity when working in the metropolis in the 1830s and 1840s, while on his annual two-month visits home he reassumed a peasant identity and culture.[36] The traditional cultural infrastructure was largely preserved at home by the women (as wives, sisters, mothers) who cultivated the smallholdings and who exerted control over key kinship rituals like weddings.[37] Paradoxically, on their return the men were both admired and derided as 'Parisians'. This, then, was not quite the traditional peasant society that historians have liked to contrast with 'modernisation'.[38] For such itinerant labourers and their families, Paris really did exist as the locus of work, gifts, expectations and fabulous tales. Nonetheless, city and country belonged to separate planes; economically and culturally, they involved different and in many ways mutually incompatible worlds. Moving across from one to another signalled a dislocation of identity rather than the metropolitan's concentration of force. Interestingly, the self-educated Nadaud began to break the pattern when he brought his wife and children to Paris for good at the end of the 1840s.

At the other end of the spectrum were the residual ideologies of the traditional landed aristocracy, a class which could claim to belong as much to the land as the city.[39] Following a ritualised calendar, they alternated between winter and spring seasons in the capital and summer and autumn on their landed estates. Politics and business alternated with the hunting season and rural festivals. Certainly, the city was perceived to have its uses, at the right time and place. Through the system of salons, formal politics and personal influence, it cemented political interests and the management of family fortunes and dynastic alliances. Yet by many aristocrats, especially those on the right, Paris was also viewed with deep suspicion as a corrosive threat to the order of the landed estate and, by extension, of society. The legitimist Comte de Falloux warmly evoked one of his neighbours as a 'country gentleman' passionately attached to his native Anjou for whom the term 'Parisian' was equivalent to an insult.[40] Neither he nor his sons had ever visited the place, and their only point of contact was the newspapers (for reports on king and court). De Falloux himself stressed his provincial formation and declared his commitment to spending part of the year in Anjou in order to refresh his roots. For men like this, encroaching emblems of the city – newspapers, cafés, the secular schoolteacher – were deeply disturbing, disrupting established patterns of deference and encouraging meritocratic self-improvement.[41] The damaging corollary was that humble folk would be fired with ambitions above their station and lured into the destructive whirlpool of the metropolis. As one aristocratic moralist put it, speaking of her own stories: 'if they keep some of those unfortunates who every year come to suffer and die in Paris to the honest toil of the fields, the author will praise God for it'.[42]

The identification of legitimist gentry with the land was intensified by the political settlement under Louis-Philippe, when many eschewed politics at the central level in disgust at the new regime. The countryside represented their blood, their heritage. But they were by no means all die-hard traditionalists. Some now cultivated a modern approach to productive agriculture or, exploiting the raw materials on their land, became dynamic and paternalistic industrialists.[43] And this entrenched position as regional *notables* was equally grounded in their dominance of the local and departmental councils, supposedly anodyne institutions which in fact allowed for the accretion of resilient power bases.[44]

Obviously, it is a massive over-simplification to elide the class interests of the landed aristocracy with legitimism pure and simple. There was a broad spectrum of positions, with significant fractions adhering willingly to the constitutional monarchy. Take 'moderates' like Victor, Duc de Broglie and Charles, Comte de Rémusat, who were leading political figures and who, according to their memoirs, participated fully in the social life of the modern city.[45] But the point is that, whatever these negotiations, the underlying cultural approach of aristocrats was profoundly different from that of the metropolitan. After all, they began their analysis with the *land*, not the city. And nature, for them, signified the *social* rather than the personal – family, ancestry, the social relations of retainers and field-workers. These pre-existent meanings and values were clearly at odds with the individualising perspective of metropolitan tourism. Even as 'progressive' a Parisian as the writer George Sand, polemical proponent of romantic literature, was caught oscillating between these responses. An aristocrat in her own right, when on her estate at Nohant she tended to revert to the role of grand *châtelaine*.[46] In this context, the pull of older power structures outweighed the appeal of *natura naturans*. Though, as we shall see later, her gender also had something to do with the case.

The picture becomes more complex when we turn to the other major social constituency confronted by *natura naturans*. This was the provincial bourgeoisie – both the established commercial and professional sectors and the growing ranks of bankers and industrialists. The latter were undoubtedly to be crucial for the take-off of industrial capitalism in France; but in cultural terms, well-to-do provincials were badly squeezed throughout the 1830s and 1840s.[47] They were caught between dominant representations of Paris as the centre of the world – to which they looked with envious eyes – and an identification with regional traditions, which placed them in a subordinate relation to the custodians of that culture, the aristocracy.[48] Given this scenario, responses varied widely.

On the one hand, there were those like Faucher and Levallois who were drawn into the magnetic aura of the capital and became thoroughgoing Parisians, sloughing off any remnants of a provincial past and life-style. Paris, after all, was a city of immigrants at every social level, not just among the peasant and working classes.[49] The personal reminiscences of the newspaper editor Henri de Villemessant were typical in insisting on the absolute break between his provincial youth and his 'real' career in the capital.[50] The narrative of the former was played for laughs, sketching a series of Daumier-like caricatures such as his grandmother with her eccentric, old-fashioned costume and bizarre habits.[51]

Others who settled in the city were not always so quick to jettison earlier identities. The republican astronomer François Arago arrived in Paris as a student in 1803.[52] As a deputy from the early 1830s, he always represented his native Pyrenees and was treated by his partisans as a local hero.[53] Yet he was also president of the municipal council in Paris for many years, and identified strongly with the interests of urban artisans. A similarly complex pattern was played out by the wine merchant and energetic town councillor Lanquetin.[54] After two decades of municipal involvement in Paris, he retired in 1857 to an estate near Mantes, where he took up agriculture. Later still, he returned to his native town of Pontarlier in the Jura, rapidly rising to an important position on the regional council. With both these men, what is at issue is the way they shifted across distinct and sometimes contradictory cultural personas at different moments and in different contexts, a process which in personal terms involved some adroit manoeuvring.

In contrast, certain sections of the provincial bourgeoisie remained profoundly mistrustful of Paris and resistant to urban influence. Some big industrial families, like the Dollfus-Mieg dynasty at Mulhouse, tended to keep separate from the capital, intermarrying with other local families who shared similar industrial interests and dominating the political and social life of their town.[55] They were seconded by regional intellectuals – notaries, lawyers, academics and journalists – who were often obsessively proud of their local traditions and inheritance.[56] The writer Charles Nodier maintained a fierce loyalty to the Franche-Comté, even though he lived and worked in the capital.[57] He detested Paris and centralisation, adopting a militant right-wing critique. Writing to a friend in 1831:

> In my state as conquered Frenchman, I have served the Restoration, as long as I saw in it a double guarantee against two detestable forms of slavery, that of Parisian democracy and that of the Empire, but centralisation has detached me from it . . . I do not wish for a Paris republic, because I know well what it will be; the tyranny of a handful of rogues enthroned on a scaffold . . . my devotion is for the Franche-Comté and for Besançon, and it will be completely exclusive.[58]

This defiant assertion of provincial autonomy cast Paris – republican and centralist – as the epitome of tyranny, while the topography of the Franche-Comté was celebrated as the 'true' heart of France: *ma patrie*. For such resistant provincials the countryside meant many things, but rarely an individualised experience of personal contemplation. For the factory owner it supplied a stream of cheap, available labour; for the antiquarian, the evidence of historical tradition. For the religious, nature signified God's pervasive mark; and for town-dwellers generally it meant those ritualised occasions of small-town social life – the Sunday-afternoon promenade or carriage drive.[59]

This schematic map of social responses to city and country – some of them rooted in class, others in the cultural traditions of the provinces – defines the field against which metropolitan nature had to operate. In many cases, these varied responses co-existed in Paris itself and even in the same individual. When the successful Auvergnat wood merchant of the Rue Saint-Denis invested his hard-earned savings in a rustic cottage at Belleville, we might speculate on the mix of cultural intentions at work – the functional prescriptions of health jostling against shrewd land speculation, the urban emphasis on leisure and contemplation undercut by echoes of an older peasant routine.

Some of these complexities and ambiguities come into focus when we turn to one archival source which clearly registers quantitatively the impact of nature. Working through the archives of notaries' files, property advertisements, wills, and so on, it is not always possible to prove the predominance of an individualising ideology. What does come through is the social breadth of involvement in the countryside, but also the overlap, the meshing together of distinctive class-cultural codes. Let us look at the evidence. One owner of an impressive country estate was the lawyer J. B. N. Parquin, who died in 1839.[60] Fifteen years before, he had purchased an historic mansion – Le Vivier-des-Ruines – at the village of Guignes in Seine-et-Marne, which he lovingly restored. Himself a local man, he had gone to Paris to pursue a successful legal career, rising to become head of the bar for two consecutive years.[61] During the 1820s and 1830s he lived close by the Louvre, just south of the dynamic new quarters. The acquisition of Le Vivier in 1824 renewed his association with his region, but from the position of metropolitan power and influence. We might also speculate that the geographical location of the residence itself indicated an investment in a rural retreat. The Seine-et-Marne was rapidly becoming a classic terrain for *maisons de campagne*. Thus, Parquin's was a triumphant return, reflected too in his membership of the *conseil général*. However, the property represented more than status or a *maison de campagne*; he took an antiquarian delight in the rich history impregnated in the building. This 'he gave over to our national history and archaeology' and he was more than happy to entertain collectors and scholars who came to admire his work.[62] After his death, the estate was sold to another member of the departmental council for the considerable sum of 300,000 francs – an indication of its extent and importance.

An equally impressive success story – this time in business – was symbolised by the estate and *maison de campagne* at Chartrettes. Again in the placid countryside of the Seine-et-Marne, this belonged to Pierre-Robert Roussel until his death in 1840.[63] The grounds were extensive, encompassing outbuildings, gardens with fishponds, vineyards, a lodge with its own garden, and agricultural land. The house, on the other hand, was relatively modest. Roussel was one of three brothers from Rouen who had jointly established a thriving cloth business in Paris's Rue Saint-Honoré from 1801.[64] As with Parquin, the location of this Parisian address is indicative that his economic success predated the urban transformations of the 1820s. He had already bought his country domain at Chartrettes by the time of his marriage in 1819, and it was to become his primary address by 1823.[65] Outliving his wife and business associates, he seems to have passed the last ten years of his life in complete retirement, although, significantly, he held on to some Parisian property, living off the revenues. Roussel having left no children, his inheritance was claimed and fought over by an extensive network of relatives from his wider family. Twenty-eight claimants were listed, many of whom had been far less successful economically than the three brothers who went to Paris.[66] In fact, the majority of the family had remained in and around Rouen. Some of them were *propriétaires*, and presumably prosperous. The majority were employed in Rouen's traditional cloth industry, one or two as merchants or manufacturers, but two branches of the family had not advanced beyond the level of skilled manufacturing labour – weavers, dyers, cloth-shearers and needlewomen. Between these artisan/proletarian families, locked into the industrial life of Rouen, and Pierre-Robert Roussel, whose commercial career took him first to success in Paris and then to civilised retirement on an estate overlooking the Seine, the cultural and class distance was immense.

Roussel and Parquin were early examples of the kind of wealth, dynamism and expertise that constituted a key input into metropolitanism. And for both, the house in nature seems to have been a key sign of personal success. The cloth merchant's decision to steer well clear of the Rouen region, where his relations – burghers some, but virtual proletarians others – were much in evidence, was no accident. Instead, his choice was of an estate not too far from Paris, of a dwelling that was modest rather than sumptuous, and of grounds that twinned productivity with decorativeness. In short, here was a refusal of the provinces together with a careful negotiation of land ownership to construct a very personal retreat. Parquin, on the other hand, with the acquisition of an historic château and his move on to the local *conseil général*, was working for a position as established landowner and *notable*. Even his antiquarianism might suggest identification with an aristocratic, establishment past. In fact, though, the way he approached traditionalism resonated with the enthusiasm of the city man. Carefully renovating the château, discussing the finer points of French history – these were the relaxing pastimes that filled the leisure hours of our eminent lawyer. In this respect, it is relevant that Parquin was far more concerned with the picturesque appearance of his property than with exploiting the possibilities of the industrial clay also found on his land.[67]

Not all rural retreats changed hands at anything like 300,000 francs. Staying in the same region, let us explore the cultural resonance of other more modest transactions. In November 1847, the twice-widowed Mme Guiney sold her property at the village of Recluses in the Seine-et-Marne to two Parisian merchant businessmen.[68] The main building consisted of a comfortable but unimposing block with four rooms on the ground floor and an attic floor above, but there were outhouses too, and grounds that took in vineyards and woodland. Mme Guiney had it from her first husband, who, along with his sister, inherited the estate from his father, Antoine Mielle, a Parisian café owner. He had acquired it back in 1819 (paying by instalments) from Dr Joseph Delachenil, also a Parisian. In the space of under thirty years, the same property passed through the hands of three typical representatives of the city – the professional, the service entrepreneur and the commercial businessman. What of the new owners? Given that the old widow retained the right during her lifetime to walk in the garden and store wine in the cellars, and given that the house itself was hardly generous enough to cater for two establishments, then the obvious inference is that this was to be an occasional home or rustic retreat. Sited as it was in the Seine-et-Marne, it certainly fulfilled all the requirements – rest, refreshment, pictorial views – of a *maison de campagne*.

Finally, from the records of the same Fontainebleau notary comes an even more modest story.[69] In August 1847, Charles Lecocq and his wife, of Changy near Fontainebleau, sold a house to the Parisians Charles Teissier and his wife for 4,000 francs. Lecocq had put up the building himself, on ground exchanged for land inherited from his father. It consisted of three rooms on the ground floor and one room above, a cellar, outhouses (wood store and stable), garden and well. This would seem to have been a dwelling purpose-built by a local for the seasonal visitor. It contained sufficient attributes of comfort and ease – like the stable and wine-cellar – to cater for civilised requirements, yet was hardly large enough or imposing enough to make a permanent home. The position right at the edge of the Fontainebleau forest marked the beginning of the urban colonisation of that wilder, more 'primitive' nature. As important, it was situated close by the railway station on the Paris–Lyon line and was thus ideal for easy access to Paris. In the capital, the Teissiers lived in the Rue de Grenelle Saint-Honoré, in the traditional commercial centre, where he was a manufacturer of embroidery. They were certainly not wealthy; the 4,000 francs was paid off in instalments over a four-year period.

The most striking conclusion to emerge from these narratives is the breadth of urban class fractions which invested in some form of rural property and experience. What is far less easy to gauge, given the dearth of private memoirs, is how far they shared the structure of personalised response typified by professionals like Michelet. Clearly, some Parisians, while attracted to the idea of the country retreat, found it in practice to be a confusing and hostile place. Witness a comic story told by that urban sophisticate, the cultural entrepreneur Dr Véron.[70] The 'hero' was a Parisian merchant of the Rue Saint-Denis. After a lifetime of toil in the commercial heart of the city, he had amassed a sufficient fortune to become a property owner deep in the countryside. Here, he would 'finish his days far from the noise of the world and business'. What he required was a 'country house and a fertile estate'. Once installed, he set about improvements: 'here, some new plantations; there, earthworks; the old stables are to be transformed into an inhabitable wing; new stables to be built; some workshops, pavilions and cottages to be erected; in sum, great activity of work and men for at least twelve or fifteen months.'[71] After this period, little remained to be done. The estate was in good order; *ennui* began to set in, and with it regrets: 'his thoughts and desires turn back towards Paris and his stores, to his back room behind the shop where he worked with such merry gusto at becoming rich'. Egged on by rural neighbours eager to profit from his improvements, suddenly he could bear it no longer and, 'in a paroxysm of disgust and nostalgia, he must have Paris, he must have a new life that is active, noisy and occupied'.[72]

The moral of the tale: nature was not for everyone! *Natura naturans* made only partial sense to this Saint-Denis businessman. Not all Parisian bourgeois drew the same kinds of connection in their heads between pictorial views and the environment that made nature a special force. Cultural formations are rarely homogeneous or totalising in their effects; they encompass all manner of fractures, refusals and resistances.

2   Culture or nature? Masculinity and femininity

If nature fed into metropolitan *class* relations, it was equally implicated in the production of gendered identities. If men were placed at the centre of urban existence, so too nature – an urban construct – seemed addressed to man as *his* resting-place, *his* meditative reflection upon *his* own person. Women were not so much excluded as categorised within it in tightly-defined ways. In the process, both masculinity and femininity were worked up and fixed through a series of parallel identifications and oppositions. Gender difference was sharpened in and through these complementary relations.

In the accounts we have examined, nature was frequently *feminised*, though in different guises – mother, lover, mistress. The equation worked equally the other way round. That is, women were often perceived by metropolitan men as an integral part of nature, a property or signifier of natural bliss. The argument had a double movement. Women were closer to nature in their physiological make-up, they could be seen to embody its non-rational purity and innocence. At the same time, nature was secure for women as an enclosed and protective haven. These were not just arguments endorsed in nature tracts and pamphlets. The educational tradition deriving from Jean-Jacques Rousseau was equally insistent on women's affective and non-intellectual nature.[73] Further, from mid-century if not before, such theories began to be promoted by secularists and republicans – Michelet, Auguste Comte, Ernest Legouvé – who now drew on the authority of modern science to argue for women's domestic role. It was, of course, precisely at this moment that feminists also took up and debated similar concerns.[74] Unlike the situation in Britain, though, it is arguable whether a fully-fledged ideology of domesticity and complementary roles was effectively implemented until the republican settlement of the 1870s.[75] However, what is clear is that the 1830s and 1840s already saw the discourse of nature, with its connotations of privacy, sensation and refreshment, becoming crystallised around gender difference.

Michelet is illuminating once more. On his first Fontainebleau trip of 1841 with Mme Dumesnil, the cultivated wife of a Rouen banker, his journal recorded a number of intimate vignettes. At the *Nid de l'Aigle*, 'we discussed the influence that studies of nature might have on my work: *She advances towards you, breasts full and hands full of flowers*'.[76] Michelet's ambiguity was deliberate – was this nature or Mme Dumesnil? The image condensed a sensualised representation with the self-conscious echo of artistic codes – woodland nymphs and the like. And the effect was to undercut any notion of an equal, intellectual partnership. Instead, Mme Dumesnil was inserted into the overall 'natural' framework intended to nourish and complement the author himself. Some nine years later, similar equations were reproduced on a trip to the same forest with his young second wife, after the sudden death of their baby son.[77] Again, the sojourn in the intimacy of the forest glades supposedly furnished the context for the re-establishment of her health and vigour. Yet it was as much the historian's own emotional strength and vitality that was confirmed in the encounter:

> It gave me such pleasure to see her trot before me across the soft grass of that wilderness. She found a grass-snake and vowed to terrify all her friends with the description of the monsters she had seen. In a moment she became gay, her gaiety as delicate as the lovely weather with which we were then favoured, the sky a veiled grey-blue; mischievous, jumping up on a rock from which you could see the Seine and the railway line, agreeably lit up in contrast to the austere, thickly-wooded and rocky landscape around us. I was delighted to see her, something so rare, *in her full nature*.[78]

The obvious point to draw out is the constant slippage between Mme Michelet and nature. She was child-like in her innocence, with her stories of grass-snakes and monsters. She was implicitly likened to an animal or bird, jumping from rock to rock, chattering inconsequentially. Her nature mirrored that of the countryside itself. Beyond that, though, it could be argued that these perceptions were crucial in establishing the distance and difference by which masculinity was to be measured. Built into the historian's observations of femininity was the assertion of his gendered identity, one that was rational, centred, in control.

It would be unwise to build general conclusions on the basis of one particular case. But it does suggest some of the potential interrelations between the sense of self-definition in nature forged by men and their perceptions of private, domestic and even sexualised pleasure. Two other examples reinforce the point. Listen to journalist and critic Jules Janin, writing in 1847 to his young wife, Adèle, while she was visiting her parents' estate at Gaillon in the Eure:

> I wonder what you are doing at this moment, in this lovely morning sun? It seems to me that I see you in a short skirt, your lovely little legs exposed to the four winds of the heavens, your charming feet in those broken-down slippers, and your little muzzle plunged into the cold water while the sunlight plays about on your shoulders, dazzling as a mirror.[79]

Marital intimacy, the emergent codes of private life, seemed to be generated here through imagery that both infantilised his wife and transformed her into an extension of the natural world. And implicit in both kinds of description was a sexualisation of her body, a projection of the writer's desires. Janin's own sense of masculinity was reinforced through a hierarchical relation which placed Mme Janin under his tutelage and protection.

Finally, turn to the painter Théodore Rousseau. After preliminary negotiations to marry George Sand's adopted daughter, Augustine, ended in failure and bitterness, he set up a mistress, Elisa Gros, in his rented cottage at Barbizon.[80] She, like him, originated in the Jura, and through the codes of the artist's biographies was frequently depicted as being on the edge of mental illness.[81] Savage in his indictment of clever women corrupted by modern living (like Sand), Rousseau treated his mistress with a mixture of paternalistic affection for a 'wounded creature' and a titillating incitement to frivolity.[82] For if Elisa Gros was to be protected as the 'senseless thing' of nature, she was also, in her child-like 'simplicity', in her naïve delight in baubles and sweetmeats, an object of sexual desire. In the eyes of the artist, Gros oscillated between the innocent child and the sexualised mistress. Both images, of course, fed into the confirmation of his masculine persona.

For these men, nature represented an intimate domain, and they often identified the experience of the countryside with femininity and heightened emotions – romance, sexuality or convalescence. In the process, gender differences were intensified. For, in so far as women were 'naturalised', written into the scripts of the natural, then that strongly-centred sense of self forged in nature became all the more securely bound up with masculinity.

But what of the women themselves? To what extent and in what ways did such discourses address them? Were there positive appropriations to be made, or merely awkward resistances and refusals? What follows is necessarily schematic and tentative. To go further would demand considerably more research on the relation between nature and bourgeois femininity. Scanning the letters and memoirs of two women whose accounts have been preserved, the writers George Sand and Marie d'Agoult, it is striking how rarely the experience of nature assumed a major role. There were exceptions of course; professedly devout women such as the mystic writer Eugénie de Guérin, who celebrated nature in terms of a traditional deism, as cause for wonder and prayer and as a source of revelation.[83] In more secular circles, women's responses to the rural were much more ambivalent.

Take an obvious figure – George Sand. According to different contexts and circumstances, her responses to the natural world fluctuated widely, structured both by gendered *and* class codes. As a partisan of romantic literature, she sited a key episode of one of her earliest novels, *Lélia* (1833), in the evocative setting of the Fontainebleau forest. Yet nature, for Sand, primarily referenced *home*, the ancestral estate of Nohant, near Le Châtre in the Berry, where she was brought up as a child and which she successfully reclaimed after her definitive separation from her husband.[84] Nohant was always being conjured up in terms of childhood memories, family history, loyal old retainers: 'It was then that I began to regret Nohant . . . I would have rested there, facing those same horizons that had confronted my earliest vision, among the friends of my childhood; I would have spied out the chimneys of Nohant pouring out smoke behind the trees planted by my grandmother.'[85] This, of course, was the patrician language of the gentry, with its stresses on memory, continuity and an ordered social vision. It was the imagery of her inherited class, which did not always sit easily with her republican convictions.

On the other hand, a trip to Fontainebleau in the summer of 1837 seemed to exhibit all the signs of metropolitan tourism. 'Broken up with fatigue and overwhelmed with grief' after the death of her mother, Sand, together with her son Maurice, came to recuperate in this 'regular little Switzerland'.[86] 'We are snugly settled', she wrote, 'in a small inn overlooking the forest. We ride daily on horses and donkeys, bathe and catch butterflies. I am not sorry that he should have some holidays.'[87] Though the underlying rationale of the excursion was undoubtedly the strain of her mother's death, Sand never referenced the soothing effect of the countryside on *her* spirit and emotions, insisting instead on her son's need for a holiday.

Yet at other moments Sand did seem to engage positively with ideologies of nature, and in ways that were potentially disruptive of burgeoning codes of female weakness and vulnerability. After all, participation in physical pursuits and games could embrace an assertion of strength and autonomy. The writer, for instance, repeatedly harped on about her sick and weakened frame, her inability ever quite to feel well. But weigh that very conventional construction against comments following a visit to Venice in 1834 which concluded with a detour into the Alps: 'I walked as much as twenty-four miles a day, and found that that kind of exercise was most wholesome for me, physically and morally . . . my nose is so sunburnt that I look altogether *lovely*'.[88] On this occasion, the sickly and enfeebled novelist seemed to have had no difficulty in rising from her day-bed and tramping across the countryside in adventurous style. The theme of the 'tramp' and the cheerful unconcern at sunburn marked out a persona which, while proper to nature, was nonetheless deeply disruptive of conventional codes of feminine propriety. Sand, who often used men's clothes and a pipe at this period to move in all-male company, was skilful in juggling different personas to subvert gendered perceptions of herself. In her handling of nature, as in other areas of her public life and career, she negotiated a path which brought her maximum freedom to manoeuvre. If that sometimes meant the assertion of old-established aristocratic codes, and sometimes a take-up of bourgeois femininity (she was indeed a devoted mother), it also allowed for distinctive appropriations of *natura naturans* through a celebration of vigorous exercise and unbecoming sunburn.

A similar heterogeneity of response characterised the letters and memoirs of Marie d'Agoult, later known as the writer Daniel Stern. Again, for this traditional aristocrat nature initially signified the possession and control of the countryside. Letters from the early 1830s written on her estate at Croissy talked frequently of '*my* lake' and '*my* good peasants'.[89] Then, surrendering all claims on 'society' in a romance with the musician Liszt which almost parodied contemporary romantic fiction, nature became the hiding-place and the sympathetic setting for her love.[90] Here, nature assumed the colours of an essentially literary preoccupation. Finally, virtually abandoned by the composer and newly returned to Paris, where she was to forge her own literary reputation, d'Agoult participated in the full range of metropolitan culture. Her take-up of the nature dimension, though, was never more than lukewarm. In August 1840, Paris was becoming 'more odious than ever' and, like so many others, she planned a visit to Fontainebleau with her two daughters.[91] Perhaps more pertinent, this was also the opportunity for a rare reunion with her lover. Her personal commentary revealed little sense of renewal or rejuvenation. Either she was ill, or bored, or, when walking in the forest, her thoughts turned romantically to Liszt.[92] Nature itself had little coherence in her world-view.

Of course, the most immediate thing to note about d'Agoult is that, like Sand, she was an aristocrat. It was patrician culture that initially shaped her experience. On the other hand, as an educated woman she was also interpellated by the structures of romantic literature. Literary imaginings, linked to her passion for Liszt, outweighed the appeal of metropolitan perceptions of nature. Beyond that, what is evident in both writers is the lack of consistency or coherence, the sense of an experience that was fragmented rather than unified, though one that could on occasion be turned to their own advantage. Their stories are probably unusual rather than typical; but they do seem to hint, as we might expect, at the mediated and often awkward relation of *natura naturans* to women themselves.

3   Conclusion

This section has been something in the way of an experiment: the weaving together of theory and history to deliver an argument about identity and power. Fundamental to the enterprise has been the insistence on a materialist analysis of subjectivity. This is the linchpin because, in terms of its effects, *natura naturans* was not, by and large, experienced through public institutions and state programmes; it was essentially lived out at the level of the personal and the individual. It has been our contention, however, that this personalised domain was not in any real sense private, or sealed off from public discourse, but was actively bound into the broader network of relations structuring nineteenth-century French society. In short, what we are dealing with is the *production* of the personal in historically specific terms, the construction of a certain persona in and through distinctive ideological mechanisms. That is to say, identity does not pre-exist social situations; it takes shape and significance according to the languages of the social.

The dialogue with nature was carried by two complementary yet differentiated dynamics – the pictorial and the environmental – which delivered a strongly-centred sense of self. By means of our three biographies, it has been possible to show this structure of experience in operation as part of the culture of metropolitanism. Biography here has furnished a means, not of reasserting the essential coherence of individuals, but of probing the complex pattern of connections between public and private. But this has also contributed to a wider argument about the crystallisation of class relations under Orleanism. What we have been charting is one of the cultural mechanisms in the exercise of hegemony. In making such a claim, it is important to tread with care. Metropolitanism, and *natura naturans*, are not bourgeois ideologies in any simple or direct sense. Rather, nature, in particular, both spoke to and was advanced by key urban strata – most typically, professionals – which gained influence and weight within the power bloc out of proportion to their numbers and economic strength. Undercutting other class-related discourses on town and country, by mid-century *natura naturans* had become both highly visible and widespread. The reasons for its success lay in its ability both inside and beyond the power bloc to draw other philosophies and class fractions into its symbolic orbit. But 'success' was often partial and temporary; for what went on in people's heads was always more complex, juxtaposing contradictory personas and identities.

Finally, as always, gender complicates the issue of class and culture. Though women were frequently identified with nature and the natural world, it was to *men* that the nature experience was primarily addressed. But not to men as some pre-formed category that was already 'there'. Rather, it can be argued that such discourses were instrumental in mapping out and firming up a new, tightly patriarchal version of masculinity. What women themselves got out of nature – health and romance apart – is altogether more ambiguous. This was an area of awkward refusals and negotiations as much as simple leisure and pleasure.

PART FOUR

Provincial resistances: the Fontainebleau story

The local context

Introduction

Listening to the tales of confident metropolitans steeping themselves in rural refreshment, it is easy to believe that the Parisian invasion of the countryside was inexorable. For Barbizon, read all the other countless locations linked to the capital by the tentacles of an ever-expanding rail network – Chantilly and Compiègne to the north, Saint-Germain-en-Laye to the west, the valleys of the Seine and Marne. The appetite for colonisation seemed insatiable. Now, it has been a leitmotif of our account to argue that here was an ideological formation endowing certain sections of the bourgeoisie with a confidence and sureness to compete with the claims of established aristocrats or non-urban *notables*. Mid-century, metropolitans as much as anyone stood in symbolic terms at the centre of the world. And so impressive was their take-up of rural areas, so steady their progress into the suburbs and beyond, that it is tempting to read the implementation of this dominant ideology as smooth and conflict-free. In reality this was far from the case. There was to be no easy fit between the creation of an urban vision of the countryside and its full working-out in and through tourism. Just as in the case of *Carnaval*, where we identified the *barrière* as the site for sharp class-cultural conflicts, so too it can be argued that the appropriation of the provinces in general for *natura naturans* involved all kinds of negotiations and refusals. Those contradictions become quite clearly visible when we return to our case study of Fontainebleau.

Of all the many districts around Paris where nature tourism blossomed, Fontainebleau was the epitome. Uniting the historical appeal of a royal palace with the picturesque beauty of the forest, Fontainebleau was – and remains for many Parisians – a name to conjure with, the essence of the rural excursion. Criss-crossed by trails, look-out posts and picnic spots, the forest even now bears the insignia of a hundred and fifty years of tourism – something of a record! We have already seen how the artists of Barbizon, along with littérateurs and the press, did much to build up that reputation. But they were only one side of the equation. To stop there is to accept colonisation at face value. What Fontainebleau itself produced was a dense network of provincial ideologues and entrepreneurs with different interests and aspirations. They told quite another story.

> Oh artists, you lucky band,
> For whom Paris is the Pantheon,
> Won't you visit this year,
> The villa of Napoleon?
> Take up your brushes, tools and cash,
> Hasten to the railway terminal,
> And may the steam delirious
> Bring you on its steel infernal.
>
> So soon as autumn rumbles on,
> You flee the mighty city,
> Come into my forest deep,
> And taste in peace its liberty.[1]

This halting doggerel was by Alexis Durand, local worker-poet, and published in the *Abeille de Fontainebleau* in 1846. It was a modest hymn that put together the usual litany of themes: the centrality of Paris, the *rite de passage* of train travel, personal meditation in the forest. Yet, in the context of local economics and cultural politics, Durand's rhyme touched on quite different resonances and carried other social implications. Which points to the way language, when transposed from one context to another, could articulate an alternative view of things. The fluidity of meanings helped open up room for manoeuvre around the realisation of nature. Durand himself, with his home-grown literary brew, was a leading protagonist of tourism in the Fontainebleau media of the 1840s. He worked hard to promote the attractions of the region to outsiders and natives alike. His narrative is part of a rich local archive which forms the substance of our concluding section. But our interest in Fontainebleau is not motivated by antiquarianism. Rather, it moves us away from the point of view of the Parisian visitor or nature painter to that of the locals. Now we are beginning to look from the other end of the telescope. Seen from the angle of vision of a small provincial town, the making of *natura naturans* embraced all kinds of negotiations around *regional* priorities and interests. At times such interests were stubbornly resistant to metropolitan hegemony, but more often they took the form of negotiated compromises. Fontainebleau offers some striking accounts of that process in action.

We have already encountered the hamlet of Barbizon, but the important settlements in this area of the Seine-et-Marne were Melun to the north of the forest and Fontainebleau near its southern fringe. Melun was the slightly larger town, the departmental capital and local centre of commerce, housing the headquarters of the prefect and the *conseil général* (the departmental council).[2] It enjoyed relatively good communications with Paris by regular coach services and steamboat well before a direct rail link was opened up at the end of the 1840s.[3] Fontainebleau, on the other hand, was only the administrative seat of one of the sub-prefects of the department, with a population of just about eight thousand in the early 1840s. Despite a distinguished history connected with the royal château and the forest, it had sunk since the Restoration into a sleepy provincial backwater, with little industry and primitive communications.[4] In 1820, one commentator remarked on the impoverished state of the town: 'half the houses are shut up' and 'a crowd of labourers are languishing in the centre' because of lack of work.[5] Twenty years later, the situation seemed little improved:

> Fontainebleau is hardly what you would call an industrial town and it is impossible to name any important manufacture there apart from a porcelain factory, whose products – in the *rocaille* style – were noted at the last industrial exhibition (1839); the exploitation of quarries in the forest, which sends paving stones to Paris, and tree-felling form two branches of industry which employ many hands.[6]

Apart from the raw materials extracted from the forest by the quarrying and the state-run forestry business, the whole area had little to offer except agriculture.[7] Here, the large and profitable estates on the fertile plains encroached upon the smallholdings of peasants and field-workers in villages clustering round the forest's less fertile edges.[8] For instance, the census returns for 1846 showed that of eighty-three households in Barbizon only one farmer (*cultivateur*) boasted a servant. In the larger village of Chailly, further out on the rich plain of Brie, there were several farmers with domestics and one gentleman proprietor, Martial Parent-Duchâtelet, brother of the Parisian hygienist.[9]

On first glance, the predominance of agrarian capital might seem to have shaped the political structure of the region in favour of conservatism. Landowners and traditional aristocrats certainly held the reins of political power. Paul-Philippe, Comte de Ségur, farmed at Thoméry just outside Fontainebleau, and sat in the *Chambre de Pairs* (the upper chamber) along with another fourteen aristocrats resident in the department. His son, Paul de Ségur, also a big landowner, represented the district of Fontainebleau in the Chamber of Deputies between 1842 and 1848, combining this with a seat on the regional *conseil général*.[10] However, the situation in reality was more complicated, with little simple correspondence between economic class interests on the land and a conservative political power base. Though the de Ségurs were one of the oldest noble families in the country, this particular branch, with a distinguished military ancestry, had rallied early to Napoleon and the imperial regime.[11] Paul-Philippe fought in the Russian campaign and was renowned as one of the most heroic of Napoleon's young officers. His military career having ended when he was thirty-five, he wrote a loyal history of the last years of the Empire, gaining election to the Académie Française in 1830.[12] The de Ségurs were discreetly part of the liberal opposition during the Restoration, characteristically rallying, like so many former Bonapartists of the upper ranks, to the Louis-Philippe régime which made Paul-Philippe a peer in his own right. An earlier representative of the Fontainebleau district between 1830 and 1835, Comte Antoine-Jean Durosnel, was equally a loyal supporter of the Orleanist government and a recent peer.[13] But he too could point to a proud record of military service under Bonaparte. In the years between Durosnel and Paul de Ségur, the area elected the local industrialist Louis Lebeuf, possibly as an opposition candidate since he stood again in 1848 on a moderate republican ticket.[14] It should come as no surprise, though, to find that Lebeuf could and did claim an army connection as former *aide de camp* to the republican general Lafayette in 1830.[15] Following through the military link, in 1848 it was Oscar Lafayette, big local landowner and grandson of the same famous general, who was temporarily appointed as provisional governor of the Seine-et-Marne.[16] The point is, then, that although political representation at the central and departmental levels was dominated by the landed establishment, there was an equally strong Bonapartist tradition in the region which registered the strong military heritage, especially around Fontainebleau. This could split either into loyalty to the Orleanist monarchy or moderate republican opposition.[17]

At the district level, similar fractures and tensions emerge. The town councils of Melun and Fontainebleau were dominated by a clique of small-town proprietors and professionals, the latter chiefly from the legal profession and judiciary.[18] But, as so often, the relatively homogeneous appearance of the local power bloc concealed sharp political antagonisms and competing social interests. According to one outsider's shrewd analysis in 1842, Fontainebleau divided into different factions organised around the twin pillars of the palace and the army.[19] Like Melun, this was a garrison town, and Bonapartist memories lived on among the many ex-servicemen who had settled there. After all, 1814 had produced one last moment of fleeting notoriety in its glorious history when Napoleon, retreating towards Paris, passed his last few days before abdication in the palace (the 'villa' of Durand's 1846 poem) at Fontainebleau.[20] Thus: 'since 1814, the soldiers of the Empire have come here to die slowly and quietly. Fontainebleau is a sublime Hôtel des Invalides ... These valiant knights of Napoleon make up, if not the largest, the most glorious and lively section of the population.'[21]

Counterposed against the knights of the Empire was, if we stay with the same account, a tight-knit group of die-hard monarchists who dated from Restoration days: 'They live among themselves, tightly squashed together like ducks trying to keep warm, without, I believe, any connection with the bourgeoisie, still less with the 'nobles' of the Empire'.[22] Third, there was a service sector also depending, initially at least, on the palace and its visitors. These were the wealthier commercial interests of the town, castigated as

> *rentiers* by birth, or rather merchants, innkeepers and restaurateurs become *rentiers* for good or evil. In general they have the best houses and the best cuisine – but little else. They are of course devoted protectors and lovers of the fine arts; you will find some old crust in their home which they admire inordinately because it has cost them a lot and sometimes a masterpiece which they scorn because they got it on the cheap.[23]

'Independents' in politics – that is, Orleanists or 'fair-weather' republicans – they formed the fraction with most to gain economically from the development of commerce and tourism. The sardonic reference to their cultural aspirations also hinted at the potential tie-up between local wealth derived from trade and allegiance to metropolitan values. Here were *commerçants* who twinned the old-style provincial economics with artistic and cultural pretensions.

But this scathing critique was hardly impartial. The commentator was none other than our old friend Auguste Luchet. He in his own person represented the final important constituency in Fontainebleau: the Parisians who came to admire, to visit and to settle. Born a Parisian, the polemical republican writer was an occasional visitor to the town in the late 1830s and early 1840s; his novels were printed there by Jacquin, Bonapartist printer-editor of the local newspaper.[24] After a period of exile for attacks in one of these books on the sanctity of the family, he settled in Fontainebleau in 1847.[25] In the revolutionary year of 1848, he was briefly appointed administrator of the palace (now thrown open to the people) through connections with the socialist Louis Blanc, and he himself stood unsuccessfully as a radical republican candidate for the Constituent Assembly in the spring of that year.[26] It is worth remembering that his account was informed not only by left-wing politics but also, as with his earlier analysis of the city, by the centralist bias of the Parisian constructing the provinces as exotic, peripheral and inferior.

A stagnant economy with clear divisions between the landed gentry and small-town *notables*, sharp political infighting among competing cliques behind a façade of provincial torpor – these factors set some of the conditions for the provincial response to the metropolitan invasion. And it is here that we can build a new dimension into our argument about the construction of Parisian nature. That process was not merely imposed from above by the excursions of the Parisian bourgeoisie. Nor was it simply the result of those artists who colonised Barbizon and other places round the forest. The production of nature was worked for and promoted by rival factions within the provinces in the light of their own interests and priorities. Monarchist librarians at the palace and Bonapartist ex-servicemen were to be as involved in developing the cultural potential of their region as the get-rich-quick hoteliers so despised by Luchet.

2   The press and provincial culture

Making sense of local social relations in Fontainebleau means becoming acquainted with some of the key institutions channelling communication. As in Paris, the newspapers – the *Abeille de Fontainebleau* and the *Indicateur de Seine-et-Marne* (the latter based at Melun) – were powerful mechanisms of cultural dissemination. As in Paris, newspapers were critical arbiters of metropolitan culture, representing to their audience a particular image of the city and of provincials' relation to it. Through their pages and in the identities of their contributors, we can begin to piece together something of the map of local bourgeois aspirations.

Both papers were weeklies and were founded or resuscitated in the 1830s. Unlike most Parisian and major provincial journals, they did not show their political colours. Their contents were, as the *Indicateur* proclaimed: 'literary, industrial, agricultural, administrative, judicial, with legal announcements and miscellaneous items'.[27] The paper pushed the point home by announcing smugly: 'Politics is excluded from this newspaper'. It was a disingenuousness that concealed a cosy conservatism, snuggling up to the establishment; witness the fact that the paper's proprietor-editor, A. C. Michelin, just happened to be the official printer for the prefecture at Melun.[28] But the guise of political neutrality also made good market sense, given the ready availability of Paris's political dailies in the department. In fact, both the *Indicateur* and the *Abeille* profited from a quasi-official status, as they were charged with the dissemination of announcements from the prefecture and from the regional and local councils. This was inscribed, too, in their right to carry legal advertisements for their respective districts. The many column-inches given over to accounts of legal business and advertisements registered the social and political weight wielded locally by the judiciary and the legal profession.

But of course these newspapers contained rather more than a reflection of establishment interests, whether official or professional. They had a cultural agenda too, carried through the genres of journalistic reportage and entertainment. In their miscellany sections, including news and items of general interest, and in their expansive literary coverage, they drew heavily on the kinds of codes pioneered in Paris by Girardin with *La Presse*. Columns entitled 'Lettres Parisiennes', poetry, novellas and statistical titbits on the spread of Parisian dailies or the national railway system were part of the staple diet.[29] Moreover, as in the capital's papers, advertisements played a prominent role both in selling and in financing the paper. Luchet, with his eye on the Fontainebleau situation, commented:

> The newspaper which once was a rostrum has become a shop-counter, a boutique in which the subscriber is daily sold three pages of copied novels, of politics culled from published books, of waiting-room literature. These three pages are merely a pretext to make the reader swallow the fourth – bizarre adverts of every kind . . . from those for the great books which are our pride, the eternal torch of our civilisation, to shameful quackery and esoteric chimeras.[30]

It would seem that antipathy to the culture of the market has a history almost as long as that of socialism itself !

In replicating the style of the new, cheaper Parisian journalism, literary advertisements, miscellaneous curiosities and serialised novellas presented the capital according to metropolitan priorities. Advertisements for books like Sue's *Mystères de Paris* reinforced the centrality of the city, in terms of the permanent threat of misery, criminality and danger, while for the literary *Journal des Femmes* what was evoked was the sparkling quality of Parisian society.[31] Its blurb was frothy and effervescent. Yet it was also working with a newer domestic ideology represented as homely domesticity: 'It is full of the wit and charm of piquant conversations garnered from the cosy comfort of the fireside'.[32] Up-to-the-minute Parisian consumerism was on offer too, as an advertisement for a sumptuous draper's emporium in the *Abeille* of January 1844 made clear. 'Everyone', the back page trumpeted, 'who sends in a request will immediately receive a collection of samples. If preferable, we will send out the material itself for selection'.[33] And for those making a trip to the capital, why not try the Hôtel des Petits Champs, handy, as the blurb put it, 'for business, situated in the quarter of the Bank, and close by the Palais-Royal, the Tuileries and the stock exchange'?[34]

The regional press, along with Parisian dailies, made available urban commodities, fashions, literature and culture to the prosperous inhabitants of the Seine-et-Marne. Newspaper-reading, however, did not necessarily encourage total identification with Paris. The circulation of urban discourses worked hand-in-hand with a construction of local events and news – whether an isolated murder or the coming of gas lighting to Melun – as particular, immediate and tangible. In other words, the newspapers mediated between Paris and the provinces by stressing, in their content, layout and publicity, the centrality of Paris, its pervasiveness but also its *distance* from their own constituencies. And this did not always work to the advantage of the city. At times, the eulogy of Parisian civilisation was undercut by a moral critique. In 1840, the *Indicateur* ruefully remarked:

> Paris, it is France, Europe, the whole world . . . There is no fashion except at Paris. There is no real glory but at Paris . . . Go and speak to a Frenchman of the provincial newspaper and he will treat you like a wild man, a fisherman, a homeopathic fanatic, a provincial – provincial! – the worst insult that exists . . . And yet this journalism of which he makes such a joke, how beautiful and noble it is compared to Parisian journalism – that *filthy and dissolute hotchpotch* – for whereas the first works for glory, the second works for profit . . . In Paris one lives and dies for money.[35]

Yet even this brave attempt to reverse dominant power relations was caught in their remorseless logic. For the passage went on to mock the naïve self-importance of the provincial proprietor/editor-cum-journalist, with his pride in 'my newspaper'.

In the same way, the negotiated relationship between Paris and the regions informed the many literary items penned by locals which regularly filled the column-inches. At one level, of course, literature signalled Paris. But in this local context its presence also worked in other ways, and principally as a signifier for the civilising properties of the provincial paper. Maurice Agulhon has argued that in the *cercles* or men's clubs – a key cultural/political institution, rapidly proliferating throughout France in the 1830s and 1840s – there was frequently little distinction drawn between reading literature and reading the papers.[36] That is to say, the appearance of literary items and even gossip could be used by audiences to validate newspaper-reading as an improving or educative activity. This was precisely the kind of culture that de Tocqueville railed against in 1848 when describing the Montagnard radicals in parliament, who

> spoke a jargon which was properly speaking neither untutored nor educated French, but shared the faults of both, for it was full of vulgarities and bold rhetoric . . . evidently these people were no more the product of the bar than of the salon; I believe they had practised their manners in the cafés and nourished their intellect solely on the literature of the newspapers.[37]

We shall have cause to become acquainted with a homegrown Fontainebleau Montagnard in due course. The interesting thing about de Tocqueville's diatribe is the perception that the literary paraphernalia of the metropolis, circulated via press and cafés, could be appropriated by provincials to form the basis of an oppositional language.

Many of the poetic contributors to our particular journals had this double perspective. One eye was firmly fixed on Paris culture, reflecting their aspiration to be 'real' littérateurs; the other presented a slightly self-demeaning provincial humility. And it was here that nature came into view, doubly accented as a fit subject for high-grade poetry and as a local source of pride in its density of picturesque interest. Of those writing occasionally for the *Indicateur*, perhaps the most striking was Denis de Thézan, who celebrated the picturesque history of the area and the beauties of nature in an extravagantly romantic style.[38] The most regular literary contributor to the *Abeille* was Alexis Durand, whose rhyming doggerel we have already tasted. His inspiration *par excellence* was the epic qualities of the Fontainebleau forest.[39] Obviously, the constant harping on the natural environment has to be set in relation to Parisian literary consumerism. Yet, at the same moment, to write as an inhabitant of Fontainebleau was to announce cultural aspirations specific to the provinces. Given his prominence in the *Abeille* and his role in the glorification of the forest, let us pause for a moment to consider Durand's particular contribution. It is a story which vividly illuminates the class alliances and ambiguities punctuating provincial investment in the countryside.

3   The carpenter-poet, the judge and the librarian:
     local literary ideologues

Sometime in 1834 or 1835, Clovis Michaux, the *procureur du roi* (state prosecutor), newly arrived in Fontainebleau, had need of a carpenter.[40] Impressed by a local man, Durand, he employed him on a number of domestic jobs. As a result, Durand had occasion to visit Michaux's library – an opportunity he clearly relished. Several times the artisan spoke of his love for poetry, but the attorney's ears were blocked by prejudice: 'I made the mistake of only seeing in him an artisan, though very polite, and I did not penetrate this surface appearance'.[41] In June 1835, Michaux was visited by Etienne Jamin, clerk at the palace of Fontainebleau and author of a recent guide to this historic château, which, incidentally, was prefaced with a poem penned by Michaux himself.[42] Jamin came to seek out the prosecutor's opinion on a fragment of poetry he had unearthed, entitled *Le Bouquet du Roi* – the name of a famous oak in the forest. As it turned out, this poem had been composed by none other than the carpenter, Durand. Shocked and impressed, Michaux sought out the artisan, asking him, 'When and how did you wake up a poet?'[43] In response, the carpenter told his tale.

Born in 1795, the son of a brewer who died when he was a child, Durand had been apprenticed to a master cabinet-maker in Paris. It was from this early stage that he dated his interests in the arts. After setting out on the *tour de France* (the traditional apprenticeship circuit for skilled artisans) he had volunteered to fight for Napoleon, returning to his trade with the fall of the Empire in 1814. Like many other inhabitants of Fontainebleau, he retained some kind of Bonapartist allegiance through to the 1840s.[44] A total autodidact, he began studying at twenty, first teaching himself Latin and then Italian. Being in a skilled trade which involved tramping the country as part of its structures of apprenticeship, combined with experience of Napoleonic soldiering, opened up to Durand possibilities of travel and education over and above what was generally possible for one of his class.[45] Finally, in the 1820s, he settled back in his native town of Fontainebleau, married, and established a carpentry business. It was at this point that he became involved with the epic dimensions of the forest, and his ambitions fixed on making it the subject of a grandiose poem. This he had eventually managed in the years 1833–35.

Under the auspices of Michaux, who wrote to the editor, Durand's poetic fragment was published in 1835 in the *Chronique de Seine-et-Marne*, the only local paper then thriving. It carried an introduction by the prosecutor who claimed Durand as his protégé: 'I am happy and proud to reveal to the public the existence of a man who will honour his native land. Fontainebleau, which little knows it, has within its walls a poet, and this poet is one of its children.'[46] Michaux's explicit aim here was to advertise for subscribers to help publish the full volume of Durand's poetry, for the sake of art, civilisation and the glory of the town. The current deputy for the district, Durosnel, showed a copy to the King, who put himself at the head of the subscriber's list, while Michaux received enthusiastic homages to the carpenter from his legal and literary peers.[47] Durand was praised by the poet Béranger, walked the forest with Chateaubriand, and was elected a corresponding member of the literary Académie Eroicienne based at Evreux in Normandy.[48] As a crowning glory, the *Forêt de Fontainebleau: Poème en quatre chants* was published locally in 1836, dedicated to Michaux. It is the preface to this work which furnishes us with the thoroughly improving tale of the carpenter and his discovery.

Worker-poets were a distinctive phenomenon in 1830s and 1840s France.[49] In a period when instruction was neither universal nor compulsory, they epitomised the benefits that literary civilisation could deliver in terms of education and social progress. As such, they were claimed by competing classes and political interests. Implicit in the definition of worker-poets was the notion that they were emblematic of the universal power of literature to civilise but untainted by the disadvantages of that culture. In other words, they had not ceased to *work*, to labour; they had not lost their sense of class belonging. For some proletarian autodidacts and political militants, worker-poets represented a vanguard of the class, offering hope and inspiration in their expression of popular dreams and aspirations.[50] Could the timid Durand be considered the rustic equivalent of those organic intellectuals of the *barrière* dance-halls recently uncovered by Jacques Rancière? The themes of Durand's writing did not overtly confront the central concerns of working-class experience. That, though, is not necessarily the issue. It may well be that in the very aspiration to speak in an epic tongue, in the attempt to hold together the grandeur of classic literary form with an artisanal persona, his work represented a peculiar variant on Rancière's 'proletarian dreamers'.[51]

On the other hand, worker-poets could equally be claimed by other political constituencies. 'Progressive' ideologues within the Orleanist camp hailed them as a potent example of harmonious class relationships mediated by literature. Here was a reworked version of paternalism whereby the worker became the protégé of the caring employer-patron. The ways in which Durand and his poetry were appropriated by Michaux point to a strategic attempt, albeit on a microcosmic scale, to cement social relations in the face of contemporary class dislocations. The political rioting of the early 1830s, especially in Paris, along with emergent economic militancy in industrial cities like Lyon, were shadowy presences in this celebration of social harmony.[52] As Michaux openly avowed in his preface:

> The author of the poems of the forest of Fontainebleau belongs to this labouring class which seems to be completely restricted and tied down by the bonds of material and prosaic life. But those bonds could not hold him. While his muscular arms were devoted to the hard work gaining him his daily bread, his thoughts, raised high above the cold realities of this wordly existence, caused him to contemplate nature with love, and from the moment he believed himself beloved of nature, he could behold society without bitterness and without envy.[53]

It was no coincidence that Clovis Michaux became so prominent in promoting the worker-poet. As state prosecutor for Fontainebleau he was, together with the sub-prefect and the mayor, one of the most senior and influential officials in the town.[54] A man with wide professional and metropolitan connections, he was politically aligned with the Orleanist establishment. An ardent Bonapartist in his youth, his career had been promoted by rapid allegiance to the constitutional monarchy.[55] Michaux was thus typical of many – especially in the judiciary and the prefectoral administration – who made the switch from Bonapartism to Orleanism. However, he was not only an important political and professional representative of the central state. Through his personal interests, he also intervened actively in the organisation of local cultural relations. Himself an amateur littérateur and member of several *sociétés savantes*, he had already published his own poem called *A Fontainebleau* in a local agricultural journal.[56] It was part of this which cropped up as the poetic preface to Jamin's palace guide of 1834.

Jamin, whom we shall re-encounter as a major early contributor to the tourist literature on the forest, also needs sketching. By his own (exaggerated) account 'a former teacher at the University', he progressed from clerk in the caretaker's lodge in the mid-1830s to secretary in the service of the royal library some ten years later.[57] Identifying strongly with metropolitan values, Jamin was the eager subaltern to Michaux's projects. Like Durand, he was a regular writer for the *Abeille* and the *Indicateur* on a variety of themes.[58] In 1842, Luchet characterised him as a lackey of the regime for his over-enthusiastic praise of recent and mediocre restoration work at the château.[59] For our republican polemicist, the erudite Jamin typified the servile voice of the Orleanist camp within Fontainebleau.

The links between Michaux, Jamin and their worker protégé, Durand, illuminate a tightly-woven network of dependent power relations principally secured through literary culture. Another event brings out the further ramifications of these shifting skeins of dependence. In 1839 Fontainebleau opened its doors to a public library, largely on the initiative and with the financial backing of councillor Denis Guérin. Guérin, a wealthy proprietor, who was to be mayor for much of the ensuing thirty years, was another figure from *outside* who had a powerful impact on the town.[60] A Parisian who effectively integrated himself into small-town politics and culture to become a local 'notable' (as against a metropolitan settler) he stands apart from the dominant pattern of urban-rural relations. After amassing a fortune in the capital with the patenting of a quack remedy, he retired to Fontainebleau in 1830, aged only thirty-two, and devoted his energies to worthy causes and urban improvements, assuming the status of a public benefactor. Guérin's initiatives as mayor were manifold, including mud and rubbish clearance, opening new streets, house numbering, gas lighting and paving – an environmentalist package plainly modelled on Rambuteau's approach in Paris. 'I consider', he later wrote, 'and I love the town of Fontainebleau as a great family'.[61] His practical reforms, keen interests in private welfare and educational projects situate Guérin politically as a relatively 'non-political' progressive.[62] A man who could continue in office as mayor during the July monarchy, the different phases of the Second Republic and the later period of the Second Empire clearly possessed a considerable degree of political phlegmatism. We might be tempted to see him as typical of the wealthy commerical interests among the local bourgeoisie excoriated by Luchet. But his political stance and his social position in the town were negotiated less through economic clout than philanthropic and cultural activity. Education was one area, symbolically as much as literally, where contacts were made and alliances sealed.

Guérin used his status as chief benefactor of the library to select and buy books, assisted by a small committee. This consisted of the familiar trio of Michaux, Jamin and Durand.[63] And it should come as no surprise to find that it was Michaux who presided over the opening ceremony. In his speech he pontificated on the lessons to be drawn from Durand's example and on the social benefits of the library: 'Artisans, come then with confidence to seek learning and advice ... who realises if unbeknownst to yourself there slumbers another Alexis Durand who one day will go to bed a carpenter to rise the next a poet?'.[64] The carpenter–poet himself was prepared to play the game and even to endorse it publicly. In a comic vaudeville play of 1845, dedicated to an anonymous benefactor, he celebrated benevolent class relations.[65] While the crass materialism of the bourgeoisie was castigated, progress for the poor was proposed not through material improvement but through moral and spiritual uplift. It was education, understood in terms of the cultivation of the soul, which gave men the imaginative freedom to rise above their physical state and differences of social position. Such a reverent tribute needs to be treated with caution. Clearly, for Durand himself, 'cultivation of the soul' had borne palpable fruits both economically and socially. By the 1840s, he seems to have been living off his earnings, involved in small property deals, possibly employed at the municipal library, and maintaining visibility as a local hero-poet through regular contributions to the *Abeille*.[66] From the perspective of the self-educated artisan, literary production offered real material and cultural benefits which were not necessarily recuperated within the frame of dominant ideology.

This excursion into the story of the carpenter-poet of Fontainebleau announces some of the themes running through my discussion of provincial nature tourism. The different 'celebrities', with their distinct social and economic interests, are representative of a skein of local alliances organised around the linked issues of education and literary culture. It was precisely this group – through its literary productions, from journalism to poetry and guidebooks – which took the initiative in representing Fontainebleau to visiting Parisians. Guidebooks were a case in point.

Guides to Fontainebleau

1   Meditating on the forest

In general terms, regional guidebooks were a response to the lavish picturesque publications proliferating from the early 1820s.[67] As against the often encyclopedic format of the latter, which breathlessly encompassed the historical, the geographical, the military, the anecdotal, the literary and the pictorial, local travelogues were specific and unambitious. Their aim was to stimulate interest in the royal palace and forest, and to package that interest in an easily-consumable form. In doing so, what is important for us is the way they spelt out *how* visitors should read the countryside. They acted as manuals, rather like Gay's letters for the Parisian initiate. In this sense, they actively fed into the Parisian experience of nature. Yet once again we should be aware that they did not simply pander passively to urban visitors; they were always driven by local priorities and ambitions.

The first nineteenth-century guide to Fontainebleau, of 1820, was by Charles Rémard, librarian at the château, who had already recognised the potential connection between tourism and renewed prosperity.[68] His book had a self-conscious intent; it was a deliberate attempt to stir up the kind of general curiosity that would bring back wealth and fortune to a town in the slough of economic decline.[69] The text followed the contemporary dictums of the picturesque, concentrating on an antiquarian approach to the palace, its history and architecture. When it did touch briefly on the attractions of the forest, this was specifically in terms of the sketching possibilities for the artist and the benefits of hygienic exercise for the vigorous walker. Fourteen years later, Jamin's little guide, stimulated by recent renovation work, also eulogised the historic monument. However, the poetic preface by Michaux set up quite different resonances, suggesting that here was the presence – in embryo, at least – of a very metropolitan experience of nature: 'Weary of Paris, the solitary dreamer/Alone, loves to view your old parterres in flower'.[70] This was the familiar search of the city man for solitude and refreshment conveyed through literary language.

Though not constituting a guidebook in any formal sense, Durand's poems on the forest of 1836, the *Forêt de Fontainebleau*, projected similar responses. Strong on poetic contemplation, they seem on first inspection the very opposite of a guided tour:

> Muse, let us quit this spot and, scorning the road,
> Plunge upon a path 'neath lugubrious vaults.
> I burn to arrive by the *Bouquet du Roi*;
> This noble tree always had attractions for me.
> Already I espy the proud stature,
> The last fires of day gilding its fronds . . .
> You, whose age is lost in the mists of time,
> What transports of delights I feel for your ancient shade,
> Giant of the forest, noble *Bouquet du Roi*,
> Whom the voyager's eye beholds with terror.[71]

Durand's poetry was cast in the epic form of regular classical stanzas – the only mode, he believed, grand enough to glorify his subject.[72] More pragmatically, he aimed to impress with his mastery of this complex and elevated metre. We may speculate that a Parisian audience was prompted to visit the area, titillated by the exotica of a worker-poet. Not only had Fontainebleau stirred the imagination of Senancour, Béranger and Sand; so potent was its magic that it produced its own poetic acolyte from the rough material of a carpenter! At the same time, although these banally heroic strophes were frustratingly unspecific on topography and location, the text was carefully annotated, littered with picturesque details about names, positions, history, or even, as here, the enormous girth of a tree.[73] In other words, the poem spliced together generalised meditation – the praise of solitude and reverie – and a quite precise delineation of place. That sense of place marked a subtle shift from the picturesque mode, where interest was primarily stimulated in and through antiquarian or historical vignettes. Here, anecdotal information served to make the format more materially real and, in a sense, personal to the visitor. It furnished the material setting within which meditation could signify not just a literary genre but a structure of response – visual, sensual, emotional – to the countryside. The combination was to provide a winning formula for nature tourism.

Fontainebleau's literary ideologues now began to scent something big. The next year, the 'learned' Jamin brought out his *Quatre Promenades dans la forêt de Fontainebleau*, the first real guide to the forest as such. It was no accident, of course, that it was dedicated to his friend Durand, 'inspired interpreter of the muses'.[74] The declared purpose of the book was to provide a practical complement to the poems, aiding visitors further to appreciate both them and the beauty of the forest: 'For you is the honour of painting the forest. For me, the modest concern to guide through it the admirers both of it and of you. I merely propose to teach them how to use your poem'.[75] The relationship between the two was becoming a profitable mutual admiration society! Durand replied to the dedication with the hope that it would arouse the natives of Fontainebleau from an indifference born of habit, and inspire that crowd of people who 'love solitude and reverie and for whom contemplation of a beautiful site is a source of inestimable enjoyment'.[76] Clearly, involvement in such literary productions was already endowing Jamin and Durand with a sense of their difference from and superiority to small-town society. Nature seemed to forge a channel through which they could realise élite status.

In Jamin's guide, the literary perspective was again well to the fore. He began with a long peroration concerning the influence of forests on the human imagination. Sadly, he wailed, the regularisation of most French forests had destroyed their 'poetic mystery'. Fontainebleau was the exception, which, because of its immense natural variety, had kept that 'virginal character, that natural physiognomy which was akin to the first forests of the world'. He expressed the hope that the reader, in proceeding, would open up Durand's book of poems, for in such a light the forest 'will appear at once grander, more beautiful and more mysterious'.[77] In contrast to all this general philosophical meditation, the four walks, the ostensible *raison d'être* of the text, took up a relatively small section. Of these, at least two were well known to locals. The first was to the *gorges* of Franchard, site of the popular festival of Pentecost. It took in Durand's favourite haunt, the *Bouquet du Roi*, as well as the historic hermitage, an ancient royal hunting *rendez-vous*.[78] According to Luchet's rather more cynical view five years later, 'civilisation has practically worn away these titanic gorges; it has taken half to pave Paris and its suburbs, it has opened up the rest to gentle promenades with benches and stairways'.[79] Jamin's second walk, to the *Mare aux Oevées*, was also familiar. As one of the favourite public promenades for the inhabitants of Melun, it had been much improved, so the sycophantic librarian tells us, by drainage work and regularisation undertaken on the initiative of Louis-Philippe.[80] The point is that Jamin was revealing a nature which was hardly pure, virginal or primitive to anyone who lived in the area. These were habitual Sunday outings, forming part of the ritual customs and practices of small-town society.

The walks Jamin described were neither novel nor particularly rural. But this hardly signified. What mattered for the *visitor* audience was the balance between the material reality of the promenades, as enshrined in detailed description, and the omnipresent invocation of a poetic and reflective response. This was the means by which Parisians were incited to experience the forest in terms of their subjectivities. This was how the guide acted literally as a pair of eyes, not only turning attention in particular directions but also correlating place with emotion and reverie. The combination of 'literariness' and the protocols of the picturesque worked to produce a clearly-situated sense of being in the countryside.

Nature constituted a common currency from which the intense provincial devotee and the city-weary urbanite could mutually profit. It was this that early guidebooks exploited. But the identity of terms apparently shared by both parties conceals divergences and even antagonisms. This was nowhere more clearly revealed than in the contrasting attitudes to technological progress and the popularisation of the countryside. Whereas metropolitan visitors like the Barbizon artists campaigned against the commercialism of Boisd'hyver's forestry programme and later became hysterical about day trippers and the damage they caused,[81] locals had a much more positive attitude. After all, *their* primary involvement in nature was as part of a literary culture that put them in touch with Paris. They welcomed any developments that brought the capital closer to Fontainebleau, even when that process meant devastation of the forest. Throughout the 1840s the *Abeille* commented enthusiastically on the advance of the Paris–Lyon railway, which was to pass through both Melun and Fontainebleau.[82] In 1846 Durand was sent out to inspect progress, and reported back: 'The railway! This is the subject on everyone's lips! The frenzy of every imagination! The purpose of every peregrination! The target of every speculation!'[83] Durand handled the swath of devastation caused by the intrusion of the railway as integral to the elemental grandeur which made the forest so admirable.[84] Indeed, there was romance in the delirious steam and infernal steel. Moreover, the trains were going to enable the poetic magnificence of Fontainebleau (and thereby of its poet) to be fully appreciated by tourists. Connections between travel, tourism and economic prosperity were quite clear to the *Abeille* when it polemicised in 1845 for the shortest rail route possible:

> that will bring us an economy of time of twenty minutes per trip; economy of seventy-five centimes on the cost of the journey . . . what town in France will be able to rival us for ease of communications? Fontainebleau, we have no hesitation in predicting, will become the Versailles of former ages.[85]

Celebrating the new rail link was, of course, underpinned by a canny realisation of the economic and cultural gains for provincials. The arrival of trains would break the stranglehold of earlier isolation, potentially bringing in a flow of cosmopolitan customers interested in the palace, forest and *maisons de campagne.* Fontainebleau, as Rémard had hoped some twenty years before, would become prosperous again. It would be glorious in its own right. Alongside the identification of Jamin and Durand with metropolitan literary civilisation ran an obvious determination to milk Parisians to the economic advantage of the town and themselves.

2   **Enter Denecourt: the dynamic entrepreneur**

By the end of the 1830s, a number of guides were on offer to visitors. As the editor of Luchet's book on Fontainebleau put it in 1842:

> The palace and the forest of Fontainebleau have their guides and their poet. MM. Denecourt and Jamin know by heart those marvels of which M. Alexis Durand has sung. The serious traveller, the studying artist, the man of the world in search of leisure, will not be able to find in the pages that follow anything that can replace, in respect of them, the works of MM. Jamin and Denecourt, or the verses of M. Durand.[86]

Already the urban constituencies most directly addressed by the marketing of nature were becoming clearly identified. But there was also someone new registered here, a different name slipped in among the ciceroni of the forest – Claude-François Denecourt. With Denecourt we move decisively away from the realm of literature to business. With Denecourt we meet the most dynamic entrepreneur of Fontainebleau tourism. His guidebooks, picturesque prints, maps, souvenirs and paths through the forest were to have a mammoth and enduring impact on what Parisians did on their visits.[87] Publishing his first guide in 1839, he went on to bring out eighteen editions of what he called the *Indicateur* over the next thirty years. It was Denecourt who most effectively sealed the bonds between local commercial interests, the forest and a metropolitan audience. Yet again there was no straightforward alignment between the economic production of guides and maps by Denecourt and Parisian nature ideology. Complex negotiations and mismatches of interest were much in evidence here too.

In mapping this history of Denecourt, we are drawn further into the web of small-town politics and class relations. Like Durand, he was no traditional bourgeois. Born in 1788 to a humble background, he worked his way up to become a cultural 'expert' as cicerone (or guide) as well as a highly successful businessman.[88] After extensive military service during the Napoleonic wars, he had remained in the army under the Restoration as a porter-caretaker at Versailles. His entrepreneurial skills were already at work in a profitable wholesale wine and brandy business pursued on the side. Moved to Fontai-

Claude-François Denecourt as *cicerone* and man of letters.

nebleau in 1832 in the same job, he was sacked, by his own account, for his radical political views. Unlike Durand, Denecourt drew on his Napoleonic experiences to lay claim to an oppositional politics – Bonapartist and then republican – which caused occasional clashes with the authorities. In 1848 he stood unsuccessfully, alongside his republican friend Luchet, for a seat in the Constituent Assembly. In 1851, as the Second Republic turned increasingly repressive, he was listed in police files as an inhabitant professing dangerous views.[89]

Yet it would be quite mistaken to read Denecourt as an outsider or, alternatively, as the simple 'man of nature' later portrayed by Parisian commentators. He as much as Durand invested in nature not only as a profitable consumer commodity but as the touchstone to cultural position and quasi-professional knowledge. Despite, or perhaps because of, his political views (since Fontainebleau, as we have seen, had a clique strongly loyal to Bonapartist memories), he managed to negotiate a series of deals which brought mutual benefit to him and the town. He was, for example, the sole operator authorised by Boisd'hyver to open up new paths in the forest, and he enjoyed good enough relations with the mayor to name a newly-discovered hill after Guérin in 1851.[90] Initially, Denecourt collaborated with Jamin and Durand. Later, though, alliance turned to rivalry and bitter enmity when the poet perceived Denecourt's popular commerical guides to be drowning out his more 'authentic' strophes.[91] Finally, there were the links with local business interests, café owners and hoteliers, who thrived directly as a result of his publications. In 1868 they recognised their debt to Monsieur Denecourt by bestowing a medal on the *sylvain*, as he had come to be called.[92]

What, then, was so special about Denecourt's modest *Indicateurs?* The first point is that they marked a sharp move away from literary culture towards a more populist mode of tourism. The first *Guide des voyageurs dans la forêt de Fontainebleau; choix de promenades les plus pittoresques par les allées forestières* came out in spring 1839, modestly priced at one franc fifty. In some of the introductory remarks it emulated the poetic mode of its predecessor by Jamin, proclaiming: 'I am close to forgetting that the depiction of a nature so grandiose must be the work of the painter and the poet, whose genius it sets on fire, while my mission must be limited to directing the traveller who comes to admire these beauties'.[93] However, the overall tone was far from literary. Most of the text was concerned neither with poetic evocation nor picturesque information. It consisted of a clear, direct set of instructions enabling visitors to find their way around. Unlike Jamin, Denecourt, even in this first publication, did not stick to the obvious and well-worn jaunts of the locals. Rather, he aimed to map his own itineraries through forest paths, linking one celebrated site to another. This was not easy, for although the forest was (and is) criss-crossed by straight hunting avenues dating back to Louis XIV, it was a complicated matter to chart a route that would take in suitably interesting views. Deploying skills developed during active military service, Denecourt carefully plotted his five paths so as to encompass as many panoramas and objects of curiosity as possible, displacing poetic reverie by an overwhelming plenitude of things to see.

One factor contributing to the success of his enterprise was instant press attention. In the *Indicateur* of 6 July 1839, this first guide received a broadly favourable review from Jamin himself, which is indicative of their early identity of interests.[94] Interestingly, Jamin's response was still framed in literary terms, evoking the forest of Senancour's *Obermann* and of scenic sunrises rather than describing the content of the pamphlet in any detail. In the ensuing expansion of Denecourt's business, advertisements, announcements of new publications and reviews were to furnish stalwart support.[95] Another event in the same year also proved an encouraging stimulus. That was the temporary military camp established in August on the western edge of the forest, by the village of Arbonne. The *Indicateur* was ecstatic at the attention focused on the area and the crowds filling local hotels. It trumpeted on 14 September: 'Fontainebleau has quite changed its appearance; it is no longer the little town, calm and indifferent, with its wide roads silent and sad and its desolate park . . . What an atmosphere of festivity'.[96] It even quoted reports from the major political daily, the *Journal des Débats*, to demonstrate how the military manoeuvres had brought the town into the public, that is Parisian, eye.[97] With exemplary foresight, Denecourt rushed out a supplement on the *Camp de Fontainebleau* which the newspaper encouraged all visitors to acquire.[98] The brochure provided a schematic description of the layout of the camp and of the most advantageous viewpoints from which its activities could be surveyed. An account of several paths from both Melun and Fontainebleau to the camp completed the contents. Again these encompassed some of the most dramatic, curious and attractive sights of the forest. And again the language was clear and directional, with an eye to the precise notation of distinctive landmarks in terms of colour and shape.

With the boost from the military camp, Denecourt's career as cicerone was well and truly launched. Hardly a year went by without a new and improved edition of his *Indicateur*, a new choice of walks, or an introduction to the palace as well as the forest being published under his auspices. As he became more confident and better informed, the walks were increasingly embroidered with information and historical anecdotes. Denecourt became keen on places personalised by attractive and evocative names, and he mined the device to the full.[99] Sites, trees and rocks were liberally plastered with appropriate titles – of historical personages, of artists who had painted on the spot, of animals and plant forms which they resembled. Imagination took flight, and he frequently invented associations and stories to accompany the elements he wanted to foreground. Yet, despite the increasing and often apocryphal richness of information, the organising principles of the guides remained broadly similar to those of his two publications of 1839: detailed directions, a rapid succession of named motifs, and clear, pictorial descriptions of what was to be seen on either side of the paths.

Though obviously sharing some features with Jamin's earlier guide, the structure of Denecourt's texts was distinctive. What was projected was a well-defined spatial relationship between visitor/viewer and nature, underpinned by the fact that the guides' primary function was to trace particular routes through the forest. The paths existed *as paths* only in so far as walkers were able clearly to identify trees as *Henri IV* or the *Bouquet du Roi*, rocks shaped like mushrooms or the distinctive colour-coding of the *Gorges d'Apremont* as pointers which constantly moved them forward on their way. The corollary of this naming and descriptive approach was that each path became a non-stop sequence of visual events – viewpoints, objects to admire, things to identify. Throughout, there existed an ambiguity as to whether the paths were there for the sake of the motifs to be seen, or whether the motifs were being identified to help plot the whereabouts of the path. It was a productive tension, investing both the operations of walking and looking with continual interest.

Denecourt's guides took consumer familiarity with the countryside for granted. They acknowledged that Parisian visitors already carried with them a format of personalised response that needed no forcing. And it is tempting to speculate that the relegation of élite literary connotations in favour of more precise pictorial indications registered a broadening, in economic class terms, of the audience to which nature was being addressed by the 1840s. Most important, when we probe their structures of perception, the *Indicateurs* turn out to be metropolitan in a very specific sense indeed. For, through their distinctive use of visual codes, they projected nature as a continually-changing sequence of tableaux akin to the 'moving pavement' spectacles on the boulevard – the fashions, the *objets de luxe* in shop-windows, the glances of café society.

From the early 1840s, Denecourt expanded his pictorial path-plotting. Now he received official permission to open up new walks which could penetrate the very depths of the forest, marked out by arrows and signs in blue paint.[100] This was to provide the ultimate in accessible solitude. Our cicerone blasted his way through rocks, uncovered forgotten grottoes, hacked through resistant undergrowth to reveal remote viewpoints and to build look-out towers.[101] In the search for new motifs and more of the variety for which the place was becoming so famed, he invented as much as discovered features. The process of characterisation through naming and describing was all the more vital if the public were to negotiate the increasingly intricate web of pathways. Take, for example, the path opened up in 1850 around the *Gorges d'Apremont*. Still in existence today, the walk takes several hours, can only be undertaken on foot, and involves strict attention to instructions to avoid deviation from the route.[102] On arrival at the *gorges*, the path weaves its way in and out of the rocks, sometimes virtually encircling a boulder of especially curious form and markings in order to allow investigation of all its angles. Each moment brings into focus a new view, a different framing of one motif by another.

The cultural weight of Denecourt's whole enterprise was to associate a proper appreciation of nature with initiation into the *right* ways of moving around it. It was no accident that he warned tourists in 1855 against hazarding a walk into the forest on their own:

> Do not forget that the vast forest . . . is nothing other than an immense and admirable *pêle-mêle*; . . . an intricate and picturesque labyrinth . . . it is not in giving yourselves over to chances or to one of those so-called guides who themselves know little of the forest that you will ever manage to visit it agreeably, but rather in approaching it with method and in some sense with artistry. We have talked elsewhere of how and at what expense we have acquired this art. But that matters little to the inquisitive enthusiasts who come to explore our romantic wildernesses, our primitive rocks, our ancient groves, our sacred oaks. What is essential is to furnish them with the means with which to seek these things out easily and most agreeably.[103]

Portentously, the guide laid claim to a cultural expertise equivalent to that of the nature artist. Nature, like art, had its secrets and by-laws which the visitor – implicitly defined as an outsider – could not fathom without the illuminations of a knowledgeable expert. Denecourt may not have been an aspiring littérateur like Durand. He was, of course, the personification of the provincial businessman, the representative of self-made commercial interests. But – and the point is an important one – commercial nature opened a path to cultural as much as economic power. His was an unstable position, oscillating between local personality and professional 'expert' of the forest. In this respect the path-*making* – as opposed to the publishing of guides – played a seminal role, allowing him to represent himself as the innovator, the creator of views, the revealer of secrets. Leaving aside literature, he drew his analogies with the increasingly visible landscape artist. It was a kind of cultural position that could tackle Paris on something approaching its own terms.

Commercially, the move into creating new paths proved a profitable diversification of Denecourt's business interests and increased his stranglehold over competitors. In effect, it raised the stakes in relation to potential rivals, relegating simple and easy paths to the status of the banal and ordinary. Visitors were made more reliant both on his publications and on his personally-conducted tours. Creative entrepreneur that he was, he had already begun to move in other directions which supported and extended his central activity. For example, the analogy with the landscape painter was made tangible by involvement with picturesque prints. From 1840, he edited several albums of lithographs on the Fontainebleau area and other scenic outskirts of Paris.[104] Wearing this hat, he made an appearance at the Salon exhibition of 1843. Although he never became directly involved in catering, he was careful to cultivate good relations with hoteliers in the locality. One guide of 1846 was dedicated to a M. Lez, owner of a long-established café-restaurant who just happened to be a municipal councillor. A later publication was offered to Luniot, son-in-law to Ganne, who now ran the major hostelry at Barbizon.[105] Denecourt also made sure to list in his guides available hotels, cafés and horse-and-carriage hire firms for excursions into the forest.[106] With similar shrewdness, he welcomed the arrival of the railway in 1849. This was one occasion for collaboration with Durand. Together they produced a celebratory pamphlet and then a brochure, specifically addressed to the day visitors brought by cheap *trains de plaisir*.[107]

Finally, the influx of trippers led to the marketing of new forms of souvenir. From the mid-1840s, our imaginative businessman began to produce small-scale collections of lithographs bound in jackets of sweet-scented and decorative wood from the juniper tree found in the forest.[108] But this time he was not the first in the field. In 1844, Jamin reported in the *Indicateur* on a new trinket sold by Mme Marchand, trader in curios, which she had named 'juniperines' (*genévrines*).[109] These had been shown to the King on a recent visit to the palace at Fontainebleau. Swift to capitalise on royal patronage, Mme Marchand rushed out a large-scale advertisement for her products. She recalled: 'The numerous visitors who come every year to admire the beautiful and royal residence of Fontainebleau, its vast and picturesque forest, used to be surprised to find no souvenir, no industrial product particular to this historic town'.[110] Now they would be able to take away her *genévrines*, which 'spread a slight scent of balsam to which is attributed the quality of freshening the air'.[111] Perhaps these wooden charms offered the most suitable momentos of Fontainebleau, for tourists could carry away with them wherever they went an evocative aroma of the freshness of the forest.

Sweet-smelling 'juniperines', day excursions from Paris, a proliferation of cheap, easy-to-read brochures, these were the paraphernalia of the rapidly-expanding tourist trade. Such wide-ranging commercial developments signalled the arrival, by the end of the 1840s, of an extensive urban audience – shopkeepers, clerks and the lower ranks of the bureaucracy as much as the familiar men of letters and artists. Denecourt was the most significant architect of that expansion. Building on openings made by Durand and Jamin, this self-made autodidact brought to bear shrewd entrepreneurial skills and a wealth of business interests to construct for himself an enduring persona as local celebrity.

3   Conclusion

There we close the narrative of Fontainebleau and its dignitaries. But what has this case history to tell us about nature tourism in the provinces? And, more generally, about the relation between centre and periphery in early nineteenth-century France? With its palace and forest, the town undoubtedly enjoyed an unusual position *vis-à-vis* Paris which was not necessarily replicated even in other satellite towns around the capital. Few places in France were able, at this early date, to enter so dynamically into dialogue with dominant urban values. So, we should be wary of pulling out over-generalised injunctions from this one history. What we *can* do is point to some salient trends. The most obvious conclusion to emerge is that nature involved a double dynamic, a two-way transaction between metropolitans and locals. At first sight this may look like a uniformity of interests, a harmonious celebration of the same value systems. In fact, tourism in Fontainebleau was always negotiated by distinct and active regional priorities, as much cultural as economic. This leads to a more general insistence about discursive formations or dominant ideologies that needs constant underlining. It is all too tempting, especially for text-based historians, to get fixated at the level of ideological production, to forget about implementation and effects. Fontainebleau shows up the weakness of that approach. Far from being a straightforward imposition from above, that is from Paris, the working-out of nature tourism condensed all kinds of small, yet effective, resistances and manoeuvres from below. The implications were twofold. While carving out their own identities as experts and celebrities, the guides and paths of Durand and Denecourt also actively coloured metropolitan experience. The nature invasion was by no means all one way.

If the vocabulary of the guides masked divergent cultural interests, the economic prosperity they stimulated was a more overt point of contention. It is worth remembering that the poetic Durand was caught up as much as Denecourt in the commercial regeneration of the town. Their positive attitudes to commerce invoked explicit antagonism from Parisian visitors like the Barbizon artists. For the latter, commercial exploitation of any kind (like Boisd'hyver's pine-planting strategy) introduced a rhythm totally at odds with what they had come to seek. For nature to be nature in the terms of their own discourse, it had to be left to rot and reproduce according to its own pace. They alone were to be the intrepid explorers who might penetrate this private retreat. Following that logic, settlers such as the artist Rousseau went on in the 1850s and 1860s to assail Denecourt as a 'maniacal old man' whose useless paths and ridiculous belvederes commercialised and banalised the natural panorama.[112] It was Denecourt whom they held responsible for the vulgarisation of the place, for bringing in hordes of day trippers and philistine picnickers to disrupt artists' essential peace and quiet.

From the perspective of the provinces, the cultural economy looked very different. Though equally 'devoted' to the forest, Durand and Denecourt saw no conflict between entrepreneurial activity and the marketing of nature. How could they? In their eyes, one was a precondition of the other. Without the proliferation of the economic and institutional apparatuses of tourism, without the emergent infrastructure linking modern communications and the local press to services such as maps, guides and souvenirs, Durand and Denecourt were as nothing. It was through such material structures that their own social identities were put together.

When we set the metropolitan construction of nature against this history of provincial tourism, which worked so hard to make nature presentable to the Parisians, the mismatch between central expectations and regional aspirations is striking. Far from waiting passively to be appreciated and appropriated, the provinces grasped the nettle from their own viewpoint of economic expansion and cultural status. The countryside rose up and draped itself in poetic and pictorial attitudes under the impetus of small-town littérateurs and entrepreneurs who were quite as dynamic as their Parisian compeers. In fact, it was through the *dynamism* of Denecourt and others that Parisians were able to enjoy the forest in terms of privacy, peace and tranquility. And yet, as his fame grew throughout the 1850s, our astute businessman was rewarded with Parisian literary admiration which positioned him, like the resident artists, as a symbol of the forest – the *sylvain*, simple and naïve man of the woods.[113] One of the more bizarre images came from the romantic poet Théophile Gautier:

> If you speak to the inhabitants of Fontainebleau, they will answer that Denecourt is a bourgeois, a little strange perhaps, who likes to walk in the forest. And, indeed, he seems little else; but examine him more closely and you will see mapped out beneath the vulgar features of the man the physiognomy of the wood-god: his waistcoat is wood-brown, his trousers nutty-coloured . . . his tumbled hair resembles undergrowth; his colour is greenish and it seems as if his fingers split into branches.[114]

It is altogether unclear whether Denecourt would have recognised himself in this patronising image of the primeval *sylvain*. More to the point, as the cicerone all visiting celebrities now wanted to meet, he probably would not have cared.

179

At stake here were competing claims over symbolic ownership of the forest. But there were other processes at work too. Which is where we come back to an intrinsic contradiction at the heart of nature ideology. The more powerful the vision of nature, projected partly by the metropolitan landscape artists themselves, the more popular the trip to the country. The more popular they became, the more places like the forest of Fontainebleau were perceived by those élite metropolitans to be invaded and desecrated. Widening ripples of popularity threatened, metaphorically at least, the rhythm of personalised immersion and individual contemplation that made nature so special. The ideology carried the seeds of its own destruction.

Finally, moving from culture and economics to politics, it is not too fanciful to situate the distinct inputs of our Fontainebleau ideologues in relation to broader political and class allegiances under Orleanism. This may come as something of a surprise. Throughout the book I have been consistently wary of defining the articulation of nature ideology to political discourse in any direct fashion, because it seemed that metropolitanism ran across and even defused political positions. Having said that, putting Fontainebleau under the microscope shows how the separate strategies of our two 'heroes' – Durand and Denecourt – did connect with political and social networks of different casts. Interestingly, both were from poor backgrounds, both were Bonapartists and both won for themselves a place within bourgeois society. The difference lay in the modes of 'sociality', the structures of initiation into political culture that they inhabited. These have something to tell us about the conflicting modes of political process written into the Orleanist settlement.

Take Durand first. Initially he appears the more obvious proletarian hero, a man who held together a hard-earned artisanal trade with a noble autodidacticism. But Durand is hardly complete, of course, without his friends and protectors. Michaux, Jamin and Guérin formed a close-knit and mutually supportive social grouping. Parisians, or in some sense carrying the cachet of 'Parisianness', they made for a potent mix of power and knowledge in the town. The state prosecutor, the municipal councillor wealthy from speculative enterprise, the learned clerk: here was the Orleanist ruling bloc on a microcosmic scale. Durand was to become their protégé, their friend, if not quite their equal. His advances were achieved under their guidance. In other words, the set-up drew on long established patterns of vertical patronage and governmentality. Social mobility was a function of the gift bestowed on 'men of talent' by their superiors. This was a pattern generally associated with the government of the *notables*, the remnants of the old pre-Revolutionary ruling order. But it was equally familiar – in perhaps more rumbustious and 'vulgar' forms – in the 'modern' salon of Delphine Gay. For at one level metropolitan culture was deeply complicit in these old-style social and political relations.

Denecourt moved in quite another way. While cultivating some of the same associates – Jamin, Guérin, the publishers from the local press – he was nobody's protégé. A classic small-town capitalist, he was prepared to deal with all and sundry, from café owners to forest inspectors and palace mandarins. The tone of his letters and dedications to key officials like the local police chief or Boisd'hyver might seem as servile as that of Durand's to Michaux, but the terms of the social relationships were of quite another order. For in his case capitalist enterprise went hand-in-hand with a meritocratic and egalitarian politics. Unlike Durand, whose Bonapartism dissolved into woolly sentimentality, Denecourt firmed up into a strong republican, one of the few good friends the radical Luchet had in the town. In a sense, he represented a variant of the Montagnards who so appalled de Tocqueville in the 1848 parliament. For he too was between cultures, educated not on Durand's classical diet but on a flotsam-and-jetsam of historical information and other anecdotes, much of it apocryphal. These were the signs of cultural anarchy and confusion that the political commentator feared. Yet would not de Tocqueville have endorsed his sturdy spirit of enterprise? Perhaps what was truly alarming about Denecourt was his social 'modernism'. He worked on the outskirts of traditional patronage through a skein of horizontal relationships. Both assertive business practice and nascent democratic politics fed a mode of operation where backers, associates, consumers and colleagues were treated as relative equals. And of course, as we know, these new social forms were not absent from the metropolis either. Alongside vertical patronage, they were present in Gay's salon – *par excellence* among the literary and press professionals – carrying a partial critique of older rituals and protocols. It was precisely the effect of metropolitanism as a cultural formation to disguise and blur old hierarchies and distinctions. In the provinces, on the other hand, the divisions between old and new class relations were stark. The run-up to the 1848 revolution saw horizontal forms of political communication formalised into the provincial banquet campaign, laying the trail for a nascent tradition of bourgeois republicanism. Yet nothing is simple. In Denecourt's case, it was capitalism as much as egalitarian politics that furnished the cultural means to approach Paris on equal terms.

CONCLUSION

From Luchet's savage critique of speculative capital to Denecourt's optimistic entrepreneurialism, from Gay's sophisticated urban gossip to Michelet's intense subjective reverie; these diverse commentaries have all played an important part in our nature story. Their coming together in this account has been underpinned by the theoretical protocols of the argument. To recap. This has been a book about definitions of nature as the countryside. It has argued that the 'nature' of early nineteenth-century France was an historically specific construct, a product of discourses materially grounded in the conditions of contemporary Paris. At the core of the argument has been the hypothesis that *natura naturans* constituted a structure of experience – twinning immersion with pictorialism – rather than a set of objects or themes. What that perceptual dialogue delivered, specifically among metropolitan men, was a sense of personal identity that extended and reinforced their social power.

Moving outwards to a broader scenario, the analysis of nature has formed part of a rather more speculative thesis concerning dominant class relations in early to mid-century France, and the power of metropolitan culture to inflect the power bloc. In pushing for such a position, the intention has not been simply to reassert the primacy of Paris familiar in traditional history writing: Paris as the seat of government, the hub of revolutions; Paris as the France that mattered. This would be to continue to inhabit metropolitan ideology itself. In fact, with one or two exceptions, the whole thrust of recent historiographical debate has been (correctly, in my view) to downplay the economic and political significance of the centre in favour of regional and local developments. The focus has been on the landed power base of traditional *notables*, the dynamism of provincial industrialists, the advance of proletarian class struggles in cities like Lyon, Limoges and Toulouse.[1] Yet, in a sense, the overall picture of dominant class relations to emerge from these histories is one of stalemate and fragmentation, a negative image of old corruption and patronage rubbing up uncomfortably against new industrial and professional fractions. I would argue for a rather more positive bourgeois consensus mediated through a shared cultural language. Which is where the *symbolic* grip of Paris comes in.

This, of course, involves rethinking the relation between civil society and state. In particular, I have wanted – against more functionalist accounts – to refuse the necessary priority of the economic in understanding this period. Capitalism is not the underlying common denominator here. Metropolitanism (and with it, nature) seems to have cut across economic class lines, drawing quite distinct groups – from finance capital and rising professionals to small urban businessmen and provincial consumers of the metropolitan press – into the orbit of Paris. Establishing a potent set of codes around life-style and behaviour, metropolitanism was *exclusive* as much as inclusive;

unavailable most obviously to the peasantry and urban working class, but also antithetical to the culture of the landed aristocracy and certain provincial strata. Here was a pattern of connections and disarticulations, of inclusions and exclusions, which won ideological hegemony under Orleanism. All of which is less to contradict the histories of regional development than to supplement them. For it was precisely at a period of political stagnancy, of highly uneven and disparate economic transformation, that the space was opened up for the leading role of the cultural in articulating class relations.

Finally, what more contemporary lessons, if any, are to be elicited from this history? For one thing, nature as the countryside is very much with us today as a structure of leisure and pleasure. And now, too, this appears to be an area of private life far removed from the realm of the 'political'. But there is, of course, a politics to nature, and not just a politics about extending or reducing the green belt, protecting ramblers' walkways, and so forth. It is a politics of space, of the ways in which space becomes ideologically loaded and the ways in which corresponding cultural perceptions of space actively intervene in the shaping of social relations and identities. If there is one clear message to be drawn out, it is this. Here is an area where anthropologists, geographers and cultural historians could fruitfully work together.

On a quite different tack, it may well be that there is another set of relevancies to be charted. For in mapping metropolitan culture we have touched on many of the features that continue to make France so fascinating to a certain British and American audience: café society, promenading on the boulevards and conspicuous consumption, artistic and literary bohemia. These images form part of an enduring construction of Frenchness, manifest in over a hundred years of organised tourism and ordered around pleasure, if not frivolity. Well, you may ask, what is wrong with that? The point is that such constructions do materially inflect the whole field of Anglo-French relations. We might ask ourselves, for instance, whether the motivation for delving into nineteenth-century France is anything more than a kind of metaphorical tourism. It is clear that the association of Frenchness with 'confetti culture', the arts of cooking and couture, frequently blinds us to major economic transformations or political change. What we see is what we want to see. In other words, our historical and cultural interest in France can tell us as much about ourselves, our own cultural class relations, as it does about the French. To pursue this line of thought, though, would be to embark on quite another story.

Notes

Introduction

1 My approach has been informed by a general reading of Michel Foucault, principally *The Archaeology of Knowledge*, 1972; *The Birth of the Clinic*, 1973; *Discipline and Punish: The Birth of the Prison*, 1977; and *The History of Sexuality: Volume 1, An Introduction*, 1981.

2 Of major importance in this field have been the following: the work of T. J. Clark, most recently *The Painting of Modern Life: Paris in the Art of Manet and his Followers*, 1984; J. Barrell, *The Dark Side of the Landscape: The Rural Poor in English Painting, 1730-1840*, 1980; G. Pollock, 'Vision, voice and power: Feminist art history and Marxism', *Block*, 1982, 6; L. Nead, *Myths of Sexuality: Representations of Women in Victorian Britain*, 1988; and, more generally, articles published by the periodical *Block*.

3 On space and urbanism see, for example, M. Castells, *The Urban Question: A Marxist Approach*, 1977, and D. Harvey, *Consciousness and the Urban Experience*, 1985, especially pp. 63-220.

4 This is a problem faced, though not centrally addressed, by N. Rose, 'The psychological complex: Mental measurement and social administration', *Ideology and Consciousness*, 1979, 5, pp. 5-68; and K. Jones and K. Williamson, 'The birth of the schoolroom', *Ideology and Consciousness*, 1979, 6, pp. 59-110.

5 See, for example, C. Morazé, *La France bourgeoise*, 1946, and A. Soboul, *La Révolution française*, 1964.

6 L. Althusser, 'Contradiction and overdetermination', in *For Marx*, 1969; 'Ideology and ideological state apparatuses', in *Lenin and Philosophy and Other Essays*, 1971. And, for more general glosses, see S. Hall *et al.* (eds), *On Ideology*, 1978; A. Hunt (ed.), *Class and Class Structure*, 1977; E. Laclau, *Politics and Ideology in Marxist Theory*, 1977; and J. Bloomfield (ed.), *Class, Hegemony and Party*, 1977.

7 S. Hall, 'The "political" and the "economic" in Marx's theory of classes', *Class and Class Structure*, ed. Hunt, p. 46.

8 G. Stedman Jones, *Languages of Class: Studies in English Working-Class History, 1832-1982*, 1983; J. Rancière, *La Nuit des prolétaires*, 1981.

9 Rancière, pp. 48-53.

10 Althusser, 'Ideology and ideological state apparatuses', pp. 158-83. Also see the

introduction by V. Beechey and J. Donald (eds) to *Subjectivity and Social Relations*, 1985, for an attempt to build a theoretical alliance between Althusser and Foucault around subjectivity.

The metropolitan gaze

1 A. Luchet, *Paris: Esquisses dédiées au peuple parisien*, 1830, pp. 156–7.
2 *Ibid.*, pp. 149–50.
3 The most obvious prototype was L. Mercier's *Le Tableau de Paris*, published in twelve parts between 1781 and 1788, though Luchet also referenced J. A. Dulaure, *Histoire physique, civile et morale de Paris*, 8 vols, 1821–25.
4 Luchet, *Esquisses*, pp. 64–8.
5 Take the classic statement by Pierre Thibault and Jean Le Yaouanq that 'in its overall lines Paris is going to preserve until the Second Empire its archaic and heterogeneous format' ('L'histoire de Paris', chapter 2 of *Paris et sa région*, ed. J. Bastié, 1977, p. 107). In various forms the premise informs such accounts as: A. Sutcliffe, *The Autumn of Central Paris*, 1970; Archives Nationales, *Le Parisien chez lui aux XIXe siècle, 1814–1914*, 1976; J. Gaillard, *Paris, la ville, 1852–1870*, 1977.
6 W. Benjamin, *Charles Baudelaire: A Lyric Poet in the High Era of Capitalism*, trans. H. Zohn, 1973. Though razor-sharp in foregrounding all the elements relevant to a history of Paris, the problem lies in his elision of these developments with the Second Empire, identified as the 'high era' of capitalism.
7 Typical is P. Lavedan's *Histoire de l'urbanisme à Paris*, 1975, which provides an evolutionary account of the transformation of Paris, organised around the premise that coherent planning was the key signifier for the city's development. Since the writing of this book the standard paradigms have been challenged by F. Loyer, *Paris, XIXe siècle: L'Immeuble et la rue*, 1987, a major and innovatory architectural history which devotes considerable attention to the Restoration and Louis-Philippe periods.
8 For the 'gothic' image of the city, see V. Hugo, *Notre Dame de Paris*, 1835; E. Sue, *Les Mystères de Paris*, 1843; and F. Pyat, *Le Chiffonier de Paris*, 1847. Later accounts like that of Maxime Ducamp, *Paris, ses organes, ses fonctions et sa vie dans la seconde moitié du XIXe siècle*, 1869–75, and the memoirs of Baron Haussmann dramatically exaggerated the primitive state of the whole city prior to 1850. It was representations such as these which shaped the classic interpretation by Louis Chevalier in *Classes laborieuses et classes dangereuses à Paris*, 1958.
9 J. Pronteau, *Construction et aménagement des nouveaux quartiers à Paris, 1820–1826*, 1958.
10 *Ibid.*, pp. 9, 15–16.
11 *Ibid.*, p. 16.
12 *Ibid.*, p. 11.
13 Archives Nationales, *Le Parisien chez lui*, pp. 42–4, and Loyer, *Paris, XIXe siècle*, pp. 85–97, for the style of apartment block constructed at the period.
14 Anon., *Mémoire addressé par une réunion de propriétaires, architectes et constructeurs de la ville de Paris, à MM. les membres de la commission d'enquête*, 1828, pp. 5–6.
15 Pronteau, *Construction et aménagement*, p. 24.
16 Musée Renan-Scheffer, *La Nouvelle Athènes*, 1984.
17 *Ibid.*, pp. 46–7.
18 Sutcliffe, *The Autumn of Central Paris*, p. 149. Fashion was concentrated in the Rue Vivienne, running north from the Palais-Royal to the Boulevard des Italiens and just adjacent to the Bourse. The Opéra was first situated in the Rue de Richelieu; but after the assassination of the Duc de Berry (younger son of the future king, Charles X) on

this site in 1821 it was moved to the Rue Lepeletier, running north-east of the boulevard, close by the Rue Laffitte.

19 T. Gautier, *Histoire de Romantisme*, 1874, pp. 1-2, 99-114; J. Gaudon, *Victor Hugo et le théâtre*, 1985, pp. 26-34.

20 Dr L. Véron, *Mémoires d'un bourgeois de Paris*, 1856, 3, pp. 236-7; A. Levinson, *Marie Taglioni, 1804-1884*, trans. C. W. Beaumont, 1977, pp. 42-3, 46-7. For a recent account of the Opéra, see J. Fulcher, *The Nation's Image: French Grand Opera as Politics and as Politicised Art*, 1987.

21 M. Berthold, 'Honoré Daumier et le théâtre', in Daumier, *Caricaturana*, 1982, pp. 217-18; O. Krakovitch, *Hugo censuré: La liberté au théâtre au XIXe siècle*, 1985, p. 52.

22 Véron, *Mémoires*, 3, pp. 1-2.

23 See, for example, J. Janin, *The American in Paris, or Heath's Picturesque Annual for 1843*, 1843, pp. 39-40; V. de Balabine, *Paris de 1842 à 1852*, 1914, 1, p. 10; L. Lurine, 'Les Boulevards', in *Les Rues de Paris*, ed. L. Lurine, 1844, 2, p. 347.

24 Janin, *The American in Paris*, p. 40; G. Palmade, *French Capitalism in the Nineteenth Century*, trans. G. Holmes, 1972, p. 91.

25 Vicomte de Launay (D. Gay), *Les Lettres parisiennes, 1836-1848: Oeuvres complètes*, 4, 1860-61, pp. 35-6. For a similar focus on shopping, see P. Christian, 'Rue Neuve des Petits Champs', in Lurine's *Les Rues de Paris*, 1, p. 356, on the splendid bazaar of the Maison-Delille where the 'aristocracy of beauty and elegance goes to buy its fashions'.

26 Anon., *L'Hermite de la Chaussée-d'Antin*, 1812-14, 3, p. 88.

27 *Ibid.*, p. 90. He also recommended (p. 92) the popular *Les Frères Provinciaux* at the Palais-Royal as a good place to observe 'the mobile physiognomy of this great capital'.

28 *Ibid.*, pp. 226-7.

29 P. Lavedan, *La Question du déplacement de Paris*, 1969, p. 19.

30 A. Achard, 'Chaussée-d'Antin', *Les Rues de Paris*, 1, pp. 39-40.

31 Lavedan, *La Question du déplacement*.

32 L. Hautecoeur, 'De l'échoppe aux grands magasins', *Revue de Paris*, 15 August 1933, pp. 811-41 and especially pp. 822-3 on the development of shop-windows.

33 E. Berthet, 'Rue et Passage du Caire', *Les Rues de Paris*, 1, p. 250, and A. Cler, 'Rue Lepeletier', *ibid.*, 1, p. 382.

34 Benjamin, *Charles Baudelaire*, pp. 36-7, 157-9.

35 E. Piot, *Etat civil de quelques artistes français*, 1873, p. 2, noted that since the seventeenth century one of the main concentrations of artists was around the Saint-André-des-Arts area on the left bank.

36 J. R. Taylor and B. Brooke, *The Art Dealers*, 1969, p. 26; F. Haskell, *Rediscoveries in Art*, 1976, pp. 26-37.

37 L. Whiteley, 'Art et commerce d'art en France avant l'époque Impressioniste', *Romantisme*, 1983, no. 40, pp. 66-7.

38 Anon., *Catalogue de tableaux modernes faisant parties de ceux qui composaient l'ancien commerce du M. Alphonse Giroux, père*, Vente, Hôtel Bullion, 1830.

39 *Ibid.* The highest price went to André Scheffer's *Les Glaneuses*, at 670 francs, followed by 451 and 368 for landscapes by Demarne. Though comparisons are difficult because price was calculated in relation to size and importance of genre, a reasonable price for a medium-sized Salon-exhibited painting would be around 3,000-4,000 francs.

40 Whiteley, 'Art et commerce', pp. 68, 71-2; L. Venturi, *Archives de l'Impressionisme*, 1939, 2, pp. 145-6.

41 *Almanach Bottin du commerce*, 1842, p. 345.

42 *Ibid.*

43 *Ibid.*

44 *Ibid.* Of forty-four dealers listed in 1842, around sixteen were orientated towards the new quarters, with seven on the left bank and ten located by the old luxury centre close

to the Rue Saint-Honoré.

45 Venturi, *Archives*, 2, pp. 144–63.

46 *Ibid.*, p. 145. Catholicism, though, did not necessarily bar women from active involvement in business in the first half of the century. See B. G. Smith, *Ladies of the Leisure Class: Les Bourgeoises of Northern France in the Nineteenth Century*, 1981.

47 Venturi, *Archives*, 2, pp. 151–2.

48 *Ibid.*, p. 154.

49 *Ibid.* Paul Durand-Ruel took full control of the business only with the death of his father in 1865. His own speculative initiatives contributed to the spectacular financial success of the Barbizon School in the 1870s and 1880s, and later of the Impressionists.

50 This early move into high-quality promotional marketing brought the dealer into direct competition with Goupil, which had a near monopoly over art-print publishing. Goupil retaliated with a four-volume *Les Artistes contemporains*, 1846–54.

51 The *Physiologies*, pinpointed by Benjamin (*Charles Baudelaire*, pp. 35–6) as a distinctive feature of the 1840s, were collections of popular illustrated essays. For example, the *Physiologies parisiennes*, brought out by the *Bibliothèque pour rire*, included sketches of the student, *lorette*, *flâneur*, bourgeois, creditor and debtor, and of the provincial at Paris.

52 Pluchonneau, *aîné, Paris aujourd'hui: Poème historique*, 1844, p. 12.

53 *Ibid.*, preface.

54 *Ibid.*, p. 13.

55 A. Sécond, 'Rue Notre-Dame-de-Lorette', *Les Rues de Paris*, 1, p. 131.

56 *Ibid.*, p. 136.

57 E. Guinot, 'Rue Laffitte', *Les Rues de Paris*, 1, p. 113.

58 E. Feydeau, *Mémoires d'un coulissier*, 1873, pp. 151–4.

59 Guinot, 'Rue Laffitte', p. 114.

60 For Laffitte's colourful career, see the anonymous *Souvenirs de Jacques Laffitte, raconté par lui-même*, 3 vols, 1844, and Palmade, *French Capitalism*, pp. 105–7, 112–13.

61 Comte R. Apponyi, *Vingt-cinq ans à Paris*, 1913–26, 1, p. 83.

62 Feydeau, *Mémoires*, pp. 45–9, 106–7.

63 Daumier, *Caricaturana*.

64 Dr A. Poumiès de la Siboutie, *Souvenirs d'un médecin de Paris*, 1910, p. 281.

65 Musée Renan-Scheffer, *La Nouvelle Athènes*, pp. 47–56; Sécond, 'Rue Notre-Dame-de-Lorette', pp. 138–9.

66 The most notorious example was Alexandre Dumas *père's* 'factory', with collaborators churning out plays that lifted whole scenes from other sources (M. Ross, *Alexandre Dumas*, 1981, pp. 111–14). But the careers of Alphonse de Lamartine and Victor Hugo also reveal them to have been shrewd businessmen.

67 For big financial and industrial art collectors, see A. Boime, 'Entrepreneurial patronage in nineteenth-century France', in *Enterprise and Entrepreneurs in Nineteenth and Twentieth Century France*, ed. E. C. Carter, 1976, pp. 140–50. For Laffitte's patronage of the writer Charles Nodier, see Nodier's *Correspondance inédite, 1796-1844*, ed. A. Estignat, 1931, p. 274.

68 Gautier, *Histoire du Romantisme*, pp. 20–1, on the writer Petrus Borel; pp. 31–2, on the sculptor Jehan de Seigneur; and pp. 90–8, on his own famous red waistcoat.

69 Apponyi, *Vingt-cinq ans*, 3, p. 261.

70 Gay, *Lettres parisiennes*, 4, p. 102.

71 L. Maigron, *Le Romantisme et la mode*, 1911, p. 25.

72 H. Malo (ed.), *Mémoires de Mme Dosne*, 1928, introduction.

73 Maigron, *Le Romantisme*, p. 27.

74 *Ibid.*, p. 28.

75 Luchet, *Esquisses*, p. 157.

76 Sécond, 'Rue Notre-Dame-de-Lorette', pp. 131-2, 140; Musée Renan-Scheffer, *La Nouvelle Athènes*, p. 43; and L. Czyba, 'Paris et la lorette', in *Paris au XIXe siècle*, 1984, pp. 107-22.

77 E. and J. de Goncourt, *Gavarni: L'homme et l'oeuvre*, 1925, pp. 116-19.

78 C. Baudelaire, *Selected Poems*, translated and introduced by J. Richardson, 1975, pp. 11-14.

79 H. de Villemessant, *Mémoires d'un journaliste*, 1867, 1, pp. 134ff.

80 J. Michelet, *La Femme (1859)*, 1981, p. 66.

81 Gay, *Lettres parisiennes*, 4, p. 10.

82 *Ibid.*, 5, p. 364.

83 *Ibid.*, 4, pp. 417-18.

84 T. Delort, 'Rue Pierre Lescot', in Lurine's *Les Rues de Paris*, 1, p. 72.

85 P. Jacob, 'La Cité', *ibid.*, 1, p. 142.

86 R. de Beauvoir, 'Rue de la Harpe', *ibid.*, 1, p. 96.

87 L. Daubanton, 'Rapport relatif aux entreprises de construction à Paris et à l'interruption des travaux depuis cette année', from *Mémoires statistiques de la ville de Paris*, 4, 1829.

88 *Ibid.*, p. 23.

89 *Ibid.*, p. 39.

90 Luchet, *Esquisses*, pp. 159-60; 220-8.

91 See, for example, the recent exploration of moral-environmentalist ideologies in early nineteenth-century Britain by F. Mort, *Dangerous Sexualities: Medico-Moral Politics in England since 1830*, 1987, pp. 30-61. Louis Chevalier mapped a classic account of the correlation between disease and crime in early nineteenth-century Paris in *Classes laborieuses et classes dangereuses à Paris*, 1958. The difficulty with his analysis is the biological/psychological premise that reads threatening social change as an organic result of the 'pathological' state of the city.

92 The preface to the *Recherches statistiques de la ville de Paris, 1827-1836*, 5, 1844, provides a brief history. Four volumes were brought out between 1821 and 1829, then publication was broken off due to the July revolution and the death of M. Villot, 'head of statistical research'.

93 B. Lecuyer, 'Médecins et observateurs sociaux: Les *Annales d'Hygiène publique et de la médecine légale* (1820-1850)', in CNRS, *Pour une histoire de la statistique*, 1977, 1, pp. 448-9.

94 Chevalier, *Classes laborieuses*, pp. 33-4.

95 Lavedan, *Histoire de l'urbanisme*, pp. 367-8, 377. C. Rambuteau, *Mémoires*, 1905, pp. 372-3, on new roads; pp. 375-6, on sewers; pp. 381-3, on fountains and gas lighting.

96 *Ibid.*, p. 399. On fiscal grounds, he also resisted all proposals to extend the city's tax boundary to the new fortifications (*ibid.*, pp. 368-9).

97 Lavedan, *Histoire de l'urbanisme*, pp. 361-2; A. Daumard, *La Bourgeoisie parisienne de 1815 à 1848*, 1963, p. 539. Councillors included François Arago, astronomer and secretary at the Académie des Sciences, who was also a moderate republican deputy for the Pyrenees; the banker Laffitte; the doyen of the Académie de Médecine, M.-J.-B. Orfila; the economist Horace Say; and the financier Victor Ganneron.

98 Lavedan, *La Question du déplacement*. Several municipal commissions were instituted in the late 1830s and 1840s to consider these questions.

99 *Ibid.*, p. 16. For Lanquetin's biography, see E. de Monglave and E. Pascallet, *Notice biographique sur M. Jacques-Séraphim Lanquetin*, 1856.

100 Lavedan, *La Question du déplacement*, pp. 17-20.

101 For a brief discussion of the contribution of population statistics to modes of government, see M. Foucault, 'On governmentality', *Ideology and Consciousness*, 1979, 6, pp. 16-18.

102 Lavedan, *La Question du déplacement*, p. 22.

103 A. Dumas (*père*), *Souvenirs de 1830 à 1842*, 1854-55, 3, pp. 210-13.

104 The big debate in early nineteenth-century medicine concerned the merits of the physiological theory of irritation promoted by Broussais, which was somewhat removed from the objects and methods of social medicine. See F. Dubois, *Eloges lus dans la séance publique de l'Académie de Médecine (1845-1863)*, 1864, 1, pp. 55-100; 2, pp. 22-4. Medical authority was enhanced in the late 1840s with legal moves towards clarifying the qualifications of doctors and their status both as trained *savants* and moral guardians (Chambre de Pairs, *Projet de loi sur l'enseignement et l'exercice de la médecine et de la pharmacie*, 1847).

105 R. Castel, *L'Ordre psychiatrique: L'Age d'or de l'aliénisme*, 1976, pp. 162, 218-31; though, as Castel demonstrates, the law as implemented was very much a negotiated compromise.

106 For policing and public health, see H. J. Gisquet, *Mémoires*, 1840, 1, pp. 286-7, 421-5; H. Raisson, *Histoire de la police de Paris 1667-1844*, 1844, especially pp. 378-83 on the regime of Gabriel Delessert; and more generally on the police in the period, J. Tulard, *Le Préfecture de la police sous la monarchie de juillet*, 1964.

107 M. Block (ed.), *Dictionnaire de l'administration française*, 1862, pp. 956-8.

108 A. Parent-Duchâtelet, *De la prostitution dans la ville de Paris* (1836), 1981, introduction by Alain Corbin.

109 *Ibid.*, p. 33; Lecuyer, 'Médecins et observateurs sociaux', pp. 452-5.

110 On hygienics, see E. H. Ackerknecht, 'Anti-contagionism between 1821 and 1867', *Bulletin of the History of Medicine*, 1948, 5, pp. 562-93, especially pp. 572-3, 590-1. For the discourse of alienism, see Castel, *L'Ordre psychiatrique*, pp. 104-52.

111 Dubois, *Eloges*, 2, pp. 499-500, 514-15.

112 Dr T. Dagoumer, *Du danger d'habiter trop tôt des maisons nouvellement bâties*, 1825, pp. 59-65.

113 Trébuchet, 'Rapports généraux des travaux du Conseil de Salubrité - depuis 1829 jusqu' en 1839', *Annales d'Hygiène publique et de la médecine légale*, 1841, 25, p. 79.

114 Notably Chevalier, *Classes laborieuses*, and Mort, *Dangerous Sexualities*, pp. 25-42.

115 A. Corbin, *Le Miasme et la jonquille*, 1986.

116 Gisquet, *Mémoires*, 1, pp. 457-91.

117 A.-C.-L.-V., Duc de Broglie, *Souvenirs, 1785-1870*, 1886, 4, p. 365.

118 Gaillard, *Paris, la ville*, p. 561.

119 See L. Blanc, *La Révolution française: Histoire de dix ans*, 1841-44, 2, pp. 206-10, on the different revolutionary groups following the 1830 revolution; 2, pp. 346-53, on the Société des Amis du Peuple; and 4, pp. 240-50, on republican and working-class fractions in Lyon in 1834.

120 Apponyi, *Vingt-cinq ans*, 2, pp. 424-9.

121 Written in response to a competition on the 'dangerous classes' in big cities, it received an enthusiastic review in the *Annales d'Hygiène publique* (1840, 23, pp. 230-7) from the republican alienist, Dr Ulysse Trélat, who used it as an argument for comprehensive social reform. Police accounts, on the other hand, were keen to stress the size of the problem, committed as they were to an extensive policing programme (Gisquet, *Mémoires*, 1, pp. 251-2; Raisson, *Histoire de la police*, p. 367).

122 H. Fregier, *Des classes dangereuses de la population . . . et des moyens de les rendre meilleurs*, 1840, 1, pp. 113-24, 185-91.

123 This account of press expansion derives from C. Bellanger (ed.), *Histoire générale de la presse française 1815 à 1848*, 2, 1969.

124 They ran from Chateaubriand on the right, a foreign minister under the Restoration as well as a noted writer, through Guizot and Thiers, both to be centrist presidents of the *Conseil d'Etat*, to a host of republicans, such as Armand Marrast and Etienne Arago.

125 Renewed censorship was sparked off by Fieschi's ambitious assassination attempt on

Louis-Philippe, P. H. Beik, *Louis-Philippe and the Bourgeois Monarchy*, 1965, p. 35.

126 Palmade, *French Capitalism*, pp. 85–6; Bellanger, *Histoire générale*, 2, pp. 114–16.

127 Bellanger, 2, p. 121; Benjamin, *Charles Baudelaire*, pp. 27–32; L. Minor, *The Militant Hackwriter*, 1975, pp. 78–80; Bibliothèque Nationale, Les Mystères du Rez de Chaussée, 5 June–31 July 1987.

128 L. Reybaud, *Jérôme Paturot à la recherche d'une position sociale*, 1842, p. 79.

129 Balabine, *Paris*, 1, p. 137; Gay, *Lettres parisiennes*, 5, p. 280.

130 Minor, *The Militant Hackwriter*, pp. 149–50; Bibliothèque Nationale, *Les Mystères*, p. 5.

131 Benjamin, *Charles Baudelaire*, p. 28; M. Agulhon, *Le Cercle dans la France bourgeoise, 1810-1848*, 1977, p. 78.

132 Gay, *Lettres parisiennes*, 4, pp. 182–3.

133 *Ibid.*, 5, p. 293.

134 Chevalier Jacob-Kolb, *Le Frondeur, ou Observations sur les moeurs de Paris*, 1829.

135 *Ibid.*, p. 17. See also the *Gazette des Tribunaux*, 13, March 1840, p. 463, for the story of the young provincial amazed and duped by the city.

136 Bellanger, *Histoire générale*, 2, p. 119.

137 Agulhon, *Le Cercle*, pp. 76–7, quoting a somewhat ironic account from *Les Français peints par eux-mêmes*, 1840–42.

138 L. Faucher, *Biographie et correspondance*, 1875, 1, p. xxiii.

139 G. E. Haussmann, *Mémoires*, 1890–93, 1, p. 124.

140 G. Flaubert, *Madame Bovary*, trans. A. Russell, 1971, pp. 70–1.

141 The following biography draws on P. Pellissier, *Emile de Girardin: Prince de la presse*, 1985.

142 Girardin first attempted to become deputy for Bourganeuf in the Creuse, backed by such diverse allies as Guizot and Thiers. However, his election on this and future occasions was invalidated on the grounds of 'dubious nationality', since Girardin had been born illegitimate.

143 J. Vier (ed.), *Emile de Girardin inconnu: Lettres à Mme d'Agoult*, 1949, pp. 10, 48.

144 D. Desanti, *Daniel, ou Le Secret Visage d'une comtesse romantique, Marie d'Agoult*, 1980, pp. 34–42.

145 H. Malo, *La Gloire du vicomte de Launay*, 1925, p. 57. For the powerful Mme Dosne, mother-in-law to Thiers, see her *Mémoires*, 1928, introduction by H. Malo; and X. Marmier, *Journal (1848-1890)*, 1968, 2, p. 117.

146 Véron, *Mémoires*, 5, pp. 311–12.

147 A. Houssaye, *Confessions: Souvenirs d'un demi-siècle, 1830-1880*, 1885, 2, p. 32, on Gay's political position. For the wide mix of politics at her salon, see Comte de Falloux, *Mémoires d'un royaliste*, 1888, 1, pp. 52–5.

148 M. d'Agoult, 'Mes souvenirs', *Revue des Deux Mondes*, 1927, 39, pp. 38–44, on her background and infatuation with Liszt; Desanti, *Daniel*, p. 50, on the connection with Delphine Gay.

149 Desanti, p. 45.

Natura naturans

1 J. Simon, 'Souvenirs de jeunesse', *Faisons la chaîne*, ed. P. Audebrand, 1890, pp. 3–4.

2 L. Marin, *L'Art des jardins et les mouvements de l'esprit humain*, 1970, p. 162.

3 *Ibid.*, pp. 176, 226, on Lamartine and Sainte-Beuve frequenting the garden. Also see Dumas, *Souvenirs*, 1, pp. 8-9.

4 Marquis d'Avèze (J. B. D. Mazade), *Distractions ou passetemps de l'aveugle de Luxembourg*, 1818, p. 6.

5 A. Alphand, *L'Art des jardins*, 3rd edition, 1885. The gardens were illustrated in the text less by plans than by landscape views which stressed the pictorial effects.

6 H. Meynadier, *Paris pittoresque et monumental*, 1843, pp. 105–6.

7 P. Cottin, *Thoré—Burger peint par lui-même*, 1900, p. 36.

8 See P. Grate, *Deux Critiques d'art de l'époque romantique*. 1959, pp. 137–40, for an outline of Thoré's career.

9 T. Thoré, 'Lettre à Rousseau', *Salon de 1844*, 1844, pp. xxiii–xxiv, xxix.

10 T. Thoré, *Salon de 1847*, 1847, pp. 80–1.

11 *Recherches statistiques*, 5.

12 C. Bocher, *Mémoires, 1816–1907*, 1907, 1, p. 110.

13 Avèze, *Distractions*, pp. 7–8. Bocher (*Mémoires*, 1, p. 96) also commented on the continuing popularity of the Tuileries and the Palais-Royal, though the reputation of the latter was increasingly tainted by the gambling rooms and bric-à-brac stalls surrounding it.

14 A. Gouffée, *Tivoli, ou Le Jardin à la mode*, vaudeville in one act, year 5 of the Republic (1796).

15 Anon., *L'Ancien et le nouveau Tivoli, ou Les Danses en plein air*, 1827.

16 *Ibid.*, pp. 17–25, for the range of attractions. See E. Jacomin, 'Histoire de Belleville', in *Belleville*, 1980, p. 175, for the Cossack anecdote; and Dr F.-F. Cotterel, *Promenades aériennes ou montagnes françaises*, 1817, pp. 11–18, for a detailed account of the *montagnes russes* and their health-giving properties.

17 See Bibliothèque Historique de la Ville de Paris, *Paris des illusions*, 1984, pp. 64–78, on commercial halls and gardens, though mainly after mid-century.

18 Anon., *L'Ancien et le nouveau Tivoli*, p.18.

19 Pronteau, *Construction et aménagement*, p. 16 (my emphasis).

20 Trébuchet, 'Rapports généraux', p. 75.

21 Cotterel, *Promenades aériennes*, pp. 27–32, 38–40.

22 Marquis de Salvo, *Trois Mois à Montmorency: Lettres d'une dame à la princesse de . . . à Palerme*, 1846, p. 14.

23 *Ibid.*, p. 7.

24 Though most vividly associated with the heritage of Jean-Jacques Rousseau, the city-country couplet has often been traced by literary historians as far back as Horace or Theocritus. See W. J. Keith, *The Rural Tradition*, 1975, pp. 3–10, and S. Pugh, *Garden - Nature - Language*, 1988, pp. 21–3, for familiar overviews.

25 Bastié, 'La Région parisienne', p. 100. The barrier of the *fermiers-généraux* was constructed between 1784 and 1790 (Lavedan, *Histoire de l'urbanisme*, pp. 189–93).

26 Luchet, *Esquisses*, pp. 68–74.

27 Jacomin, 'Belleville, mon village', pp. 147, 174.

28 M. Nadaud, *Mémoires de Léonard, ancien garçon maçon*, ed. M. Agulhon, 1976, pp. 142–3, 145–6, 194–5.

29 In 'Le bon temps ou la barrière des plaisirs', *Les Révoltes logiques*, Spring–Summer 1978, 7, pp. 29–30, Jacques Rancière disputes the romantic interpretation of *goguettes* or *guinguettes* as pure or autonomous working-class culture, demonstrating that they were sites where 'masters' often hired or contracted out labour. What many of the activities – including escapist songs and poetry – represented was less a 'savage culture' than a 'savage relation' to culture which produced disorder. The subversive potential written into working-class poetry, songs and other leisure forms is the central theme of Rancière's *La Nuit des prolétaires*, 1981.

30 See A. Faure, *Paris, Carême-prenant*, 1978, for an extensive account of *Carnaval*.

31 Anon., *Le Carnaval*, 1840, p. 5.

32 Apponyi, *Vingt-cinq ans*, 3, pp. 37–46.
33 This caricatured the radical sexual politics of the Saint-Simonians under the leadership of Prosper Enfantin, which involved a belief in female emancipation, the theory that God was female as much as male, and, in some cases, the espousal of 'free love'. In fact, disagreements over sexual politics split the Saint-Simonians in 1831. See A. J. Booth, *Saint-Simon and Saint-Simonism: History of Socialism in France*, 1970, pp. 132–7; J. -P. Alem, *Enfantin, le prophète aux sept visages*, 1963, pp. 63–71.
34 Faure, *Paris, Carême-prenant*, pp. 58–60.
35 F. Tristan, *Flora Tristan's London Journal, 1840*, trans. D. Palmer and G. Pincetl, 1980, pp. 75–8.
36 Anon., *Physiologie de l'opéra, du carnaval, du cancan et de la cachucha*, 1842, pp. 85–6, on *travestissement*. Also see Dumas, *Mémoires*, 2, pp. 199–210, on an extravagantly-costumed ball he organised in the early 1830s. Those who did not come disguised had to wear domino costumes supplied by the host.
37 Anon., *Physiologie de l'opéra*, pp. 54, 57; P. Gavarni, *Souvenirs du bal Chicard*, 1839.
38 Faure, *Paris, Carême-prenant*, p. 57, quoting the police chief Gisquet on the threat to public order.
39 Gay, *Lettres parisiennes*, 1843, pp. 298–301.
40 Anon., *Le Carnaval*, sold at ten centimes a copy.
41 J. Levallois, *L'Année d'un ermite*, 1870, pp. 201–2.
42 Janin, *The American in Paris*, p. 241.
43 *Ibid.*
44 The evidence for excusions ranges across a wide variety of sources within civil or private society, from early tourist guides (Anon., *Trois Jours en voyage, ou Guide du promeneur à Chantilly*, 1828, p. 1) to vaudeville plays like Henri Monnier's *Partie à la campagne*, 1841, and the memoirs of élite commentators like Balabine (*Paris, I*, pp. 36, 117).
45 Daumier, *Das Lithographische Werke*, ed. K. Schrenk, 2 vols, 1977. These series continued through the 1840s and 1850s under titles like 'Les Bons Bourgeois', 'Pastorales', 'Plaisirs de la villégiature'.
46 *Ibid.*, 1, p. 509, from *Le Charivari*, 30 May 1846.
47 D. Mornet, *Le Sentiment de la nature en France de J.-J. Rousseau à Bernardin de Sainte-Pierre*, 1980, pp. 45–63.
48 See, for example, Anon., A Tour to Ermenonville, 1785; A. Thiébaut, *Voyages à l'île des peupliers*, 1798; and Anon., *Promenade ou itinéraire des jardins d'Ermenonville*, 1811.
49 Le Normand, *Lettres à Sophie, ou Itinéraire de Paris à Montmorency*, 1813, preface.
50 *Ibid.*, p. 10.
51 See R. L. Gerardin, *De la composition des paysages, ou Des moyens d'embellir la nature autour des habitations,* 1777; C. H. Watelet, *Essai sur les jardins*, 1774. These accounts often aligned landscape composition and Rousseauesque contemplation with a stress on productive agriculture. For modern accounts of the eighteenth-century garden, see D. Wiebenson, *The Picturesque Garden in France*, 1978, and W. H. Adams, *The French Garden, 1500-1800*, 1979, pp. 111–29.
52 Thiébaut, *Voyage*, p. 108.
53 Anon., *Promenade ou itinéraire des jardins d'Ermenonville*, 1788, foreword.
54 I. du Paty, *Manuel du voyageur aux environs de Paris*, 1826, pp. 26, 53, 112–13.
55 Salvo, *Trois Mois à Montmorency*, pp. 37–9.
56 Anon., *Trois Jours en voyage*.
57 J. Lemer, *La Vallée de Montmorency*, 1847, p. vii.
58 *Ibid.*, p. viii.
59 *Ibid.*, pp. 10–14.
60 *Affiches de Paris*, May–June 1750; *Journal Général d'Affiches, annonces judiciaires, légales et avis divers*, January–February 1840. In assessing the numbers of country

residences on offer to the urban audience, I have not always stuck rigidly to the designation *maison de campagne* but have included properties which in the overall advertising context suggested an equivalent usage.

61 *Journal Général d'Affiches*, 4 January 1840, p. 13. Based in the Rue Jean-Jacques Rousseau, he also offered châteaux, farms, estates and factories. Competitors included the firm of Normand in the Rue Notre-Dame des Victoires and Esnault–Pelterie in the Rue Hauteville, all well placed for clients either from the 'liberal' aristocratic Rue Saint-Honoré or the 'modern' quarters around the Bourse.

62 J.-C. Krafft, *Maisons de campagne*, 1876. This was a republication of plans and elevations of projects designed and built in the late eighteenth century, including country houses, ornamental gardens in the informal English fashion and exotic garden decorations. The term *maison de campagne* was used very loosely in the title. Some of the buildings reproduced were clearly châteaux in terms of their size and descriptions; others – specifically named *maisons de campagne* – were much more modest one or two-storey pavilions.

63 Paty's *Manuel du voyageur* (pp. 26, 39, 53) noted the presence of attractive *maisons de campagne* not only close in at Gentilly, Passy and Belleville but also at Asnières and Auteuil. The advantages of Passy, dominating the Seine from a slight hill, were obvious: 'the pure air which you can breathe there and the magnificent viewpoint to be enjoyed have contributed to the construction of a large number of pretty houses'. As at Belleville, a set of direct connections was drawn between high ground, fresh air, physical health *and* pictorial refreshment.

64 J. Michelet, *Ma Jeunesse*, 1884, p. 356.

65 P. Boitard, *L'Art de composer et décorer les jardins*, 1834, p. 22.

66 M. Alhoy, 'Belleville, Les Près-Saint-Germain, Romainville et Menilmontant', *Les Environs de Paris*, ed. L. Lurine and C. Nodier, 1844, p. 210.

67 *L'Hermite de la Chaussée-d'Antin*, 1, pp. 59–60.

68 *Ibid.*

69 See *L'Hermite*, 3, pp. 213–9, for a satirical account of a *partie de campagne* on which everything goes wrong, from the late arrival of guests to the loss of the picnic in a carriage accident and a sudden downpour of rain while they are eating *en plein air*. In typical eighteenth-century style, the object of the trip is to visit the landscaped estate of the host's son-in-law. The guests are all 'middle-rank' types – lawyer, spice merchant, teacher, doctor, guard's officer, wealthy widow – and the Hermit insinuates that their ignorance of etiquette, their lack of cultural 'know-how' is responsible for the failure of the trip.

70 For example, Daumard's *La Bourgeoisie parisienne*, especially pp. 643–5, relies extensively on the notion of aspirational osmosis or upward mobility to explain the expansion and development of the bourgeoisie, reading out tensions or frictions within the class or in relation to other competing classes.

71 This argument cuts directly against Mornet's thesis in *Le Sentiment de la nature* that a 'modern' experience of nature was already emergent in the mid to late eighteenth century. Despite the presence of *maisons de campagne* and excursions in the eighteenth century, it is the discontinuities that are striking. At the heart of eighteenth-century nature was a discourse of social *regulation* – regulation of the landscape, productively as well as aesthetically, and regulation of the human psyche. It was a discourse explicitly addressed to the landowning class and its intellectual acolytes like Rousseau. This was very different from the mix of consumption and immersion framing nineteenth-century urban experience of the countryside.

72 *Journal Général d'Affiches*, 31 January 1840, p. 9, and 6 February 1840, p. 10.

73 *Ibid.*, 15 February 1840, p. 20.

74 *Ibid.*, 16 February 1840, p. 13; 2 January 1840, p. 11; 1 February 1840, p. 18; and 15

February 1840, p. 20.
75 Meynadier, *Paris pittoresque*, pp. 197–8.
76 *Ibid.*, p. 198.
77 *Ibid.*, p. 199.
78 E. Regnault, *Histoire de dix ans, 1840-1848*, 1884, 1, pp. 244–5.
79 J. Bastié, *La Croissance de la banlieue parisienne*, 1964, p. 178.
80 Comte d'Alton Shée, *Mes Mémoires, 1826-1848*, 1869, 2, p. 72; Balabine, *Paris, I*, p. 159; Apponyi, *Vingt-cinq ans*, 3, pp. 451–3.
81 F. Arago, *Etudes sur les fortifications considérées politiquement et militairement*, 1843. H. Chauvet, *François Arago: La plus noble figure des années 1830—1848*, 1954, p. 42, demonstrates his opposition from the early 1830s to fortifications projects.
82 Bocher, *Mémoires*, 1, p. 129, on Michelet's views; Gay, *Lettres parisiennes*, 5, pp. 95ff.
83 G. Robertet, *L'Oeuvre de M. Thiers*, 1887, pp. 620–1.
84 Apponyi, *Vingt-cinq ans*, 3, p. 452.
85 Alhoy, 'Belleville', *Les Environs de Paris*, pp. 207–8.
86 Bastié, *La Croissance*, pp. 97–146.
87 A. de Tocqueville, *Souvenirs d'Alexis de Tocqueville*, 1942, p. 72.
88 F. Bernard, *Fontainebleau et ses environs*, 1853, p. 3.
89 K. A. Doukas, *The French Railroads and the State*, 1976, pp. 18–23.
90 In the late 1830s, deputies of both left and right were deeply suspicious of railway development, sharing a mistrust of speculation and finance capitalism. See J.-P. Adam, *Instauration de la politique des chemins de fer en France*, 1972, pp. 10, 36–7. Also Chauvet, *François Arago*, p. 45, for this republican deputy's initial opposition to state involvement. For local resistances, see J. Belhabit, *La Poste et le rail en Seine-et-Marne*, 1984, pp. 1–2.
91 For the imagery of railway fever, see Poumiès de la Siboutie, *Souvenirs*, p. 281, or Feydeau, *Mémoires*, p. 6.
92 J. Duplessy, *Guide indispensable du voyageur au chemin de fer de Paris à Orléans (section de Paris à Corbeil)*, 1841, pp. 42–4.
93 By the 1850s, cheap excursion trains were available to Saint-Germain-en-Laye and Chantilly as well as Fontainebleau.
94 A. L. Joanne, *Fontainebleau, son palais, ses jardins, sa forêt et ses environs*, 1867, p. 2.
95 For example, A. J. Burkart and S. Medlik, *Tourism, Past, Present and Future*, 1974, and R. W. McIntosh and C. R. Goeldner, *Tourism: Principles, Practices, Philosophies*, 1977.
96 Wiebenson, *The Picturesque Garden*; Adams, *The French Garden*, pp. 112–13.
97 J. Adhémar, 'Les lithographies de paysage en France à l'époque romantique', *Archives de l'art français*, new period, 1938, 19, pp. 189–364.
98 Boitard, *L'Art de composer*, pp. 40–1.
99 My account of the diorama derives from H. and A. Gernsheim, *L.-J.-M. Daguerre: The History of the Diorama and the Daguerrotype*, 1968, pp. 14–38, and H. El Nouty, *Théâtre et pré-cinéma*, 1978, pp. 51–62.
100 Gernsheim, *L.-J.-M. Daguerre*, p. 19. In the turbulent years of 1831 and 1832, Daguerre was forced to reduce prices first to two francs fifty and then two francs. But he refused to go further, fearing to destroy the 'tone' of the venue.
101 *Ibid.*, p. 19.
102 *Ibid.*, pp. 30–1.
103 *Ibid.*, pp. 18, 32–3, 37.
104 Anon., *Catalogue de tableaux modernes . . . du M. Alphonse Giroux, père*.
105 'Variétés – L'Artiste et le bûcheron', *Journal des Artistes*, July 1828, 2, pp. 11–12.
106 H. Van der Tuin, *Les Vieux Peintres des Pays Bas, et la critique française*, 1948, pp. 7–11, and Haskell, *Rediscoveries*, pp. 53–60.
107 According to Charles Blanc's *Trésor de la curiosité*, 1857, 2, the prices of a relatively rare

and newly-prized landscapist like Hobbema rose from around 1,000–2,000 *circa* 1810 to over 50,000 in the 1850s. On the big collectors, see A. Boime, 'Entrepreneurial patronage in nineteenth-century France', in *Enterprise and Entrepreneurs in Nineteenth and Twentieth-Century France,* ed. E. C. Carter, 1976, pp. 140–50.

108 Whiteley, 'Art et commerce', p. 66; Van der Tuin, *Les Vieux Peintres,* p. 29.

109 Van der Tuin, pp. 33–4 and throughout. Serious attention was given to Dutch landscape in J. B. Deperthes, *Histoire de l'art du paysage,* 1822, and in a number of articles published in *L'Artiste* throughout the 1830s. But the first major monographs devoted to this area arrived in the next decade, with A. Michiels, *Histoire de la peinture flamande et hollandaise,* 1845–48, and A. Houssaye, *Histoire de la peinture flamande et hollandaise,* 1846.

110 F. Lügt, *Répertoire des catalogues des ventes publiques, 1821-1863,* 1953, 2, indicates that there were only four or five public sales of contemporary pictures a year in the 1840s, though this rose to eight in 1847 as a result of auctions mounted by the dealers Binant, Durand Ruel and Souty. According to the 'Bulletin–Chronique' of the *Cabinet de l'Amateur,* 1845, 4, p. 331, the first stirrings of collector interest in modern art were felt in that year, prompted by fears of 'old master' fakes. Philippe Burty, 'L'Hôtel des ventes et le commerce des tableaux', *Paris-Guide,* 1867, 2, p. 952, dated the turning-point to the sale of the Duchesse d'Orléans collection in 1853; while Blanc, in *Trésor,* 2, included no collection devoted to modern art before the Thévenin sale of 1851 and the Collot sale of 1852.

111 The most authoritative account is still Adhémar's 'Les lithographies de paysage', but see also, M. Twyman, *Lithography, 1800-1850,* 1970 (especially pp. 41–57 on the technical developments) and W. McAllister Johnson, *French Lithography: The Restoration Salons, 1817-1824,* 1977.

112 Twyman, *Lithography,* pp. 50–7. Particularly active were the printer-publishers Charles de Lasteyrie and Godefroy Engelmann. The connection between first-hand experience and picturesque prints was often made plain in the titles of publications, like Charles Rémond's *Vues d'Italie dessinées d'après nature et lithographiées,* 1828.

113 *Journal des Artistes,* 6 January 1828, p. 14; 13 January 1828, pp. 29–30.

114 These volumes were edited by Alphonse de Cailleux, Charles Nodier and Baron Isidore Taylor. For Taylor's leading role in this and similar initiatives, see P. de Chennevières, *Souvenirs d'un Directeur des Beaux-Arts* (1883–89), 1979, 3, pp. 33–6.

115 For example, G. Planche, *Etudes sur l'école française (1831-1852),* 1855, 1, pp. 170, 178, 189, reproducing reviews of 1831 and 1833; also C. Lenormant, *Salon de 1833,* 1833, 2, pp. 105ff., and *L'Artiste,* 1834, series 1, 7, p. 63.

116 *Journal des Artistes,* 27 April 1828, p. 261.

117 A monarchist connection was made explicit in titles such as Comte A. de Jouffroy and J. J. Jorand, *Les Siècles de la monarchie française, ou Description historique de la France depuis les premiers jours jusqu'à Louis XVI,* 1824 (Johnson, *French Lithography,* no. 145, p. 90). Also A.-J. Tudesq, *Les Grands Notables en France,* 1964, 1, pp. 212–13, 217–18, for confirmation of the legitimists' concern with tradition and the nation; and D. Lalouche, *Peintres de la Bretagne: Découverte d'une province,* 1977, for provincial and often right-wing, resistance to metropolitan exploitation of Brittany.

118 *Le Magasin Pittoresque,* 1834, 2, no. 38, pp. 303–4.

119 *Ibid.,* preface. 'The principal aim of the *Magasin Pittoresque* is to spread in profusion a mass of ideas both generally accepted and useful for everyone, ideas which are suitable for all ages and which are in common use among all classes of society'.

120 This point was made to me by Jacques Rancière in discussion of the different appropriations that could be made of the encyclopaedic traditions of knowledge derived from Diderot and associates.

121 Adhémar, 'Les lithographies de paysage', pp. 202–3.

122 E. Weber, *Peasants into Frenchmen: The Modernization of Rural France, 1870-1914*, 1977; Green, *The Nature of the Bourgeoisie*, part two, chapter 4: 'Education and the ideology of civic individualism'.

123 The link between popular Bonapartism and emergent forms of republican politics is to some extent a hunch based on contemporary memoirs. Secondary sources, on the other hand, stress the input of the revolutionary tradition and utopian socialism (G. Perreux, *Aux temps des sociétés secrètes*, 1931, pp. 1-70; J. Kayser, *Les Grandes Batailles du radicalisme*, 1961, pp. 6-14).

124 For example, two key paintings brought back from the Berry in 1842 by Théodore Rousseau were called *Under the Beeches - the curé*, and *The Pool*, making no reference to the distinctive picturesque reputation of the Berry as a remote and strange region.

125 Obviously, the literature on romantic literature and nature is too vast to enumerate here, though of surprisingly little help to the cultural historian.

126 Sainte-Beuve wrote the preface for the second edition of P. de Senancour's *Obermann* (first published in 1804) in 1833. The novel had long sections devoted to the relation between man and nature, meditating in Rousseauesque vein, and a central episode was set in the Fontainebleau forest. Sainte-Beuve identified Senancour as a kindred spirit to Jean-Jacques Rousseau, Mme de Staël and Chateaubriand, stressing his *ennui* but also his sense of the infinite. This 'heroisation' was followed up by George Sand's preface to the third edition, based on a complimentary article in the *Revue des Deux Mondes*. See G. Michaut, *Senancour, amis et ennemis*, 1909, pp. 7-12, 119-20, on the making of Senancourt as a typically romantic figure. Further, the publisher Curmer brought out a lavishly-illustrated version of Bernardin de Saint-Pierre's classic *Paul et Virginie* (1788) and *La Chaumière indienne* (1791) in 1838, with a major forward by the critic Sainte-Beuve. Once again, this situated the experience of nature at the heart of romanticism, linking individual sensibility with more general philosophical conceptions. Finally, the poet Alphonse de Lamartine, an important exponent of meditative nature poetry and extremely popular in the 1830s and 1840s, referenced Bernardin among a pleiad of heroes - Ossian, J.-J. Rousseau and Goethe - in his 'Les destinées de la poésie', *Oeuvres complètes*, 1845, 1, p. 52.

127 This draws on the arguments of C. A. and H. C. White on the development of the Salon/critic system in *Canvases and Careers: Institutional Change in the French Painting World*, 1965.

128 For attacks on the salon jury, see A. Decamps, *Le Musée de 1834*, 1834; Planche, *Etudes*, 1, 281-94.

129 See Grate, *Deux Critiques d'art*, pp. 57-9. And, for lists of critical reviews, M. Tourneux, *Salons et expositions d'art à Paris, 1801-1870*, 1919; C. Parsons and M. Ward, *A Bibliography of Salon Criticism in Second Empire Paris*, 1986.

130 The concentration among modern art historians on individual 'literary' critics who broke the rules, like Stendhal and Baudelaire, has distracted attention from the structural predominance of the hierarchy of genres as an organising principle of critical discourse up to the 1860s and beyond.

131 For the savaging of history landscape, see Planche, *Etudes*, 1, pp. 170, 178; *L'Artiste*, 1831, series 1, 1, pp. 272-3 (review by Schloecher).

132 *L'Artiste*, 1833, series 1, 1, p. 146.

133 Lenormant, *Salon de 1833*, p. 111.

134 *L'Artiste*, 1839, series 2, 2, p. 269.

135 Lemer, *La Vallée de Montmorency*, pp. 14-15.

136 On the crystallisation of the judiciary, M. Rousselet, *La Magistrature sous la monarchie de juillet*, 1937; on the growth of status of doctors and alienists, J. Léonard, *Les Médecins de l'ouest au XIXe siècle*, 1978, and Castel, *L'Ordre psychiatrique*, pp. 191-2.

137 *Loi relative aux droits de propriété des Auteurs d'écrits en tout genre, des Compositeurs*

de musique, des Peintres et des Dessinateurs: Lois et Actes du Gouvernement, no. 7, vendémiaire An II (i.e. Sept.-Oct. 1793).

138 See A. Quatremère de Quincy, *Essai sur l'idéal dans ses applications pratiques aux oeuvres de l'imitation,* 1837, for a classic, if retrospective, statement of classicising discourse. Also the Grand Palais exhibition *David à Delacroix: Peinture française, 1774-1830,* 1974, pp. 163–8, on the use of classicism for Napoleonic propaganda.

139 A. Boime, *The Academy and French Painting,* 1971, pp. 22–47, provides a detailed account of the academic training process. For a personal memoir, see E.-E. Amaury-Duval, *L'Atelier d'Ingres,* 1878.

140 Valenciennes served on the committee of academicians in 1790–91 which sought to revise the institution's statutes at the height of the Revolution.

141 Following in the footsteps of the great exemplar, Poussin, the idealising painter would 'move the soul of the spectator, and truly exalt his imagination': P.-H. de Valenciennes, *Elémens de perspective pratique à l'usage des artistes (1800),* 1973, pp. 580–1.

142 J. B. Deperthes, *Théorie du paysage,* 1818, p. 5.

143 Sainsbury Centre for Visual Arts, *Théodore Rousseau,* 1982, pp. 38–48, for a discussion of the different categories of preparatory work by this painter. For similar sketch work, see Hazlitt, Gooden & Fox, *The Lure of Rome: Some Northern Artists in Italy in the Nineteenth Century,* 1979.

144 This is to draw out an homology between the rationalist taxonomy informing art discourse and such fields as natural history, grammar and medicine. See M. Foucault, 'Cuvier's position in the history of biology', *Critique of Anthropology,* 1979, 13 & 14, 4, pp. 126–7, and *The Birth of the Clinic,* trans. A. Sheridan, 1973.

145 C. Wenzel, *The Transformation of French Landscape Painting from Valenciennes to Corot, 1787-1827,* 1979, p. 75.

146 Deperthes, *Théorie,* p. 1.

147 Archives Nationales AJ[52]193 – *Concours du Grand Prix du paysage historique (1821-1861),* pp. 170ff. See also AJ[52] 475 for the list of subjects set in the annual tree competitions between 1817 and 1861; AJ[52] 491 for the prize-winners of this competition between 1823 and 1835; and AJ[52] 71 for preliminary notes describing the subjects set.

148 The subject was usually laid out in the form of a narrative, and occasionally lines of poetry were quoted to emphasise the importance of literary imagination. Throughout the 1820s and 1830s, under the aegis of Quatremère de Quincy as secretary of the Académie des Beaux-Arts, instructions to candidates were detailed. Thereafter, the notes became much more sketchy – an indication of the fall-off in official interest in history landscape.

149 A. Sensier, *Souvenirs sur Théodore Rousseau,* 1872; Louvre, *Théodore Rousseau,* 1967; Sainsbury Centre for Visual Arts, *Théodore Rousseau,* essay by N. Green.

150 See, for example, J. P. Thénot, *Cours complet de paysage,* 1834, and *Cours complet de lithographie,* 1836. The Cabinet des Estampes in the Bibliothèque Nationale contains a collection of drawing manuals and landscape courses by the likes of C. Bourgeois, Emile Dardoize, Hubert, Guyot and others.

151 Thénot, *Cours complet de paysage,* p. 6.

152 These figures are for the 1840s and 1850s, but population in Barbizon remained relatively static. In 1846 there were eighty-three houses and two hundred and ninety-six inhabitants, in 1856 eighty-six houses and three hundred and five people. Information from the census register for Melun South, Archives Départementales, Melun, Seine-et-Marne.

153 M.-T. de Forges, *Barbizon,* 1962.

154 S. Bulgari, *Souvenirs,* 1835, pp. 11–15.

155 Forges, *Barbizon*, p. 32. Both F. Pigeory ('Barbizon – Notes et souvenirs', *Revue des Beaux-Arts*, 1854, 5, p. 230) and G. Gassies (des Brûlies) (*Guide artistique de Barbizon*, 1930, p. 11) claimed that Ganne was a grocer (*épicier*), but it is unclear whether this trade was established prior to his hostelry.

156 Bulgari, *Souvenirs*, p. 15, described the intense discussions on philosophy and art which the students indulged in after their evening meal, combining élite education with schoolboy hilarity.

157 J.-B.-G. Gassies, *Le Vieux Barbizon: Souvenirs de jeunesse d'un paysagiste*, 1907, p. 32.

158 T. Thoré, 'Par monts et par bois', *Le Constitutionnel*, 27 November 1847, p. 1, mentioned that Diaz had recently rented a cottage: 'a veritable palace for the area, two rooms on the ground floor along with a barn, an entrance court and a bit of greenery'. Sensier, *Souvenirs*, pp. 170 and 198, indicated that Rousseau also had rented a cottage during 1847.

159 Gassies, *Souvenirs*, p. 20; Forges, *Barbizon*, pp. 34–6.

160 Rousseau's reputation as a martyr was instigated by the Salon jury's refusal of his large and ambitious entry, *La Descente des vaches dans le Jura*, in 1836. This provoked a storm of critical protest, orchestrated by Gustave Planche (Planche, *Etudes*, 1, p. 282; 2, p. 38). For the next five years, Rousseau was consistently rejected by the Salon; but critics like Planche and Thoré continued to mention him, not merely keeping his name alive but feeding his reputation as outsider and martyr. See *L'Artiste*, 1838/1839, series 2, 2, p. 64; Planche, *Etudes*, 2, p. 139; and reviews by Decamps in *Le National*, 5 March 1837 and 5 March 1838.

161 Sainsbury Centre for Visual Arts, *Théodore Rousseau*, p. 19 and note 52, p. 28. In the 1830s Rousseau rented an attic in the Rue Taitbout, adjacent to the Chaussée-d'Antin. A decade later he was sharing with his friend Jules Dupré a studio in the Rue Frochot, close by Pigalle but at the northern tip of the Notre-Dame-de-Lorette quarter.

162 Rousseau became an avid collector, especially of antique medals and Japanese prints. The sale after his death also included 'old master' prints and a number of fine books (Sensier, *Souvenirs*, p. 280; Moreau-Nélaton dossier on Rousseau, Cabinet de Documentation, Louvre).

163 Archives Départementales, Melun, census register for Melun South, 1856, 10 M 149.

164 Gassies (des Brûlies) *Guide*, pp. 46–51.

165 On Jacque's many business activities, see Gassies, *Souvenirs*, pp. 140–7, 164.

166 On the traditional association of the Boisd'hyver family with the administration of the forest, see E. Bourges, *Recherches sur Fontainebleau*, 1896, p. 51, and J. Aigoin, *Fontainebleau sous le Second Empire: Souvenirs*, 1934, pp. 37–9.

167 A. S., 'La Forêt de Fontainebleau – Dévastations', *L'Artiste*, 1839, series 2, 3, pp. 290–2.

168 Thoré's 'Par monts et par bois' was published in two instalments on 27 and 28 November 1847.

169 Forges, *Barbizon*, p. 25.

170 E. Jamin, *Quatre Promenades dans la forêt de Fontainebleau*, 1837, pp. 246, 248–9, pointed to the ubiquitous presence of visiting landscapists at the foot of every tree.

171 Bernard, *Fontainebleau*, pp. 119–20.

172 A. de la Fizelière, 'Les auberges illustrées', *L'Illustration*, 1853, 22, pp. 423ff; Pigeory, 'Barbizon'. The latter played upon the rustic verses composed by the visiting artists to celebrate their distinguished members and exploits – the *Plainte de Barbizon*. See Gassies, *Guide*, pp. 17–18, for a later development of this 'song'.

173 Forges, *Barbizon*, p. 64; Gassies, *Guide*, pp. 50–1. According to an article in the Fontainebleau newspaper *L'Abeille de Fontainebleau* of 7 July 1867, an exhibition of Barbizon works was inaugurated in the *petit chalet* of M. Siron, previously a wood merchant (information from the Archives Départementales, Melun).

174 Extract from *L'Abeille de Fontainebleau*, 28 July 1867 (Archives Départementales,

Melun).

175 Extract from *L'Abeille de Fontainebleau*, 21 June 1868, (Archives Départementales, Melun). The Emperor and his retinue had already given an official stamp of approval to the natural beauties of the forest when they picnicked at the *Gorges d'Apremont* in 1863 (Forges, *Barbizon*, p. 65).

176 Forges, *Barbizon*, p. 64; Gassies, *Guide*, pp. 11-12.

177 E. and J. de Goncourt, *Manette Salomon*, 1867; H. Taine, *Vie et opinions de Frédéric-Thomas Graindorge*, 1867; G. Flaubert, *L'Education sentimentale*, 1869.

The subject in nature

1 For debate about the subject in structuralism as an empty vessel or bearer, see E. P. Thompson, *The Poverty of Theory and Other Essays*, 1978, especially pp. 199-201, and R. Johnson, 'Histories of culture/theories of ideology: Notes on an impasse', *Ideology and Cultural Production*, ed. M. Barrett, 1979. The following recent texts have been helpful in thinking through a more complex materialist approach to the subject: J. Henriques *et al.* (eds), *Changing the Subject: Psychology, Social Regulation and Subjectivity*, 1984; V. Beechey and J. Donald (eds), *Subjectivity and Social Relations*, 1985, specifically the introduction; and C. Weedon, *Feminist Practice and Poststructuralist Theory*, 1987.

2 Weedon, *Feminist Practice*, pp. 43-73, 87-91.

3 Althusser, 'Ideology and ideological state apparatuses', *Lenin and Philosophy and Other Essays*, pp. 159-83.

4 M. Foucault, *The Archaeology of Knowledge*, especially pp. 94-5, 200-2; *The History of Sexuality*, pp. 140-57; and 'What is an author?', *Language, Countermemory, Practice*, 1977.

5 The use of biography as a 'synthetic' tool draws on the precedent of R. Johnson in 'Educating the educators: "Experts" and the state, 1833-1839', in *Social Control in Nineteenth-Century Britain*, ed. A. Donajgrodski, 1977.

6 J. Michelet, *Lettres inédites (1841-1871)*, ed. P. Sirven, 1924, p. 179.

7 Faucher, *Biographie*, 1, pp. 346, 349.

8 Apart from this literary-cum-ethical meditation on nature, Levallois wrote a book on the Fontainebleau forest, *Mémoires d'une forêt* (1875), showing how it had been made famous by writers and artists.

9 *Ibid.*, pp. 201-2.

10 *Ibid.*, pp. 209-11.

11 On Levallois's idealism, see E. and J. de Goncourt, *Journal: Mémoires de la vie littéraire*, 1956-59, 2, pp. 30-1.

12 Louvre, *Théodore Rousseau*, for a spectrum of the artist's pictures, many of them using both framing and deep perspectival devices. My reading here is based on the codes projected by contemporary landscape treatises. See, in particular, J.-B. Laurens, *Théorie du beau pittoresque*, 1849.

13 Louvre, *Théodore Rousseau*, no. 40.

14 This account of Michelet draws on the following: J. Michelet, *Journal, 1828-1874*, 4 vols, 1959-76; R. Barthes (ed.), *Michelet par lui-même*, 1965; and O. Haac, *Jules Michelet*, 1982.

15 The Russian diplomat Victor de Balabine was one élite witness who went to hear Michelet in full flood against the Jesuits (*Paris*, 1, p. 136).

16 In his personal journal of the 1840s, the record of Michelet's own social round ranged from visits to the royal family and attendance at a ball held by Guizot to association with young and struggling artists like Tassaert and Couture and republican militants

such as Eugène Pelletan.

17 Faucher, *Biographie*, 1, pp. iv–xlix.

18 *Ibid.*, p. cx. Faucher initially voted for Napoleon as President in 1848, but by 1851 he was one of the leading liberal politicians to oppose the *coup d'état*.

19 J. Levallois, *Mémoires d'un critique*, 1896.

20 *Ibid.*, p. 2.

21 *Ibid.*, pp. 5–6. Bonapartist memories were revived when the ashes of Napoleon were brought up the Seine to Paris via Rouen in 1840.

22 *Ibid.*, pp. 89–92, on Levallois's 'bohemian' survival in early-1850s Paris. The *Larrousse du XIXe siècle*, 1873, 10, pp. 438–9, charts his rise to literary prominence via the post of Sainte-Beuve's secretary from 1855.

23 Levallois, *Mémoires d'un critique*, p. 297.

24 Faucher, *Biographie*, 1, pp. 201–2.

25 *Ibid.*, p. 265.

26 See, for example, Michelet, *Lettres inédites*, pp. 346–7, on the danger from cholera.

27 Michelet, *Journal*, 1, p. 503.

28 Faucher, *Biographie*, 1, pp. 266, 353.

29 Michelet's first wife Pauline, apparently badly neglected by the historian, died in 1839. Less than a year later, he had installed the ailing Mme Dumesnil in his house to aid her convalescence (Michelet, *Lettres inédites*, pp. ix–xv).

30 See Part Four for a full discussion of the provincial input into nature tourism at Fontainebleau.

31 Michelet, *Journal, 1, p. 366.*

32 Levallois, *Mémoires d'un critique*, p. 92.

33 *Ibid.*, p. 273.

34 T. Thoré, *La Recherche de la liberté*, 1845. As much as a story about nature, this brief novella was a social tract which revealed the growing influence of the socialist Pierre Leroux on Thoré's thinking.

35 Compare the *Souvenirs* of the republican businessman from Brittany, Charles Beslay, with those of the patrician Duc de Broglie. If anything, the former are more discreet than the latter. Beslay's private life seems to be encapsulated in a referece to his wedding in 1833 (C. Beslay, *Mes Souvenirs, 1830-1848-1870*, 1873, p. 136) and another to his wife's death in childbirth some eighteen months later (p. 138).

36 Nadaud, *Mémoires de Léonard*, pp. 120–2, 215. Something of a similar structure persisted for the many ex-peasants who had come to the capital as servants, artisans and small traders. Frequently, they retained their provincial roots through inherited property, to which they sometimes returned at the end of their working lives (Daumard, *La Bourgeoisie parisienne*, pp. 250–6).

37 Nadaud, *Mémoires de Léonard*, pp. 209–16.

38 The classic 'modernisation' thesis was recently restated by Weber in *Peasants into Frenchmen*.

39 Principle sources for the aristocracy have been Tudesq, *Les Grands Notables* and R. R. Locke, *French Legitimists and the Politics of Moral Order in the Early Third Republic*, 1974.

40 Comte de Falloux, *Mémoires*, 1, p. 10.

41 Locke, *French Legitimists*, pp. 149–56; Tudesq, *Les Grands Notables*, 1, pp. 218–26.

42 Comtesse V. de Gasparin, *Allons faire fortune à Paris*, 1863, p. vii.

43 Locke, *French Legitimists*, p. 62.

44 A.-J. Tudesq, *Les Conseillers généraux en France au temps de Guizot, 1840-1848*, 1967, pp. 21–32.

45 A.-C.-L.-V. Duc de Broglie, *Souvenirs*; C. Comte de Rémusat, *Mémoires de ma vie*, 1958-67.

46 See below, pp. 149–50, for a fuller discussion of Sand in relation to gender as well as class.

47 See P. N. Stearns, *Paths to Authority: The Middle Class and the Industrial Labour Force in France, 1820–1848*, 1978, for one account of the dispersed development of the industrial bourgeoisie in France. Also R. Aminzade, *Class, Politics, and Early Industrial Capitalism: A Study of Mid-Nineteenth-Century Toulouse*, 1981, for a case study of a specific area.

48 As an ambitious young sub-prefect, Haussmann served in the remote Garonne at Nérac. He found little recognisable society – families with status lived in the countryside, and the social round consisted of a series of home visits. When his mother and sisters came to stay with him, 'the sojourn of these *Parisiennes* was an event' – cause of celebrations and dancing (Haussmann, *Mémoires*, 1, pp. 122–7).

49 Daumard, *La Bourgeoisie parisienne*, pp. 164, 226–7.

50 Villemessant, *Mémoires*.

51 *Ibid.*, pp. 20–2.

52 Chauvet, *François Arago*, p. 10.

53 *Ibid.*, pp. 27–9.

54 Lavedan, *La Question du déplacement*, p. 16.

55 See H. Dollfus, *Histoire et généalogie de la famille Dollfus de Mulhouse, 1450–1908*, 1909. Also interesting from a republican perspective are the *Souvenirs de jeunesse*, 1905, of Auguste Scheurer-Kestner, pp. 18–35.

56 For involvement of local intellectuals in preserving traditions, see C. Bertho, 'L'invention de la Bretagne: Génèse sociale d'un stéréotype', *Actes de la recherche en sciences sociales*, November 1980, no. 35, pp. 45–62.

57 As with Brittany, pride in the Franche-Comté, annexed in 1678, remained particularly strong. Nodier's regionalism was shared by Proudhon, Max Buchon and Courbet among others.

58 Nodier, *Correspondance inédite*, p. 241.

59 See A. Ranc, *Souvenirs: Correspondance, 1831–1908*, 1913, p. 14, on the *bons bourgeois* of Poitiers taking their leisure among the lime trees of the Place du Pilori.

60 Information on Parquin and his estate derives from articles and advertisements in the *Indicateur de Seine-et-Marne*, 20 October 1838; 2 March, 13 and 27 July 1839.

61 *Indicateur*, 2 March 1839. According to the *Almanach Bottin du commerce* (1821, p. 525; 1832, p. 357), Parquin lived in Paris at the Rue des Deux-Ecus, now demolished. His son was a law student and one daughter had married a proprietor of the Rue Saint-Honoré.

62 *Indicateur*, 2 March 1839.

63 Information on Roussel and his estate comes from the notary's announcement of the legal sale of property in *Affiches, Annonces et Avis Divers du département de Seine-et-Marne*, 11 September 1840, and from *Etude XCVIII* – the files of the Parisian notaries Petit and Lefer in the Rue Saint-Honoré, especially *liasse* 991 (Archives Notariales, Paris).

64 *Etude XCVIII, liasse* 991 (Archives Notariales, Paris): documents deposited on 30 August 1840, which furnish the legal history of Roussel's Parisian property. Along with his brothers, François Alexandre and Pierre Felix, Pierre Robert Roussel purchased number 72, Rue Saint-Honoré on 23 floréal, year 9 of the Revolution, from Charles Louis Duplessis, who retained the usufruct on the property until his death in 1807. By the wills of his two brother-associates, who died in 1823 and 1829, Pierre Robert was the sole beneficiary of the business property. He seems to have disposed of this well before his death, though he retained another five-storey building – including shops and rented apartments – in the Rue Saint-Honoré.

65 *Ibid.* In the 1823 inventory of François Alexandre Roussel's property, Pierre Robert was already described as a *propriétaire* living at Chartrettes, information confirmed by a document dealing with the *cessation d'usufruit* of Mme Veuve Roussel (widow of François Alexandre) in 1830 (*Etude* XCVIII – Petit – *liasse* 937, 1 February 1830).

66 Roussel's father had been married three times, and the lines descended from different mothers seemed to occupy quite distinct economic class positions. The working-class branch lived and worked at Darnetal, an industrial suburb of Rouen.

67 *Indicateur*, 29 February 1840.

68 Archives Notariales, Archives Départementales, Melun – 18 E 352 – file of Gravier, 7 November 1847.

69 *Ibid.*, 18 E 351 – 2 August 1847.

70 Véron, *Mémoires*, 1, p. 103.

71 *Ibid.*

72 *Ibid.*, p. 104.

73 J. Livi, *Vapeurs de femme: Essai historique sur quelques fantasmes médicaux et philosophiques*, 1984, discussed the meshing of Rousseau's views with contemporary science to confirm women's inferiority.

74 See Michelet's *La Femme*, first published 1859; and, for a modern gloss, T. Moreau, *Le Sang de l'histoire: Michelet, l'histoire et l'idée de la femme au XIXè siècle*, 1982. The light-hearted playwright Ernest Legouvé was persuaded by his friend Jean Reynaud to lecture and write on women, arguing against the 'mad and pernicious theories of the liberated woman' (E. Legouvé, *Soixante Ans de souvenirs*, 1887, pp. 272, 276). As for Comte, his misogyny emerged sharply in an exchange of letters with John Stuart Mill (A. Comte, *Lettres d'Auguste Comte à John Stuart Mill, 1841-1846*, 1877).

75 For an expansive investigation of separate-spheres ideology in early nineteenth-century Britain, see L. Davidoff and C. Hall, *Family Fortunes: Men and Women of the English Middle Class, 1780-1850*, 1987. In France, though, the picture is less clear. Despite the polemics, the evidence would seem to suggest that outside certain devout circles (Protestant as well as Catholic) complementary roles and domesticity for women was not an absolute rule, at least before the 1870s. See Smith, *Ladies of the Leisure Class*.

76 Michelet, *Journal*, 1, p. 366.

77 *Ibid.*, 2, pp. 123-30.

78 *Ibid.*, 2, pp. 129-30 (my emphasis).

79 J. Janin, *Jules Janin: 735 lettres à sa femme*, 1973-79, 1, p. 328.

80 For an account of these abortive negotiations, see G. Sand, *Correspondance*, ed. G. Lubin, 1970, 7, pp. 731-5, 745-7, 764-70.

81 For example, T. Silvestre's obituary 'Théodore Rousseau' (in *Les Artistes français*, ed. E. Faure, 1926, 1, p. 178) talked of a 'feeble and miserable being', while Sensier (*Souvenirs*, p. 260) characterised her as 'sick and senseless'. Sensier in particular used extracts from the couple's intimate letters, with their deliberate play on childish language, to confirm her 'madness'.

82 Sand, *Correspondance*, 7, pp. 745-6, for the artist's indictment of clever women. Contrast this to his tender, if deeply patriarchal, letters to Elisa Gros (unpublished correspondence, Cabinet des Dessins, Louvre, packet 6; Sensier, *Souvenirs*, pp. 314-18.

83 E. de Guérin, *Journal et lettres*, ed. G. S. Trebutien, 1865.

84 G. Sand, *Histoire de ma vie*, 1855, 19/20. In 1831, Sand separated from her husband on grounds of incompatability, effectively leaving him in control of her inherited estate at Nohant, near Le Châtre. This she successfully reclaimed after a bitterly-fought legal battle in 1836.

85 *Ibid.*, 19, p. 210.

86 G. Sand, *Letters of George Sand*, trans. R. L. Beaufort, 1886, 1, p. 282.

87 *Ibid.*

88 *Ibid.,* 1, p. 180.

89 F. Liszt, *Correspondance de Liszt et de la Comtesse d'Agoult, 1833–1840,* 1933, 1, pp. 54, 56 (my emphases).

90 Agoult, 'Mes souvenirs', pp. 51, 60.

91 Liszt, *Correspondance,* 1, p. 385; 2, p. 14.

92 *Ibid.,* 2, pp. 20, 24, 36.

Provincial resistances

1 Alexis Durand, 'Aux Artistes', *Abeille de Fontainebleau,* 6 September 1846.

2 According to the *Almanach Bottin du commerce,* 1821, p. 978, the principal industries were 'glass and window-panes, corn, flour, wines, cotton thread, manufacture of printed cloth, wool, animals, cheese'. The predominance of agriculture-related industries and products is clear. In the mid 1840s the population of Melun was 8,950 with 677 electors for its electoral district. In fact, the largest town in the department was Meaux, to the east, with *circa* 9,000 inhabitants (*Annuaire de Seine-et-Marne,* 1844, pp. 90, 100–1).

3 In the 1820s there were three coach companies, offering five services a day between Paris and Melun each way (Paty, *Manuel du voyageur,* p. 196). There were also several steamboats working the Seine, including the *Ibrahim* (going since the mid-1830s), the *Ville de Melun* (started in 1840) and later the *Parisien* (*Indicateur,* 29 February 1840, 'Chronique', p. 1, and advertisement, p. 4).

4 *Annuaire de Seine-et-Marne,* 1844, pp. 90, 304; Bourges, *Recherches,* p. 548; Paty, *Manuel du voyageur,* p. 196. At this point (1826), there was only one coach a day between Paris and Fontainebleau. Even when the rail link via Corbeil opened in the late 1830s, the journey still took about four hours, using two coach companies between Corbeil and Fontainebleau (Duplessy, *Guide indispensable,* pp. 42–5).

5 C. Rémard, *Guide de Fontainebleau,* 1820, p. 140.

6 Duplessy, *Guide indispensable,* p. 46. The little porcelain factory dated back to the eighteenth century. In the 1830s it was owned by Jacob Pillet and employed about eighty workers, expanding to three times that number over the next decade (Société des Amis de la Forêt de Fontainebleau, *Claude-François Denecourt,* p. 57). Also see L. Lurine, 'Fontainebleau', in *Les Environs de Paris,* ed. Lurine and Nodier, pp. 417–18.

7 The biggest industrial manufacturer was Louis Lebeuf, with a porcelain factory at Montereau in the far south of the department, which employed around 1,000 workers (*Almanach Bottin du commerce,* 1832, p. 720; *Indicateur,* 8 April 1848, p. 4). Also the villages of Thoméry and By on the hillsides above the Seine, just outside Fontainebleau, were famous for their *chasselas* grapes (Jamin, *Quatre Promenades,* pp. 253–4). For general confirmation of the economic infrastructure of the department, see P. Bernard, *Economie et sociologie de la Seine-et-Marne 1850–1950,* 1953, pp. 96–106.

8 Gassies, *Souvenirs,* pp. 108–9.

9 Archives Départementales, Melun – census returns for Melun South, 1868 – 10 8 83. In 1844, Duchâtelet donated a fifteen-volume work on the *Cérémonies et coutumes religieuses de tous les peuples du monde* to the library at Melun, a gift indicative of his status as a local grandee (*Indicateur,* 9 November 1844).

10 *Annuaire de Seine-et-Marne,* 1844, pp. 66, 77, 101. The *conseil général* was dominated by the establishment. There were seven peers, three judges and seven proprietors. Paul de Ségur, who farmed at Lorrez le Boccage, sat on the council for Moret. See also Bourges, *Recherches,* p. 542, on the list of deputies for Fontainebleau in the nineteenth century.

11 Vicomte de Ségur-Cabanac, *Histoire de la maison de Ségur,* 1908, pp. 45, 61–9. Paul-Philippe's father, Louis-Philippe, had been ambassador to St Petersburg, but had rallied

to the Empire, becoming *maître de cérémonies*. It is also relevant that this branch of the family was Protestant.

12 Anon., *Biographies du XIXe siècle - Général de Ségur*, undated, pp. 123-55. The Comte de Ségur was author of *Un aide de camp de Napoléon: Mémoires du Général Comte de Ségur*, 3 vols, 1894-95. His father had also been a member of the Académie Française, but Philippe was elected in March 1830, in replacement of M. de Lévis, for his historical writing (Vapereau, *Dictionnaire universel des contemporains*, 1858, p. 1580).

13 Antoine-Jean Durosnel (1771-1849) was born in Paris and embarked on a military career, rising through the army to become general of a brigade at Austerlitz and to be made *Comte de l'Empire* by Napoleon in 1808. He supported Napoleon on his abortive return from Elba, and consequently was regarded with suspicion under the Restoration, retiring from the army in 1816 at forty-five. He was elected deputy for the Seine-et-Marne as a government candidate in 1830, 1831 and 1834 (Balteau, *Dictionnaire de biographie française*, 1970, 12, p. 797).

14 Bourges, *Recherches*, p. 356; *Indicateur*, 8 April 1848, p. 4. Lebeuf was a regent of the Bank of France as well as a leading industrialist, and sat on the *conseil général* in the 1840s. He was in favour of free trade, and argued in his 1848 election address that only a republic could restore order in the interior of the country and strength abroad.

15 *Indicateur*, 8 April 1848, p. 4.

16 *Indicateur*, 1 April 1848, p. 2. Oscar Lafayette had been elected an opposition deputy in 1846 for Meaux. Another Lafayette, George, the son of the famous general, had also been a representative of the department and stood again in 1848.

17 On Bonapartist opposition and revolutionary plots from the early 1820s, see A. Jardin and A.-J. Tudesq, *La France des notables (1815-1848)*, 1973, 1, pp. 64-6; on the split between liberals who rallied to the Orleanist regime and the new republican opposition in the early 1830s, *ibid.*, pp. 136-41.

18 *Annuaire de Seine-et-Marne*, 1844, p. 120. At Fontainebleau there were three retired military figures, seven representatives of the legal profession and magistracy, three proprietors, one doctor and eight men in business, commerce and trade.

19 A. Luchet, *Souvenirs de Fontainebleau*, 1842, pp. 54-6. This left-wing analysis of the social composition of the town was confirmed later by the right-wing Aigoin in *Fontainebleau*.

20 P. Comte de Ségur, *Du Rhin à Fontainebleau: Mémoires*, 1913, pp. 429-90.

21 Luchet, *Souvenirs*, p.53.

22 *Ibid.*, pp. 56-7.

23 *Ibid.*, p. 58. Luchet did draw a distinction between the bourgeois merchants who had retired to the town - about whom he was vitriolic - and the 'bourgeois indigènes' - to whom he was more indulgent, regarding them as gentle and harmless. The latter supported the constitutional monarchy because, in a town without industry or commerce, the military garrison furnished their livelihood.

24 F. Hébert, 'Auguste Luchet (1805-1872): Etude bio-bibliographique': Supplements to *Abeille de Fontainebleau*, 1913, Archives Départementales, Melun. (The archive at Melun is incomplete and has to be complemented by the original articles in the *Abeille.*) Luchet, the son of a minor civil servant, became a *carbonaro* and a freemason in the 1820s, while studying medicine under Broussais, which he then abandoned for journalism. In the 1830s he wrote for left-wing newspapers like *Le Temps* and *Le Bon Sens* and started writing popular plays with Felix Pyat and, later, novels. His first novel, *Frère et Soeur* (1838) - an attack on the bourgeois family - was published in Fontainebleau, probably because Luchet's editor, Souverain, was friendly with the Fontainebleau printer Jacquin, and books published outside Paris might more easily escape the censors.

25 Hébert, 'Auguste Luchet': Supplements of 31 January and 21 February 1913. He went

into exile in Jersey for five years from 1842. The offending novel was *Nom de famille* which was seen to attack the monarchy and public morality. Exile was preferable to two years of prison and a thousand-franc fine.

26 Hébert, 'Auguste Luchet': Supplement of 3 January 1913; *Indicateur*, 18 April 1848. His was the most radical programme of all the candidates, demanding 'absolute equality of rights, relative equality of taxes, absolute freedom', free education for all, etc. He received 10,102 votes. For Luchet as provisional governor and administrator of the chateau in 1848, see *Abeille de Fontainebleau*, 5 March 1848, p. 4.

27 The *Indicateur* was revived in September 1838, after some years of neglect, as a weekly Saturday paper. It assumed its standard format and heading from October of that year. The *Abeille de Fontainebleau* was founded by Emile-Antoine Jacquin, who in 1835 took over the printing business of Huré at Fontainebleau and with it a *Feuille judiciaire de l'arrondissement*, which he transformed into the *Abeille* in 1840 (M. Beauvilliers, *Fontainebleau: Etudes d'histoire locale*, 1896, pp. 175, 180). Also see Jean Watelet, *Bibliographie de la presse française: Seine-et-Marne, 1865-1944*, 1976, pp. 7–10. Watelet points out that, unlike those of many provincial cities, the newspapers of the Seine-et-Marne were mainly non-political, registering both the desire of local printer-publishers to get their businesses known via the steady trade in legal announcements and the penetration by Parisian papers.

28 In the *Almanach Bottin du commerce* for 1835, p. 803, Michelin was listed as the official printer-publisher to the prefecture. Jacquin was the son of Baron Jacquin, one of the most valiant generals of the First Empire (Bourges, *Recherches*, preface, p. vii). According to Watelet (*Bibliographie de la presse*, p. 10), the *Abeille* was frankly Bonapartist. This was certainly true from mid-century, when it rallied to the Empire, but the political allegiance of the paper was far from explicit in the 1840s. In the 'Faits Divers' section of 25 February 1844, the *Abeille* talked sympathetically about the Arago brothers, from a well-known republican family; while, a week before, there was also an enthusiastic report on the pro-government deputy Paul de Ségur, who had secured 1,000 francs for the local charity office. The paper also carried official announcements from the prefect and *conseil général* which clearly restricted its capacity to criticise.

29 The *Indicateur* introduced a column called 'Lettres Parisiennes' from 1843. An example of titillating statistical information was provided by the 'Fait Divers' of the *Abeille* on 21 January 1844, which informed readers of the numbers of travellers using the Paris-to-Corbeil and Paris-to-Orléans trains the previous December, and listed all the different kinds of newspapers and periodicals available in Paris. See also, 'Faits Divers', 2 June 1844, on the amount of railway track laid throughout France.

30 Hébert, 'Auguste Luchet': eleventh article (undated) in the series of Supplements (Archives Départementales, Melun), quoting from Luchet's novel *Nom de famille*.

31 *Abeille de Fontainebleau*, 22 October 1843, for an advertisement for Sue's *Mystères de Paris* at fifty centimes a part; 2 June 1844, for an illustrated edition of the same; and 20 October 1844, for an illustrated edition of Hugo's *Notre-Dame de Paris*. Advertisements, especially for Sue, were regularly repeated throughout 1845.

32 *Ibid.*, 22 October 1843.

33 *Ibid.*, 21 January 1844, pp. 3, 4. The shop concerned was the *Maison du coin de rue*, 8, Rue Montesquieu, which had just incorporated four additional 'immenses galeries'.

34 *Ibid.*, 27 November 1842.

35 *Indicateur*, 8 February 1840, pp. 2–3.

36 Agulhon, *Le Cercle*, pp. 73–7.

37 Tocqueville, *Souvenirs*, p. 107.

38 See *Indicateur*, 13 and 20 October 1838, for Denis de Thézan's picturesque account of the château of Le Vivier–les Ruines, near Guignes; also 'Pochade', *Indicateur*, 10 August 1839, pp. 2–3, on the forest of Fontainebleau.

39 See, for example, 'La Route de Franchard', *Abeille de Fontainebleau*, 26 May 1844, pp. 2–3, on a walk through the forest; or 'Promenade au chemin de fer', *Abeille de Fontainebleau*, 12 April 1846. There was also a certain M. Barthelemy who contributed poetry and prose.

40 J.-B. Alexis Durand, *Forêt de Fontainebleau: Poème en quatre chants,*1836, preface by Clovis Michaux, p. v. Michaux was appointed to the post in Fontainebleau in 1832. Durand's story is derived from this preface.

41 *Ibid.*, p. vi.

42 E. Jamin, *Fontainebleau: Notice historique et descriptive sur cette résidence royale*, 1834.

43 Durand, *Forêt de Fontainebleau*, p. vi.

44 *Ibid.*, pp. vii–viii. He was later to write a poem celebrating Napoleon called *Napoléon à Fontainebleau: Choix d'épisodes*, 1850.

45 On the *tour de France* and its structures of apprenticeship, see A. Perdiguier, *Le Livre de compagnonnage*, 1841, and *Mémoires d'un compagnon* (1854–55), 1964.

46 Clovis Michaux, letter to the editor-in-chief of the *Chronique de Seine-et-Marne*, 10 July 1835, published as a preface to the 'Bouquet du Roi' poetic fragment by Durand (Archives Départementales, Melun).

47 Durand, *Forêt de Fontainebleau*, pp. xvii–xix.

48 *Ibid.*, pp. xxi–xxiv. Other members of the Académie Eroicienne referenced by Michelet in *Le Peuple* were Chateaubriand, Lamartine and Ancelot.

49 On worker-poets during the July monarchy, see J. Touchard, *La Gloire de Béranger*, 1968, 2, pp. 116–34.

50 Nadaud, *Mémoires de Léonard*, pp. 319–32, praised the self-improvement typified by those like Agricol Perdiguier or indeed himself – though of course Nadaud, later a moderate republican Third Republic deputy, is often seen as having 'sold out' his class.

51 Jacques Rancière, in *La Nuit des prolétaires*, 1981, makes a convincing case for the importance of worker-poets and equivalent cultural practices in marking out a complex, contradictory and multi-accented cultural space within and for the working class.

52 L. Blanc, *La Révolution française: Histoire de dix ans, 1830-1840*, 1841–44, 3, pp. 203–25, on 'guerre civile' at Lyon resulting from economic crisis in 1832; 4, pp. 100–24, on the insurrection in Paris following the funeral of Général Lamarque, 1832; 5, pp. 175–99, on the economic uprising in Lyon, 1834 and consequent violence in Paris.

53 Durand, *Forêt de Fontainebleau*, p. xxv.

54 The real name of Michaux (1788–1874) was Nicholas-Louis. He changed it to the poetic Clovis in 1827 to avoid confusion with a literary competitor of the same name. He was *procureur du roi* in Fontainebleau between 1832 and 1845 (Rousselet, *La Magistrature*, p. 465). Indicative of his status, Michaux was vice-president of the local education committee and one of the directors of the *caisse d'épargne* (*Annuaire de Seine-et-Marne*, 1844, pp. 198, 282).

55 C. Michaux, *Poésies posthumes*, 1875, biographical notice by L. A. Bourguin, pp. iii–viii. Ten days after the battle of Waterloo, Michaux wrote a passionate letter to Carnot, as member of the provisional government, demanding that he should share the fate of his hero, Napoleon. Not surprisingly, he lost his position under the Restoration. Between 1830 and 1832, he showed himself a strong partisan of law and order by helping to put down the Parisian riots as a member of the National Guard. The position of *procureur du roi* was compensation for his earlier destitution.

56 *Ibid.*, pp. ix–xii. He had earlier published a book of poetry in Paris called *Les Douze Heures de la nuit* (1825). Apart from his poem on Fontainebleau, he translated Horace's *Odes* into French and wrote a piece dedicated to Béranger called *L'Homme*. He was acquainted with the poet through a lawyer friend, Berville, who was also a

partisan of poetry. For these broad cultural connections, see also Eugène de Pradel, *Visite à Béranger*, 1836. According to T. Lhuillier, *Seine-et-Marne: Essai de bibliographie départementale*, 1857, p. 64, Michaux's poem on Fontainebleau was published in the *Bulletin de la Société de l'Agriculture de l'Aube*, 1835, 7, p. 116.

57 Jamin, *Fontainebleau: Notice historique*, foreword; *Annuaire de Seine-et-Marne*, 1844, p. 284. Etienne Jamin (1795–1871) had, according to an alternative biographical account, been a teacher at the boys' college at Fontainebleau. He also helped edit the *Chronique de Seine-et-Marne*, founded by the printer Huré. At the palace, he never rose further than assistant steward and assistant librarian, though he was credited with great knowledge and was friendly with Alexandre Dumas *père* (Beauvilliers, *Fontainebleau*, pp. 139–40, 152–3, 180).

58 In the *Indicateur*, Jamin wrote reviews of Durand's poems (4 April 1840) and articles on Casimir Delavigne (23 December 1843) and the King's visit to Fontainebleau (11 May 1844). To the *Abeille de Fontainebleau* he contributed reports on recent books acquired for the palace library (15 September 1844) and on the problems currently suffered by bakers (29 September 1844).

59 Luchet, *Souvenirs*, p. 22.

60 For information on Guérin's life at Fontainebleau, see Bourges, *Recherches*, pp. 15–20. He was mayor from 1842 to 1852 and 1858 to 1871. He was also a member of the *conseil général* for twenty-six years.

61 D. A. Guérin, *Compte rendu de l'administration municipale de Fontainebleau*, 1852, p. 7. According to Aigoin, *Fontainebleau*, p. 35, his fortune was largely based on the success of a product called *Racahout des Arabes*.

62 As a private benefactor, he was director of the *caisse d'épargne*, founder and president of the charitable Société de Secours Mutuels de Saint-Roch, regional delegate of the *conseil de l'instruction publique*, and member of the administrative council for the *collège communal* (Bourges, *Recherches*, p. 20; *Annuaire de Seine-et-Marne*, 1844, pp. 198, 282).

63 *Indicateur*, 29 February 1840. For the establishment of the library, see Guérin, *Compte rendu*, p. 15, where he claimed to have obtained and donated 2,000 classic works in 1837: 'My plan was to approach all our contemporary literary and scientific celebrities in order to obtain a gift of their works'. By the early 1850s the library had 6,000 books, including gifts from the king and queen, Casimir Delavigne, Guizot, Hugo, Lamartine and Scribe.

64 C. Michaux, *Discours prononcé pour l'inauguration de la Bibliothèque publique de Fontainebleau*, 9 August 1839, p. 19. This initiative was reinforced by Guérin's establishment of a school for adults in 1841 (Guérin, *Compte rendu*, p. 16).

65 A. Durand, *Le Poète Artisan: scènes de la vie ouvrière*, verse comedy in three acts, 1845, dedicated to a M. Champion, member of the *légion d'honneur* – probably Clovis Michaux.

66 In the Lhuillier *Essai de bibliographie départementale,* p. 34, Durand was listed as *bibliothécaire* as well as *menuisier*, suggesting that he was employed at the municipal library. The files of the Fontainebleau notary Eugène Lecuyer show Durand to have been involved in property transactions, selling a house and then land at the village of Bourron in April and June of 1847 (Archives Départementales, Melun: Archives Notariales, 18 E 349/350). Finally, in an open letter of 4 September 1849, published in the *Indépendant de Seine-et-Marne*, (formerly the *Abeille*) the cicerone Denecourt accused Durand of having become a *rentier* (Archives Départementales, Melun).

67 Apart from Paty's *Manuel du voyageur*, which we have already considered, such picturesque publications included: J. B. Richard, *Description topographique des environs de Paris,* 1826; R. Saint-Edme, *Paris et ses environs … Dictionnaire historique, topographique et militaire des environs de Paris,* 1826; G. Touchard-Lafosse,

Histoire des environs de Paris dans un rayon de 30 à 40 lieues, 4 vols, 1834–35.

68 Dr A. Comieu, 'Notice biographique sur Charles Rémard de Château-Thierry, Biblioth-écaire du château de Fontainebleau, 1766–1828': extract from the *Annales de la Société Historique et Archéologique de Château-Thierry*, 1885 (Archives Départementales, Melun). This biography makes it clear that Rémard came to Fontainebleau from Paris in 1794 as a bookseller, and wrote a bizarre poem called *Chézonomie*, published in 1806. In 1813, he was named librarian at the palace.

69 Rémard, *Guide*, pp. 138–40.

70 Luchet, *Souvenirs*, p. 54.

71 Durand, *Forêt de Fontainebleau*, pp. 49–50.

72 For the self-educated provincial, only classical metre signified 'real' literature (*ibid.*, pp. xii–xiii). Further, Durand's work stood in the tradition of an earlier poem on the forest, Richard Castel's *La Forêt de Fontainebleau*, 1805. It is also clear that Durand's literary mentors – Jamin and Michaux – themselves favoured the standard classical literary tradition in their own writing.

73 *Ibid.*, p. 50.

74 Jamin, *Quatre Promenades*, non-paginated foreword.

75 *Ibid.*

76 *Ibid.*, p. iv.

77 *Ibid.*, p. 17.

78 *Ibid.*, pp. 186–205. Passages from Durand were liberally quoted, as were sections from Guilbert's *Histoire de Fontainebleau* of 1731. Guilbert provided historical information and anecdotes on the hermit at Franchard, and also on the many crosses and wells found in the forest.

79 Luchet, *Souvenirs*, p. 71.

80 Jamin, *Quatre Promenades*, pp. 208–17 and especially pp. 213–15 on improvements.

81 See, for example, the draft of an address to the Emperor by the landscapist Rousseau. This demanded the protection of the forest in the name of art, eulogised its wild and antique splendour and attacked the forestry administration for its concentration on profit. It also attacked the subsidies handed out to tourist operators and guides for useless paths and belvederes (unpublished correspondence of Rousseau, Cabinet des Dessins, Louvre, packet 2).

82 For example: *Abeille de Fontainebleau*, 14 April 1844, 15 September 1844, 13 October 1844, 23 March 1845, 21 September 1845, 12 July 1846, 9 August 1846, 10 October 1847, etc.

83 *Abeille de Fontainebleau*, 12 April 1846.

84 *Abeille de Fontainebleau*, 16 March 1845. The anonymous article (probably by Durand) commented that the prefect had authorised the inspector of the forest, Boisd'hyver to cut a swath through the forest in preparation of the railway line. The writer commented that numerous spectators came to watch 'the majestic undulation of this grandiose line'. See also A. Durand, *Quatre Promenades historiques et pittoresques* 1851, p. 126: 'Behold the masterpiece of modern machinery. The sublimity of human invention is present too in the employment of steam'.

85 *Abeille de Fontainebleau*, 23 March 1845.

86 Luchet, *Souvenirs*, p. 3, from the foreword provided by the editor, Reuillier. Guides were also mentioned by Pradel, *Visite à Béranger*, and by Castellan, *Fontainebleau*, p. ii. Also see *Indicateur*, 24 August 1839, for a letter from 'un ami des cicérones' which praised Jamin's guide and Durand's poetry.

87 For a detailed account of all Denecourt's activities, see Société des Amis, *Claude-François Denecourt*.

88 Denecourt's autobiography was narrated in his *Indicateur de Fontainebleau*, 10th edition, 1855, pp. 45–51. Also see Bourges, *Recherches*, pp. 391–8, and Société des

Amis, *Claude-François Denecourt*, pp. 26-9.

89 Société des Amis, *Denecourt*, pp. 28 and 31, nos. 7 and 8.

90 *Ibid.*, p. 33, nos. 25 and 27; p. 34, no. 29; and p. 42, no. 80, for letters and dedications to establishment figures like Théophile Lhuillier (head of the police department at the Melun prefecture), Louis de Ségur (deputy in the 1870s) and Boisd'hyver. See also p. 28 for the *Mont Guérin*.

91 *Ibid.*, p. 60, no. 161, for evidence that Jamin sold Denecourt the rights on his *Quatre Promenades*, which became the second part of the latter's *Nouvel Indicateur de Fontainebleau* of 1843. In 1849, Denecourt collaborated with Durand on the occasion of the opening of the train station. The latter produced a poem called 'La Légende de Némerosa' to go with Denecourt's *Itinéraire d'une charmante promenade au débarcadère* (*ibid.*, p. 28). Further, a guide published three years earlier, *Le Palais et la forêt de Fontainebleau*, 3rd edition, 1846, though bearing only Denecourt's name inside, included Durand as author on the outside cover. Certainly, the introductory note – 'L'Auteur aux voyageurs' – reads like the poet. However, Durand was already becoming ambivalent about this business competition. In the *Abeille de Fontainebleau*, 28 December 1845, the littérateur, having praised Denecourt's latest guide in an article two weeks previously, now criticised his hyperbolic language and historical inaccuracies. In 1849, Denecourt's open letter published in the *Indépendant de Seine-et-Marne* of 4 November directly referenced attacks on him by Durand and returned the insults, accusing him of jealousy (Archives Départementales, Melun). Finally, the publication by Durand of his own *Quatre Promenades historiques et pittoresque* in 1851 was an obvious attempt to beat Denecourt at his own game and reclaim his leading position as interpreter of the forest.

92 Société des Amis, *Claude-François Denecourt*, p. 29.

93 C.-F. Denecourt, *Guide du voyageur dans le palais et la forêt de Fontainebleau*, 1840, p. 6. This 1840 edition was identical with the first publication of 1839, merely combining the initial brochures on the forest and the palace in one book.

94 *Indicateur*, 6 July 1839, article by E. J. – presumably Jamin.

95 For example, *Abeille de Fontainebleau*, 12 October 1845; 14 and 28 December 1845.

96 'Variétés', *Indicateur*, 14 September 1839.

97 *Ibid.*

98 C.-F. Denecourt, *Camp de Fontainebleau*, 1839, price one franc.

99 Many trees, rocks, etc. in the forest already had names, and writers such as Jamin and Castellan had played up their picturesque effects, dwelling on the romance of historical associations. However, Denecourt turned such naming into a fine art. For example, in his *Promenades dans la forêt*, 1844, he included a section called: 'Alphabetical Nomenclature of everything contained in the forest that is remarkable or picturesque, such as its rocks, its beautiful spots, its numerous viewpoints, its ancient glades, its extremely curious trees'. The list included about one hundred and seventy-five items. See E. Michel, *La Forêt de Fontainebleau*, 1909, p. 19, for Denecourt's tendency to embroider apocryphal stories.

100 Michel, p. 18; Société des Amis, *Claude-François Denecourt*, pp. 14, 27, 46.

101 Société des Amis, *Denecourt*, p. 53. In 1853 he completed a look-out tower, first called *Point du vue de Paris* then swiftly changed to *Fort de l'Empereur*, by whom it was inaugurated in that year, and finally to *Tour Denecourt*, in 1878.

102 Information based on a walk carried out by the author on 24 May 1981.

103 Denecourt, *L'Indicateur de Fontainebleau*, 1855, pp. 2-3.

104 Société des Amis, *Claude-François Denecourt*, p. 38. He also published maps (*ibid.*, p. 45).

105 C.-F. Denecourt, *Le Palais et la forêt*, 3rd edition, 1846, (Archives Départementales, Melun); Société des Amis, *Claude-François Denecourt*, p. 42, no. 88.

106 C.-F. Denecourt, *Itinéraire descriptif du palais de Fontainebleau*, undated, but 1846 according to maps included which are dated. Useful addresses of hotels, cafés, hire firms, bookshops, post-boxes and curio shops are listed at the end. Ten hotels are listed and four principal cafés, including the Café Lez.

107 See above, note 91. Cheap excursion trains started from 1850, only a year after the line was opened. The trip took between an hour and an hour and a half from Paris (Bernard, *Fontainebleau et ses environs*, pp. 3, 6).

108 *Abeille de Fontainebleau*, 12 October 1845.

109 *Indicateur*, 11 May 1844.

110 *Indicateur*, 22 June 1844.

111 *Ibid.* She also sold *draguées de St. Roch*, made from the fruits of the juniper covered in sugar, and said to fortify the stomach and the nerves, facilitate digestion and remove the odour of cigars.

112 See above, note 81.

113 See Pigeory, 'Barbizon', pp. 229-30, for a description of Denecourt as the Pausanius of the forest, 'antiquarian, historian and raconteur'. But the most extensive and elaborate tribute to Denecourt was paid in a publication organised by Ferdinand Desnoyers in 1855 and including essays by forty-two writers and poets, *Hommage à C.-F. Denecourt*. Writers such as Lamartine, Sand, Hugo, Béranger, Luchet, Champfleury and Gautier were involved, and a feast of twenty littérateurs was held in July 1855 at a Paris café to present a magnificently bound copy of the book to Denecourt (Société des Amis, *Claude-François Denecourt*, p. 47, no. 104).

114 Société des Amis, *Denecourt*, p. 19.

Conclusion

1 See P. N. Stearns, *Paths to Authority: The Middle Class and the Industrial Labor Force in France, 1820-1848*, 1978, and R. Aminzade, *Class, Politics and Early Industrial Capitalism: A Study of Mid-Nineteenth-Century Toulouse*, 1981. The obvious exception is D. H. Pinkney, *Decisive Years in France, 1840-1847*, 1986.

Bibliography

Primary sources

I Archives

1 *Archives Nationales*

Series AJ^{52} – Académie des Beaux-Arts:
(a) Programme of courses at Ecole des Beaux-Arts, AJ^{52} 41
(b) Posters for courses at Ecole des Beaux-Arts, AJ^{52} 60
(c) Notes for competitions of history landscape, 1822–1863, AJ^{52} 71
(d) Competition for the *Grand Prix du paysage historique*, 1821–1861, AJ^{52} 193
(e) Competition for the *Grand Prix du paysage historique*, 1821–1861, AJ^{52} 439
(f) Organisation and administration of the Ecole des Beaux-Arts, including observations on the *Grand Prix du paysage historique* by Baltard, 1821, AJ^{52} 439
(g) List of subjects for tree competition, 1817–1861, AJ^{52} 475
(h) Minutes on prize-givings for painting and sculpture, 1829–1836, AJ^{52} 475
(i) Prize-winners of the *Grand Prix du paysage historique*, 1823–1835, AJ^{52} 491

Series AP – Private Archives:
(a) Pagnerre papers, 67 AP
(b) Jules Simon papers, 87 AP

2 *Archives Notariales, Paris*

Etude II – Berceau, rue Saint-Honoré, 1846, *liasses* 1042 and 1043
Etude XVIII – Poignart, rue de Richelieu, 1832, *liasse* 1176
Etude XVIII – Roquebert, rue de Richelieu, 1840, 1841 and 1860, *liasses* 1205, 1208, 1212, 1299, 1300 and 1310
Etude XCVIII – Petit and Lefer, rue Saint-Honoré, 1823, 1830 and 1840, liasses 901, 937 and 991
Etude CXII – Thion de la Chaume, rue de Faubourg Montmartre/rue Laffitte, 1846 and 1854, *liasses* 1152, 1153, 1157, 1235, 1236
Etude CXV – Clairet, boulevard des Italiens, 1840–1841, *liasses* 1317

3 Cabinet de Documentation, Louvre

(a) Moreau-Nélaton dossier on Jean-François Millet
(b) Moreau-Nélaton dossier on Théodore Rousseau
(c) Théodore Rousseau autograph letters

4 Cabinet des Dessins, Louvre

Théodore Rousseau correspondence – eight packets of unedited and mainly unpublished material

5 Archives Départementales, Melun

(a) Census returns for Fontainebleau:	1846,	10	8	73
	1851,	10	M	101
(b) Census returns for Melun South:	1846,	10	8	83
	1851,	10	M	119
	1856,	10	M	149

(c) Archives Notariales, *études* of Gravier of Fontainebleau, 1846–1847, 18 E 351 and 18 E 352
(d) Miscellaneous items

II Dictionaries

Annuaire de Seine-et-Marne, 1844.
Balteau, J., *Dictionnaire de biographie française*, 14 vols, 1933–.
Almanach Bottin du commerce, 1821, 1832 and 1842.
Curinier *Dictionnaire national des contemporains*, 5 vols, 1899–1906.
Dictionnaire biographique de Seine-et-Marne, 1893.
Didot Annuaire du commerce, 1849, 1850, 1852, 1854, 1868 and 1876.
Didot/Bottin Annuaire et Almanach du commerce, 1880.
Grand Larousse universel du XIXe siècle, 17 vols, 1864–90.
Grand Larousse encyclopédique, 10 vols, 1960–64.
Hoefer, *Nouvelle biographie générale*, 46 vols, 1855–66.
Lermina, *Dictionnaire universel illustré, biographique et bibliographique de la France contemporaine*, 2 vols, 1884–85.
Lügt, F., *Répertoire des catalogues des ventes publiques, 1821-1863*, vol 2, 1953.
Mireur, Dr H., *Dictionnaire des ventes d'art faites en France et à l'étranger pendant les XVIIIe et XIXe siècles*, 7 vols, 1901–12.
Vapereau, L. G., *Dictionnaire universel des contemporains,* 1858, 1870, 1892–93, 1895.

III Newspapers, journals and periodicals

Abeille de Fontainebleau
Affiches, Annonces et Avis Divers du département de Seine-et-Marne
Affiches de Paris
Annales d'Hygiène publique et de la médecine légale
L'Artiste
Cabinet de l'Amateur de l'Antiquaire
Chronique des Arts et de la Curiosité
Gazette des Tribunaux
L'Indicateur de Seine-et-Marne
L'Informateur de Seine-et-Marne
Journal des Artistes
Journal des Femmes
Journal Général d'Affiches, annonces judiciaires, légales et avis divers
Magasin Pittoresque

IV Other published sources

Agoult, M. Comtesse d' (Daniel Stern), *Mémoires, 1833-1854*, Paris, 1927.

Agoult, M. Comtesse d' (Daniel Stern), *Mes Souvenirs, 1806-1833*, Paris, 1877.

Agoult, M. Comtesse d' (Daniel Stern), 'Mes souvenirs', *Revue des Deux Mondes*, 1927, 39, pp. 26-75.

Aigoin, J., *Fontainebleau sous le Second Empire: Souvenirs*, Fontainebleau, 1934.

Alphand, A., *L'Art des Jardins,* 3rd edition, Paris, 1885.

Alton Shée, E. Comte d', *Mes Mémoires, 1826-1848,* 2 vols, Paris, 1869.

Amaury-Duval, E.-E.. *L'Atelier d'Ingres*, Paris, 1878.

Ancelot, V., *Un Salon de Paris, 1824 à 1864*, Paris, 1866.

Anon., *L'Ancien et le nouveau Tivoli, ou Les Danses en plein air*, Paris, 1827.

Anon., *Biographies du XIXe siècle - Général de Ségur*, Paris, undated.

Anon., *Le Carnaval*, Paris, 1840.

Anon., *Catalogue de tableaux modernes faisant partie de ceux qui composaient l'ancien commerce du M. Alphonse Giroux, père*, Paris, 1830.

Anon., *Congrès médical de 1845. Instruction générale pour MM. les membres du congrès*, Paris, 1845.

Anon., *Les Français peints par eux-mêmes: Paris*, 5 vols, Paris, 1840.

Anon., *Les Français peints par eux-mêmes: Provinces*, 3 vols, Paris, 1841-42.

Anon., *L'Hermite de la Chaussée-d'Antin*, 5 vols, Paris, 1812-14.

Anon., *Mémoire adressé par une réunion de propriétaires, architectes et contructeurs de la ville de Paris, à MM. les membres de la commission d'enquête*, Paris, 1828.

Anon., *Physiologie de l'opéra, du carnaval, du cancan et de la cachucha*, Paris, 1842.

Anon., *Promenade ou itinéraire des jardins d'Ermenonville*, Paris, 1788.

Anon., *Promenade ou itinéraire des jardins d'Ermenonville*, Paris, 1811.

Anon., *Recherches statistiques de la ville de Paris, 1827-1836*, 5, Paris, 1844.

Anon., *Répertoire itinéraire et analytique de Paris*, Paris, 1812.

Anon., *Souvenirs de Jacques Laffitte, raconté par lui-même et puisés aux sources les plus authentiques*, 3 vols, Paris, 1844.

Anon., *A Tour to Ermenonville*, London, 1785.

Anon., *Traité de la composition et de l'ornement des jardins*, 2 vols, Paris, 1839.

Anon., *Trois Jours en voyage, ou Guide du promeneur à Chantilly, Mortefontaine et Ermenonville*, Paris, 1828.

Anon., *Vente Baroilhet*, preface by Charles Blanc, Paris, 1855.

Apponyi, Comte R., *Vingt-cinq ans à Paris, 1826-1850: Journal du Comte Rodolphe Apponyi, attaché à l'ambassade d'Autriche-Hongrie à Paris*, 4 vols, Paris, 1913-26.

Arago, F., *Etudes sur les fortifications considérées politiquement et militairement*, Paris, 1843.

Avèze, Marquis d' (J.B.D. Mazade ?), *Distractions ou passetemps de l'aveugle du Luxembourg*, Paris, 1818.

Balabine, V. de, *Paris de 1842 à 1852: Journal de Victor de Balabine, I: 1842-1847*, 2 vols, Paris, 1914.

Baschet, A., 'Les ateliers de Paris, no. 6: Théodore Rousseau', *L'Artiste*, 1854, 5th series, 12, pp. 97-8.

Baudelaire, C., *Art in Paris, 1845-1862: Salons and Other Exhibitions*, translated and edited J. Mayne, London, 1965.

Beauvilliers, M., *Fontainebleau: Etudes d'histoire locale*, Fontainebleau, 1896.

Bernard, F., *Fontainebleau et ses environs*, Paris, 1853.

Bernard, F., *Petit guide à l'étranger à Paris*, Paris, 1855.

Bernardin de Saint-Pierre, J.-H., *Paul et Virginie* with *La Chaumière indienne*, Paris, 1838.

Beslay, C., *Mes Souvenirs, 1830-1848-1870*, Paris, 1873.

Blanc, A. A. P. C., *Les Peintres français au dix-neuvième siècle*, Paris, 1845.

Blanc, A. A. P. C., *Le Trésor de la curiosité tiré des catalogues de vente*, 2 vols, Paris, 1857.

Blanc. L., *La Révolution française: Histoire de dix ans, 1830-1840*, 5 vols, Paris, 1841–44.

Block, M. (ed.), *Dictionnaire de l'administration française*, 3rd edition, Paris, 1862.

Bocher, C., *Mémoires, 1816-1907*, 2 vols, Paris, 1907.

Boitard, P., *L'Art de composer et décorer les jardins,* Paris, 1834.

Bourges, E., *Recherches sur Fontainebleau,* Fontainebleau, 1896.

Broglie, A.-C.-L.-V., Duc de, *Souvenirs, 1785-1870*, 4 vols, Paris, 1886.

Broglie, I. G. A., Duchesse de, *Lettres de la duchesse de Broglie, 1814-1838*, Paris, 1896.

Bulgari, S., *Souvenirs*, Paris, 1835.

Burty, P., 'L'Hôtel des ventes et le commerce des tableaux', *Paris-Guide*, 2, Paris, 1867.

Burty, P., *Maîtres et petits maîtres*, Paris, 1877.

Castellan, A. L., *Fontainebleau: Etudes pittoresques et historiques sur ce château*, Paris, 1840.

Challemel, P.-J., *Exposition de l'industrie française en 1844*, Paris, 1845.

Chambre de Pairs, *Projet de loi sur l'enseignement et l'exercice de la médecine et de la pharmacie*, Paris, 1847.

Chennevières, P. de, *Souvenirs d'un Directeur des Beaux-Arts* (1883–89), Paris, 1979.

Comieu, Dr A., 'Notice biographique sur Charles Rémard de Château-Thierry, bibliothécaire du château de Fontainebleau, 1766–1828': extract from *Annales de la Société Historique et Archéologique de Château-Thierry*, Château-Thierry, 1885.

Copper, E., *Art et la loi*, Paris, 1903.

Cotterel, Dr F.-F., *Promenades aériennes ou montagnes françaises, considérées sous la rapport de l'agrément et de la santé*, Paris, 1817.

Cottin, P., *Thoré-Bürger peint par lui-même*, Paris, 1900.

Coxe, H. (John Millard), *The Gentleman's Guide in his Tour of France*, London, 1817.

Dagoumer, Dr T., *Du danger d'habiter trop tôt des maisons nouvellement bâties*, Paris, 1825.

Daubanton, L., *Du déplacement de la population de Paris*, Paris, 1843.

Daubanton, L., 'Rapport relatif aux entreprises de construction à Paris et à l'interruption des travaux depuis cette année': extract from *Mémoires statistiques de la ville de Paris*, 4, Paris, 1829.

Daumier, H., *Caricaturana*, Paris, 1982.

Daumier, H., *Das lithographische Werke*, edited K. Schrenk, 2 vols, Munich, 1977.

Decamps, A., *Le Musée de 1834*, Paris, 1834.

Decamps, A., 'Salon de 1837', *Le National*, 5, 14, 25 March, and 7, 27 and 30 April, 1837.

Decamps, A., 'Salon de 1838', *Le National*, 5 and 18 March, 7 April and 1 May, 1838.

Denecourt, C.-F., *Camp de Fontainebleau*, Fontainebleau, 1839.

Denecourt, C.-F., *Guide du voyageur dans le palais et la forêt de Fontainebleau*, Fontainebleau, 1840.

Denecourt, C.-F., *L'Indicateur de Fontainebleau*, 10th edition, Fontainebleau, 1855.

Denecourt, C.-F., *Le Palais et la forêt de Fontainebleau*, 3rd edition, Fontainebleau, 1846.

Denecourt, C.-F., *Promenades dans la forêt*, Fontainebleau, 1844.

Deperthes, J. B., *Histoire de l'art du paysage, depuis la renaissance des beaux-arts jusqu'au dix-huitième siècle . . .*, Paris, 1822.

Deperthes, J. B., *Théorie du paysage, ou Considérations générales sur les beautés de la nature que l'art peut imiter*, Paris, 1818.

Desnoyers, F. (ed.), *Hommage à C.-F. Denecourt*, Paris, 1855.

Dollfus, H., *Histoire et généalogie de la famille Dollfus de Mulhouse, 1450-1908*, Mulhouse, 1909.

Dosne, S., *Mémoires de Mme Dosne, L'Egérie de M. Thiers*, edited H. Malo, Paris, 1928.

Dubois, F., *Eloges lus dans la séance publique de l'Académie de Médecine (1845-1863)*, 2 vols, Paris, 1864.

Ducamp, M., *Paris, ses organes, ses fonctions et sa vie dans la seconde moitié du XIXe siècle*, 6 vols, Paris, 1869–75.

Dumas, A. *(père)*, *Souvenirs de 1830 à 1842*, 4 vols, Paris, 1854–55.

Duplessy, J., *Guide indispensable du voyageur au chemin de fer de Paris à Orléans (section de Paris à Corbeil): suivi d'un notice historique et descriptive du château et de la forêt de Fontainebleau*, Paris, 1841.

Durand, J.-B. A., *Forêt de Fontainebleau: Poème en quatre chants*, Fontainebleau, 1836.

Durand, J.-B. A., *Napoléon à Fontainebleau: Choix d'épisodes*, Fontainebleau, 1850.

Durand, J.-B. A., *Le Poète-Artisan - Scènes de la vie ouvrière*, Fontainebleau, 1845.

Durand, J.-B. A., *Quatre Promenades historiques et pittoresques*, Fontainebleau, 1851.

Falloux, A.-F.-P., Comte de, *Mémoires d'un royaliste*, 2 vols, Paris, 1888.

Faucher, L., *Biographie et correspondance*, 2 vols, Paris, 1875.

Faucon, T., *Hippolyte de Villemessant par un témoin de sa vie*, Paris, 1879.

Feydeau, E., *Mémoires d'un coulissier*, Paris, 1873.

Fizelière, A.de la, 'Les auberges illustrées', *L'Illustration*, 22, July – September 1853, pp. 423–6.

Flaubert, G., *Madame Bovary: A Story of Provincial Life*, translated A. Russell, Harmondsworth, 1971.

Fregier, H., *Des classes dangereuses de la population dans les grandes villes et des moyens de les rendre meilleurs*, 2 vols, Paris, 1840.

Gasparin, V., Comtesse de, *Allons faire fortune à Paris*, Paris, 1863.

Gassies, J.-B.-G., *Le Vieux Barbizon: Souvenirs de jeunesse d'un paysagiste*, Paris, 1907.

Gautier, T., *Histoire du romantisme*, Paris, 1874.

Gautier, T., *L'Art romantique*, Paris, 1872.

Gautier, T., *Les Beaux-Arts en Europe*, 2 vols, Paris, 1855–56.

Gavarni, P., *Souvenirs du bal Chicard*, Paris, 1839.

Gay, D. (Mme Delphine de Girardin), *Les Lettres parisiennes, 1836-1848*, vols 4 and 5 of *Oeuvres complètes*, Paris, 1860–61.

Gerardin, R. L., *De la composition des paysages, ou Des moyens d'embellir la nature autour des habitations*, Geneva and Paris, 1777.

Gisquet, H. J., *Mémoires de M. Gisquet, ancien préfet de police*, 4 vols, Paris, 1840.

Goncourt, E. and J. de, *Gavarni: L'homme et l'oeuvre*, Paris, 1925.

Goncourt, E. and J. de, *Journal: Mémoires de la vie littéraire*, 4 vols, Paris, 1956–59.

Gouffée, A., *Tivoli, ou Le Jardin à la mode*, Paris, An V (1796).

Guérin, D. A., *Compte rendu de l'administration municipale de Fontainebleau*, Fontainebleau, 1852.

Guérin, E. de, *Journal et lettres*, edited G. S. Trebutien, Paris, 1865.

Haussmann, G. E., Baron, *Mémoires*, 3 vols, Paris, 1890–93.

Houssaye, A., *Confessions: Souvenirs d'un demi-siècle, 1830-1880*, 6 vols, Paris, 1885–91.

Houssaye, A., *Histoire de la peinture flamande et hollandaise*, Paris, 1846.

Jacob-Kolb, Chevalier, *Le Frondeur, ou Observations sur les moeurs de Paris et des provinces au commencement du XIXe siècle*, Paris, 1829.

Jamin, E., *Fontainebleau: Notice historique et descriptive sur cette résidence royale*, Fontainebleau, 1834.

Jamin, E., *Quatre Promenades dans la forêt de Fontainebleau*, Fontainebleau, 1837.

Janin, J., *The American in Paris, or Heath's Picturesque Annual for 1843*, Paris, 1843.

Janin, J., *Les Gaîtés champêtres*, Paris, 1851.

Janin, J., *Jules Janin: 735 lettres à sa femme*, Paris, 1973–79.

Joanne, A. L., *Les Environs de Paris illustrés*, Paris, 1856.

Joanne, A. L., *Fontainebleau, son palais, ses jardins, sa forêt et ses environs*, Paris, 1867.

Krafft, J.-C., *Maisons de campagne*, Paris, 1876.

Lagenevais, 'Salon de 1849', *Revue des Deux Mondes*, August 1849, pp. 559–93.

Lalos, J., *De la composition des parcs et des jardins pittoresques*, Paris, 1824.

Lamartine, A. de, *Correspondance de Lamartine*, 4 vols, Paris, 1881–82.

Lamartine, A. de, *Oeuvres complètes*, 8 vols, Paris, 1845.

Laurens, J.-B., *Théorie du beau pittoresque*, Montpellier, 1849.

Lecarpentier, C. T. F., *Essai sur le paysage*, Paris, 1817.

Legouvé, E., *Soixante Ans de souvenirs*, Paris, 1887.

Lemer, J., *La Vallée de Montmorency - promenades sentimentales, histoire, paysages, monuments, moeurs et chroniques*, Paris, 1847.

Le Normand, *Lettres à Sophie, ou Itinéraire de Paris à Montmorency, à l'hermitage et à l'île des peupliers en passant par Chantilly*, Paris, 1813.

Lenormant, C., *Salon de 1831*, Paris, 1831.

Lenormant, C., *Salon de 1833*, 2 vols, Paris, 1833.

Levallois, J., *L'Année d'un ermite*, Paris, 1870.

Levallois, J., *Mémoires d'un critique*, Paris, 1896.

Levallois, J., *Mémoires d'une forêt*, Paris, 1875.

Lhuillier, T., *Seine-et-Marne: Essai de bibliographie départementale*, Meaux, 1857.

Liszt, F., *Correspondance de Liszt et de la Comtesse d'Agoult (1840-1864)*, 2 vols, Paris, 1933–34.

Luchet, A., *Paris: Esquisses dédiées au peuple parisien*, Paris, 1830.

Luchet, A., *Souvenirs de Fontainebleau*, Fontainebleau, 1842.

Lurine, L. and Nodier, C. (eds), *Les Environs de Paris: paysage, histoire, monuments, moeurs, chroniques et traditions . . .*, Paris, 1844.

Lurine, L. (ed.), *Les Rues de Paris: Paris ancien et moderne, origines, histoire, monuments, costumes, moeurs, chroniques et traditions . . .*, 2 vols, Paris, 1844.

Marmier, X., *Journal (1848-1890)*, 2 vols, Paris, 1968.

Ménière, Dr P., *Journal de Dr. P. Ménière*, Paris, 1903.

Meynadier, H., *Paris pittoresque et monumental*, Paris, 1843.

Michaux, C., *Discours prononcé pour l'inauguration de la Bibliothèque publique de Fontainebleau*, Fontainebleau, 1839.

Michaux, C., *Poésies posthumes*, Paris, 1875.

Michelet, J., *La Femme* (1859), Paris, 1981.

Michelet, J., *Journal, 1828-1874*, 4 vols, Paris, 1959–76.

Michelet, J., *Lettres inédites (1841-1871)*, ed.P. Sirven, Paris, 1924.

Michelet, J., *Ma Jeunesse*, Paris, 1844.

Michiels, A., *Histoire de la peinture flamande et hollandaise*, 4 vols, Brussels, 1845–48.

Monglave, E. de and Pascallet, E., *Notice biographique sur M. Jacques-Seraphim Lanquetin*, Paris, 1856.

Monnier, H., 'Partie à la campagne', *Scènes de la ville et de la campagne*, Paris, 1841.

Montigny, L., *Le Provincial à Paris*, 3 vols, Paris, 1825.

Musset, A. de, *La Confession d'un enfant du siècle*, Paris, 1973.

Nadaud, M., *Mémoires de Léonard, ancien garçon maçon*, edited M. Agulhon, Paris, 1976.

Nodier, C., *Correspondance inédite, 1796-1844*, edited A. Estignat, Paris, 1931.

Parent-Duchâtelet, A., *De la prostitution dans la ville de Paris, considérée sous la rapport de l'hygiène publique, de la morale et de l'administration* (1836), edited A. Corbin, Paris, 1981.

Paty, I. du, *Manuel du voyageur aux environs de Paris*, Paris, 1826.

Perdiguier, A., *Le Livre de compagnonnage*, Paris, 1841.

Pigeory, F., 'Barbizon - Notes et souvenirs', *Revue des Beaux-Arts*, 5, 1854, pp. 229-34.

Piot, E., *Etat civil de quelques artistes français*, Paris, 1873.

Planche, G., *Etudes sur l'école française (1831-1852)*, 2 vols, Paris, 1855.

Pluchonneau, *aîné, Paris aujourd'hui: Poème historique des monuments érigés, achevés ou embellis de la capitale*, Paris, 1844.

Pommiès, A., *Le Chemin de fer de Lyon et la campagne du chemin de fer d'Orléans*, Melun, 1844.

Poumiès de la Siboutie, Dr A., *Souvenirs d'un médecin de Paris*, Paris, 1910.

Pradel, E. de, *Visite à Béranger*, Paris, 1836.

Quatremère de Quincy, A., *Essai sur l'idéal dans ses applications pratiques aux oeuvres de l'imitation*, Paris, 1837.

Raisson, H., *Histoire de la police de Paris, 1667-1844*, Paris, 1844.

Rambuteau, C., *Mémoires*, Paris, 1905.

Ranc, A., *Souvenirs: Correspondance, 1831-1908*, Paris, 1913.

Rémard, C., *Guide de Fontainebleau*, Fontainebleau, 1820.

Rémond, C., *Vues d'Italie dessinées d'après nature et lithographiées*, Paris, 1828.

Rémusat, C., Comte De, *Mémoires de ma vie*, 5 vols, Paris, 1958-67.

Reybaud, L., *Jérôme Paturot à la recherche d'une position sociale*, Paris, 1842.

Robertet, G., *L'Oeuvre de M. Thiers*, Paris, 1887.

Rousseau, J.-J. *Julie, or The New Eloise*, translated and abridged J. H. McDowell, London, 1968.

Saint-A., P., *Dictionnaire historique, topographique et militaire de tous les environs de Paris*, Paris, 1820.

Salvo, Marquis de, *Trois Mois à Montmorency: Lettres d'une dame à la princesse de . . . à Palerme*, Paris, 1846.

Sand, G., *Correspondance*, edited G. Lubin, 16 vols, Paris, 1964-81.

Sand, G., *Elle et lui*, 2 vols, Paris, 1859.

Sand, G., *Le Mare au diable* with *François le champi*, Paris, 1962.

Sand, G., *Letters of George Sand*, trans. R. Ledos de Beaufort, London, 1886.

Scheurer-Kestner, A., *Souvenirs de Jeunesse*, Paris, 1905.

Ségur, P., Comte de, *Du Rhin à Fontainebleau: Mémoires*, Paris, 1913.

Ségur-Cabanac, Vicomte de, *Histoire de la maison de Ségur*, Paris, 1908.

Senancour, P. de, *Obermann: Lettres publiées par M. . . . ,* 2nd edition, preface by Sainte-Beuve, 2 vols, Paris, 1833.

Sensier, A., Souvenirs sur Théodore Rousseau, Paris, 1872.

Silvestre, T., *Les Artistes français*, ed. E. Faure, 2 vols, Paris, 1926.

Simon, J., 'Souvenirs de jeunesse', *Faisons la chaîne*, edited P. Audebrand, Paris, 1890.

Sue, E., *Les Mystères de Paris*, Paris, 1843.

Thénot, J. P., *Cours complet de lithographie*, Paris, 1836.

Thénot, J. P., *Cours complet de paysage*, Paris, 1834.

Thiébaut, A., *Voyage à l'île des peupliers*, Paris, An VII (1798).

Thoré, T., 'Par monts et par bois', *Le Constitutionnel*, 27 and 28 November 1847 .

Thoré, T., *La Recherche de la liberté*, Paris, 1845.

Thoré, T., *Salons de T. Thoré, 1844-1848*, Paris, 1868.

Tocqueville, A. de, *Souvenirs d'Alexis de Tocqueville*, Paris, 1942.

Tristan, F., *Flora Tristan's London Journal, 1840*, trans. D. Palmer and G. Pincetl, London, 1980.

Valenciennes, P.-H. de, *Elémens de perspective pratique à l'usage des artistes. Suivis de réflexions et conseils à un élève sur la peinture et particulièrement sur le paysage* (1800), Geneva, 1973.

Véron, Dr L., *Mémoires d'un bourgeois de Paris*, 5 vols, Paris, 1856.

Villemessant, H. de, *Mémoires d'un journaliste*, 6 vols, Paris, 1867-84.

Vincard J., *aîné, Mémoires épisodiques d'un vieux chansonnier Saint-Simonien*, Paris, 1878.

Watelet, C. H., *Essai sur les jardins*, Paris, 1774.

Secondary sources

Ackerknecht, E. H., 'Anti-contagionism between 1821 and 1867', *Bulletin of the History of Medicine*, 1948, no. 5, pp. 562–93.

Ackerknecht, E. H., 'Hygiene in France, 1815–1848', *Bulletin of the History of Medicine*, 1948, no. 2, pp. 118–34.

Adam, J. P., *Instauration de la politique des chemins de fer en France*, Paris, 1972.

Adams, W. H., *The French Garden, 1500–1800*, New York, 1979.

Adhémar, J., 'Les lithographies de paysage en France à l'époque romantique', *Archives de l'art français*, 1938, new period, 19, pp. 189–364.

Agulhon, M., *Le Cercle dans la France bourgeoise, 1810–1848: Etude d'une mutation de sociabilité*, Paris, 1977.

Agulhon, M., *Marianne au combat: L'Imagerie et la symbolique républicaine de 1789 à 1880*, Paris, 1979.

Althusser, L., *For Marx*, translated B. Brewster, London, 1969.

Althusser, L., *Lenin and Philosophy and Other Essays*, translated B. Brewster, London, 1971.

Aminzade, R., *Class, Politics and Early Industrial Capitalism: A Study of Mid-Nineteenth-Century Toulouse*, Albany, NY, 1981.

Anon., *Paris au XIXe siècle: Aspects d'un mythe littéraire*, Lyon, 1984.

Archives Nationales, Paris, *Le Parisien chez lui au XIXe siècle, 1814–1914*, Paris, 1976.

Aron, J. P., (ed.), *Misérable et glorieuse: La Femme au XIXe siècle*, Paris, 1980.

Barral, P., *Les Perier dans l'Isère au XIX siècle d'après leur correspondance familiale*, Paris, 1964.

Barrell, J., *The Dark Side of the Landscape: The Rural Poor in English Painting, 1730–1840*, Cambridge, 1980.

Bastié, J., *La Croissance de la banlieue parisienne*, Paris, 1964.

Bastié, J., 'La région parisienne – Croissance et organisation', in *L'Urbanisation française*, Centre de Recherche d'Urbanisme, Paris, 1964, pp. 98–125.

Baudelaire, C., *Selected Poems*, translated and introduced J. Richardson, London, 1975.

Beauroy, J. (ed.), *The Wolf and the Lamb: Popular Culture in France from the Old Regime to the Twentieth Century*, Saratoga, California, 1977.

Beechey, V. and Donald J. (eds), *Subjectivity and Social Relations*, Milton Keynes, 1985.

Beik, P. H., *Louis-Philippe and the Bourgeois Monarchy*, Princeton, 1965.

Belhabit, J., *La Poste et le rail en Seine-et-Marne*, Meaux, 1984.

Bellanger, C. (ed.), *Histoire générale de la presse française*, vols 2 and 3: *1815–1940*, Paris, 1969 and 1972.

Benjamin, W., *Charles Baudelaire: A Lyric Poet in the Era of High Capitalism*, translated H. Zohn, London, 1973.

Bernard, P., *Economie et sociologie de la Seine-et-Marne, 1850–1950*, Paris, 1953.

Bertho, C., 'L'invention de la Bretagne: Génèse sociale d'un stéréotype', *Actes de la recherche en sciences sociales*, November 1980, no. 35, pp. 45–62.

Bertrand, L., *Lamartine*, Paris, 1940.

Bibliothèque Historique de la Ville de Paris, *Paris des illusions*, Paris, 1984.

Bibliothèque Nationale, *Les Mystères du Rez de Chaussée*, Paris, 1987.

Bloomfield, J. (ed.), *Class, Hegemony and Party*, London, 1977.

Boime, A., *The Academy and French Painting in the Nineteenth Century*, London, 1971.

Bouret, J., *The Barbizon School and Nineteenth-Century French Landscape*, translated J. Brenton, London, 1973.

Braibant, C., *Guide historique des rues de Paris*, Paris, 1965.

Burkart, A. J. and Medlik, S., *Tourism: Past, Present and Future*, London, 1974.

Carter, E. C. (ed.), *Enterprise and Entrepreneurs in Nineteenth and Twentieth Century France*, Baltimore, 1976.

Castel, R., *L'Ordre psychiatrique: L'Age d'or de l'aliénisme*, Paris, 1976.

Castells, M., *The Urban Question: A Marxist Approach*, translated A. Sheridan, London, 1977.

Chauvet, H., *François Arago: La plus noble figure des années 1830-1848*, Paris, 1954.

Chevalier, L. (ed.), *Le Choléra: La Première Epidémie collective du XIXe siècle*, Paris, 1958.

Chevalier, L., *Classes laborieuses et classes dangereuses à Paris pendant la premiere moitié du XIXe siècle*, Paris, 1958.

Clark, T. J., *The Absolute Bourgeois: Artists and Politics in France, 1848-1851*, London, 1973.

Clark, T. J., *Image of the People: Gustave Courbet and the 1848 Revolution*, London, 1973.

Clark, T. J., *The Painting of Modern Life: Paris in the Art of Manet and his Followers*, London, 1984.

Corbin, A., *Le Miasme et la jonquille: L'odorat et l'imaginaire social aux XVIIIe-XIXe siècles*, Paris, 1986.

Daumard, A., *La Bourgeoisie parisienne de 1815 à 1848*, Paris, 1963.

Davidoff, L. and Hall, C., *Family Fortunes: Men and Women of the English Middle Class, 1780-1850*, London, 1987.

Department of Art, Brown University, Rhode Island, *Early Lithography, 1800-1840*, Providence, Rhode, Island, 1968.

Desanti, D., *Daniel, ou Le Secret Visage d'une comtesse romantique, Marie d'Agoult*, Paris, 1980.

Doukas, K. A., *The French Railroads and the State*, New York, 1976.

Dumesnil, R., *Le Réalisme et le naturalisme*, Paris, 1955.

Duncan, C., 'Happy mothers and other new ideas in French art', *Art Bulletin*, 1973, 56, no. 101, 1973, pp. 570-83.

El Nouty, H., *Théâtre et pré-cinéma*, Paris, 1978.

Ellis, V., *Tourism*, Cambridge, 1976.

Faure, A., *Paris, Carême-prenant: Carnaval à Paris au XIXe siècle, 1800-1914*, Paris, 1978.

Forges, M.-T. de, *Barbizon*, Paris, 1962.

Foucault, M., *The Archaeology of Knowledge*, translated A. Sheridan Smith, London, 1972.

Foucault, M., *The Birth of the Clinic: An Archaeology of Medical Perception*, translated A. Sheridan, London, 1973.

Foucault, M., *Discipline and Punish: The Birth of the Prison*, translated A. Sheridan, London, 1977.

Foucault, M., *The History of Sexuality: Volume 1, An Introduction*, translated R. Hurley, Harmondsworth, 1981.

Foucault, M., *Language, Countermemory, Practice*, translated D. F. Bouchard, London, 1977.

Foucault, M., *Madness and Civilisation: A History of Insanity in the Age of Reason*, translated R. Howard, London, 1971.

Foucault, M., 'On governmentality', trans. P. Pasquino, *Ideology and Consciousness*, 1979, 6, pp. 5-21.

Fulcher, J., *The Nation's Image: French Grand Opera as Politics and as Politicized Art*, Cambridge, 1987.

Gaillard, J., *Paris, la ville, 1852-1870*, Paris, 1977.

Galerie du Fleuve, Paris, *Aspects du paysage néo-classique en France de 1790 à 1855*, Paris, 1974.

Gassies (des Brûlies), G., *Guide artistique de Barbizon*, Paris, 1930.

Gaudon, J., *Victor Hugo et le théâtre: Stratégie et dramaturgie*, Paris, 1985.

Gernsheim, H. and A., *L.-J.-M. Daguerre: The History of the Diorama and the Daguerrotype*, New York, 1968.

Gille, B., *La Banque et le crédit en France de 1815 à 1848*, Paris, 1959.

Girard, M., *Le Libéralisme en France de 1814 à 1848: Doctrine et mouvement*, 4 vols, Paris, 1966–1967.

Goeldner, G. R. and McIntosh, R. W., *Tourism: Principles, Practices, Philosophies*, Columbus, Ohio, 1984.

Grad, B. and Riggs, T., *Visions of City and Country: Prints and Photographs of Nineteenth-Century France*, Worcester, NY, 1982.

Grana, C., *Bohemian versus Bourgeois: French Society and French Men of Letters in the Nineteenth Century*, London, 1964.

Grand Palais, Paris, *L'Art en France sous le Second Empire*, Paris, 1979.

Grand Palais, Paris, *David à Delacroix: Peinture française, 1774–1830*, Paris, 1974.

Grate, P., *Deux Critiques d'art de l'époque romantique: Gustave Planche et Théophile Thoré*, Stockholm, 1959.

Green, N. P., *The Nature of the Bourgeoisie: Nature, Art and Cultural Class Formation in Nineteenth-Century France*, unpublished PhD thesis, CNAA, 1986.

Green, N. and Mort, F., 'Is there anyone here from education (again)? Radical art and education for the 1990s', *Block*, 1987/88, 13, pp. 20-7.

Green, N. and Mort, F., 'Visual representation and cultural politics', *Block*, 1982, 7, pp. 59–68.

Haac, O. A., *Jules Michelet*, Boston, 1982.

Hadjinicolaou, N., *Art History and Class Struggle*, translated L. Asmal, London, 1978.

Hall, S. *et al.*, *Culture, Media, Language*, London, 1980.

Hall, S. *et al.*, *On Ideology*, London, 1978.

Harvey, D., *Consciousness and the Urban Experience*, Oxford, 1985.

Haskell, F., *Rediscoveries in Art: Some Aspects of Taste, Fashion and Collecting in England and France*, London, 1976.

Hautecoeur, L., 'De l'échoppe aux grands magasins', *Revue de Paris*, 15 August 1933, pp. 811–41.

Hayward Gallery, London, *Jean-François Millet*, essay and catalogue by R. L. Herbert, London, 1976.

Hazlitt Gallery, London, *Théodore Rousseau: 'Le Grand Refusé'*, London, 1961.

Hazlitt, Gooden & Fox, London, *The Lure of Rome: Some Northern Artists in Italy in the Nineteenth Century*, London, 1979.

Hébert, F., 'Auguste Luchet (1805–1872): Etude bio-bibliographique', 13 parts in supplements to the *Abeille de Fontainebleau*, 1913.

Henriques, J. *et al.* (eds), *Changing the Subject: Psychology, Social Regulation and Subjectivity*, London, 1984.

Horowicz, B., *Le Théâtre d'Opéra*, Paris, 1946.

Hunt, A. (ed.), *Class and Class Structure*, London, 1977.

Jacomin, E., 'Histoire de Belleville', in *Belleville*, 1980.

Jardin, A. and Tudesq, A.-J., *La Frances des notables (1815–1848)*, 2 vols, Paris, 1973.

Johnson, D., *Guizot: Aspects of French History, 1787–1874*, London, 1963.

Johnson, R., 'Educating the educators: "Experts" and the state, 1833–1839', in *Social Control in Nineteenth-Century Britain*, ed. A. Donajgrodski, London, 1977.

Johnson, R., 'Histories of culture / theories of ideology: Notes on an impasse', in *Ideology and Cultural Production*, ed. M. Barrett, London, 1979.

Johnson, R. *et al.*, *Making Histories: Studies in History Writing and Politics*, London, 1982.

Johnson, W. McA., *French Lithography: The Restoration Salons, 1817–1824*, Kingston, Ontario, 1977.

Jones, K. and Williamson, K., 'The birth of the schoolroom', *Ideology and Consciousness*, 1979, 6, pp. 59–110.

Keith, W. J., *The Rural Tradition: William Cobbett, Gilbert White, and Other Non-Fiction Prose Writers of the English Countryside*, Hassocks, Sussex, 1975.

Krakovitch, O., *Hugo censuré: La Liberté au théâtre au XIXe siècle*, Paris, 1985.

Kunsthalle, Bremen, *Zurück zur Natur: Die Kunstlerkolonie von Barbizon*, Bremen, 1977.

Laclau, E., *Politics and Ideology in Marxist Theory: Capitalism - Fascism - Populism*, London, 1977.

Lalouche, D., *Peintres de la Bretagne: Découverte d'une province*, Rennes, 1977.

Landes, D. S., 'French enterpreneurship and industrial growth in the nineteenth century', *Journal of Economic History*, 1949, 9, no. 1, pp. 45-61.

Lavedan, P., *Histoire de l'urbanisme à Paris*, Nouvelle Histoire de Paris, Paris, 1975.

Lavedan, P., *La Question du déplacement de Paris*, Paris, 1969.

Lecuyer, B., 'Médecins et observateurs sociaux: Les *Annales d'Hygiène publique et de la médecine légale* (1820-1850)', CNRS, *Pour une histoire de la statistique*, 1, Paris, 1977.

Léonard, J., *Les Médecins de l'ouest au XIXe siècle*, Paris, 1978.

Lethève, J., *Daily Life of French Artists in the Nineteenth Century*, translated H. Paddon, London, 1972.

Levinson, A., *Marie Taglione, 1804-1884*, translated C. W. Beaumont, London, 1977.

Levy, M.-F., *De Mères en filles: L'Education des françaises, 1850-1880*, Paris, 1984.

Lhomme, J., *La Grande Bourgeoisie au pouvoir, 1830-1880: Essai sur l'histoire sociale de la France*, Paris, 1960.

Lincoln, A., 'Through the undergrowth: Capitalist development and social formation in nineteenth-century France', *People's History and Socialist Theory*, edited R. Samuel, London, 1981.

Livi, J., *Vapeurs de Femmes: Essai historique sur quelques fantasmes médicaux et philosophiques*, Paris, 1984.

Locke, R. R., *French Legitimists and the Politics of Moral Order in the Early Third Republic*, Princeton, 1974.

Louvre, Paris, *Théodore Rousseau, 1812-1867*, Paris, 1967.

Loyer, F., *Paris, XIXe siècle: L'Immeuble et la rue*, Paris, 1987.

McWilliam, N. and Parsons, C., ' "Le Paysan de Paris": Alfred Sensier and the myth of rural France', *Oxford Art Journal*, 1983, 6, no. 2, pp. 38-58.

Maigron, L., *Le Romantisme et la mode*, Paris, 1911.

Maison de Balzac, Paris, *Le Spectacle et la fête au temps de Balzac*, Paris, 1978.

Malo, H., *La Gloire du vicomte de Launay*, 2 vols, Paris, 1925.

Marin, L., *L'Art des jardins et les mouvements de l'esprit humain*, Paris, 1970.

Marx, K., *Selected Writings*, edited and translated D. McLellan, Oxford, 1977.

Massey, D., *Spatial Divisions of Labour: Social Structures and the Geography of Production*, London, 1984.

Mayeur, F., *L'Education des filles en France au XIXe siècle*, Paris, 1979.

Merriman, J. M. (ed.), *French Cities in the Nineteenth Century*, London, 1982.

Michaut, G., *Sainte-Beuve avant les "lundis"*, Paris, 1909.

Michaut, G., *Senancour, amis et ennemis*, Paris, 1909.

Michel, E., *La Forêt de Fontainebleau*, Paris, 1909.

Minor, L., *The Militant Hackwriter: French Popular Literature, 1800-1848*, Bowling Green, Ohio, 1975.

Miquel, P., *Le Paysage français au XIXe siècle, 1824-1874: L'Ecole de la nature*, vols 1-3, Neufchâtel, 1975.

Morazé, C., *La France Bourgeoise*, Paris, 1946.

Moreau, T., *Le Sang de l'histoire: Michelet, l'histoire et l'idée de la femme au XIXe siècle*, Paris, 1982.

Mornet, D., *Le Sentiment de la nature en France de J.-J. Rousseau à Bernardin de Saint-Pierre*, Geneva and Paris, 1980.

Mort, F., *Dangerous Sexualities: Medico-Moral Politics in England since 1830*, London, 1987.

Musée des Beaux-Arts, Orléans, *Théodore Caruelle d'Aligny, 1798-1871, et ses compagnons*,

Orléans, 1979.

Museum of Fine Arts, Boston, *Barbizon Revisited,* essay and catalogue by R. L. Herbert, Boston, 1962.

Musée Renan-Scheffer, Paris, *La Nouvelle Athènes,* Paris, 1984.

Nead, L., *Myths of Sexuality: Representation of Women in Victorian Britain,* Oxford, 1988.

Pailleron, H.-L., *La Vie Littéraire sous Louis Philippe: François Buloz et ses amis,* Paris, 1930.

Palmade, G., *French Capitalism in the Nineteenth Century,* translated G. Holmes, Newton Abbot, 1972.

Parker, R. and Pollock G., *Old Mistresses: Women, Art, and Ideology,* London, 1981.

Parsons, C. and Ward, M., *A Bibliography of Salon Criticism in Second Empire Paris,* Cambridge, 1986.

Pellissier, P., *Emile de Girardin: Prince de la presse,* Paris, 1985.

Perret, P., *Un Demi-Siècle d'histoire populaire contemporaine (1830-1880),* Paris, 1886.

Perret, H. and Ribeill, G. (eds), *Le Journal intime de Caroline B.,* Paris, 1985.

Pinkney, D. H., *Decisive Years in France, 1840-1847,* Princeton, 1986.

Pollock, G., 'Revising or reviving realism', *Art History,* 1984, 7, no. 3, pp. 359-68.

Pollock, G., 'Vision, voice and power: Feminist art history and Marxism', *Block,* 1982, 6, pp. 2-21.

Pronteau, J., *Construction et aménagement des nouveaux quartiers à Paris, 1820-1826,* extract from *Histoire des entreprises,* Paris, 1958.

Pugh, S., *Garden - Nature - Language,* Manchester, 1988.

Rancière, J., 'Le bon temps ou la barrière des plaisirs', *Les Révoltes logiques,* Spring–Summer 1978, no. 7, pp. 25–66.

Rancière, J., *La Nuit des prolétaires,* Paris, 1981.

Regnault, E., *Histoire de dix ans, 1840-1848,* 2 vols, Paris, 1884.

Reverdy, A., *L'Ecole de Barbizon: Evolution des prix des tableaux, 1850-1960,* Paris, 1970.

Rifkin, A., 'Ingres and the Academic Dictionary: An essay on the social formation of stupefaction', *Art History,* 1983, 6, no. 2, pp. 153-70.

Rifkin, A., 'No particular·thing to mean', *Block,* 1983, 8, pp. 36–45.

Robichon, F., 'Le panorama, spectacle de l'histoire', *Le Mouvement social,* 1985, 131, pp. 65–86.

Rosenthal, L., *L'Art et les artistes romantiques,* Paris, 1928.

Rose, N., 'The psychological complex: Mental measurement and social administration', *Ideology and Consciousness,* 1979, 5, pp. 5–68.

Ross, M., *Alexandre Dumas,* Newton Abbot, 1981.

Rousselet, M., *La Magistrature sous la monarchie de juillet,* Paris, 1937.

Sainsbury Centre for Visual Arts, Norwich, and Hazlitt, Gooden & Fox, London, *Théodore Rousseau,* essay and catalogue by N. Green, London, 1982.

Salle des Fêtes, Barbizon, *Barbizon au temps de Millet,* Barbizon, 1975.

Shepherd Gallery, New York, *Forest of Fontainebleau, Refuge from Reality: French Landscape, 1800-1870,* New York, 1972.

Sewell, W. H., *Work and Revolution in France: The Language of Labor from the Old Regime to 1848,* Cambridge, Mass., 1980.

Simmel, G., 'The metropolis and mental life', *Cities and Societies: The Revised Reader in Urban Sociology,* edited P. K. Hatt and A. J. Reiss, Glencoe, 1961.

Sloane, J. C., *French Painting Between the Past and Present: Artists, Critics and Traditions, from 1848-1870,* Princeton, 1951.

Smith, B. G., *Ladies of the Leisure Class: Les Bourgeoises of Northern· France in the Nineteenth Century,* Princeton, 1981.

Smith, N., *Uneven Development: Nature, Capital and the Production of Space,* Oxford, 1984.

Soboul, A., La Révolution française, 2 vols, Paris, 1964.

Société des Amis de la Forêt de Fontainebleau, Fontainebleau, *Claude-François Denecourt,* Fontainebleau, 1975.

Stearns, P. N., *Paths to Authority: The Middle Class and the Industrial Labor Force in France, 1820-1848,* Urbana, 1978.

Stedman Jones, G., *Languages of Class: Studies in English Working-Class History, 1832-1982,* Cambridge, 1983.

Sutcliffe, A., *The Autumn of Central Paris: The Defeat of Town Planning, 1850-1970,* London, 1970.

Tagg, J., *The Burden of Representation: Essays on Photographies and Histories,* Basingstoke, 1988.

Tagg, J., 'Power and photography', Part I, *Screen Education,* Autumn 1980, no. 36, pp. 17-55.

Taylor, J. R. and Brooke, B., *The Art Dealers,* London, 1969.

Thibault, P. and Le Yaouanq, J., 'Histoire de Paris', in *Paris et sa région,* ed. J. Bastié, Paris, 1977.

Thompson, E. P., *The Poverty of Theory and Other Essays,* London, 1978.

Touchard, J., *La Gloire de Béranger,* 2 vols, Paris, 1968.

Tourneux, M., *Salons et expositions d'art à Paris, 1801-1870: Essai bibliographique,* Paris, 1919.

Tudesq, A.-J., *Les Conseillers généraux en France au temps de Guizot, 1840-1848,* Paris, 1967.

Tudesq, A.-J., *Les Grands Notables en France, 1840-1848: Etude historique d'une psychologie sociale,* 2 vols, Paris, 1964.

Tulard, J., *La Préfecture de la police sous la monarchie de juillet,* Paris, 1964.

Twyman, M., *Lithography, 1800-1850: The Techniques of Drawing on Stone in England and France and their Application in Works of Topography,* London, 1970.

Van der Tuin, H., *Les Vieux Peintres des Pays-Bas, et la critique français en France de la première moitié du XIXe siècle,* Lille, 1948.

Venturi, L., *Les Archives de l'Impressionisme,* 2 vols, Paris, 1939.

Vier, J. (ed.), *Emile de Girardin inconnu: Lettres à Mme d'Agoult,* Paris, 1949.

Watelet, J., *Bibliographie de la presse française: Politique de l'information générale, Seine-et-Marne, 1865-1944,* Paris, 1976.

Weber, E., *Peasants into Frenchmen: The Modernization of Rural France, 1870-1914,* London, 1977.

Weedon, C., *Feminist Practice and Poststructuralist Theory,* Oxford, 1987.

Weisberg, G., *The Realist Tradition: French Painting and Drawing, 1830-1900,* Cleveland, 1980.

Wenzel, C., *The Transformation of French Landscape Painting from Valenciennes to Corot, 1787-1827,* Pennsylvania, 1979.

White, C. A. and H. C., *Canvases and Careers: Institutional Change in the French Painting World,* New York, 1965.

Whiteley, L., 'Art et commerce d'art en France avant l'époque Impressioniste', *Romantisme,* 1983, no. 40, pp. 65-75.

Wiebenson, D., *The Picturesque Garden in France,* Princeton, 1978.

Wirth, L., *On Cities and Social Life: Selected Papers,* Chicago, 1964.

Wolff, J., *The Social Production of Art,* London, 1981.

Zeldin, T., *France, 1848-1945,* 5 vols, Oxford, 1979-1981.

Index

Avèze, Marquis d' (J. B. D. Mazade ?), 68

bals, 32, 35, 52, 73, 77
Balzac, H. de, 11, 46, 55, 63
banking, 13, 22, 31-2, 33; *see also* finance capitalism, speculation
Barbizon, 116-20, 149, 154, 155, 156, 170
barricades, 52
barrière, 72, 76, 83, 85, 109, 133, 154
Barrot, O., 63
Baudelaire, C., 35
Beaujon, 18, 72
Beauvoir, R. de, 43
Belgiosjoso, C. T. Princesse de, 33
Belleville, 50, 76, 77, 84, 85, 90
Benjamin, W., 12, 24
Béranger, P. J. de, 32, 163, 168
Bernard, F., 119
Berry, 118, 149
Berville, 26
Besançon, 143
Biarritz, 131
Binant, 26
biography, 129-30, 134-8, 152
bitumen pavements, 17, 22, 29-30, 43, 52
Blanc, L., 158
bohemians, 117, 118, 120, 134, 135
Bois de Boulogne, 12, 88
Bois de Vincennes, 12, 72, 88
Boisd'hyver, M. de, 118, 170, 173, 178, 181
Bonapartists, 52, 102, 157, 158, 164, 173, 180-1
Bordeaux, 17
Boulevard Bonne-Nouvelle, 96
Boulevard des Italiens, 10, 13, 37, 43, 75
Boulevard Saint-Denis, 52
bourgeoisie, 6, 86, 120, 129, 136, 139, 154, 166
  haute, 23
  hegemony of, 5, 86, 152, 155, 184-5
  petite, 85-6, 90, 177
  provincial, 142-3, 158, 159, 165, 184
Bourse, 13, 22, 24, 26, 27, 96, 160
Boutillier-Demontières, 84
boutique, 24
Bovary, Emma, 61
Bressuire, valley of, 132
Brie, plain of, 156
brigands, 18, 42

Brittany, 100
Broglie, V. Duc de, 51, 141
building boom, 17, 31, 74
building slump, 18, 44
building workers, 17-8, 91; *see also* working class
bureau des moeurs, 49
Buttes Chaumont, 69

Cabat, L., 119
Café de Paris, 10
cafés, 22, 141, 161
Café Tortoni, 10, 13, 20, 23, 37, 52, 93, 96
  and black market in shares, 23
capitalism, 6, 25, 29
  agricultural, 141, 156
  finance 11, 13, 22, 24, 28, 31, 33; *see also* banking, speculation
  industrial, 12, 13, 29, 65, 89, 91, 92, 142
caricature, 32, 53, 81, 107
Carnaval, 77-80, 86, 154
censorship, 11, 54, 106, 134
census registers, 118, 156
cercles, 60, 76
Chabrol de Volvic, G.-J.-G. Comte de, 45-6, 72, 74
Chailly, 117, 118, 156
Chamber of Deputies, 59, 61, 157
Chamber of Peers, 156
Champs Elysées, 18, 75, 86
Chantilly, 92, 154
Chardin, 10, 13
Charles X, 62
Charton, E., 102
Chartrettes, Seine-et-Marne, 144
Chateaubriand, F.-R. de, 163
Chaussée d'Antin, 10, 24, 26, 50, 79-80, 96
Chervin, Dr N., 50
cholera, epidemic of 1832, 46, 48, 51, 53, 136
Chronique de Seine-et-Marne, 163
cicerone, see Claude-François Denecourt
class; *see also*, aristocracy, bourgeoisie, working class
  conflict, 6, 74, 80, 86, 140, 143, 154, 163-4, 184-5
  and gender, 31, 71
  relations, 6, 13, 28, 41, 73, 97, 129-30, 139, 152, 164-6, 171

as a commodity, 5, 94, 95, 109–10
as a constructed category, 2–3, 11, 69,
   70–1, 75, 128, 159, 184
contesting definitions of, 72, 80
in the eighteenth century, 81–2, 196 n.
   71
human, 2, 82
tourism; *see* tourism
néorama, 96
Nodier, C., 143
Noel, E., 135
Nohant, 141, 149–50
Normandy, 100, 117
notables, 31, 47, 141, 145, 154, 159, 165,
   184
notaries, 87, 143, 145
Notre-Dame-de-Lorette, church of, 18, 19,
   see also Rue Notre-Dame-de-Lorette

'old masters', 25
Opéra, 13, 22, 77, 188–9 n. 18
Orleanists, 27, 86, 158, 164
   power bloc of, 134, 139, 164, 180
   regime of, 29, 31, 46, 52, 70, 102, 106,
      152, 157, 185; *see also*
July monarchy, Louis-Philippe regime
Ozy, A., 35

Palais-Royal, 13, 160, 194 n. 13
panorama, 96
Parent-Duchâtelet, A., 49
   De la prostitution dans la ville de Paris
      (1836), 49
Parent-Duchâtelet, M., 156
Paris; *see also* metropolitan ideology
   arrondissements of, 13, 44, 46, 47
   displacement of population in, 24, 47
   histories of, 5, 12–13, 76, 86, 184, 188
      n. 7 and 8
   immigrant labour in, 50, 91, 140
   modernity of, 11, 17, 22, 25, 28, 30, 43,
      53, 63, 66, 75, 92
   municipal council in, 46–7
   new quarters of, 13–14, 25, 26, 27, 28,
      40, 42, 44, 47, 51
   parks and gardens in, 18, 68, 69, 72–6
   population growth in, 44
   as spectacle, 5, 10–11, 25, 40, 48, 75, 95,
      175
   urban poor in, 42, 44–5, 46, 52, 59; *see*

also 'underclass'
   violence in, 51–2
Paris Commune (1871), 89
Paris-Lyon line, 92, 146, 170
Parquin, J. B. N., 143, 144, 145
Passage de l'Opéra, 21, 24
Passage de Panorama, 24
Passy, 84
Pẽna, N., de la, 70, 93, 118, 119
Pereire brothers, 33
Père Lachaise cemetery, 85
périphérique, 89
personal experience, 7, 71, 120, 184, 185;
   see also subjectivity
perspective, 101, 102, 112, 113, 115, **122**
philosophes, 81; *see also* intellectuals
Physiologies parisiennes, 28, 190 n. 51
picturesque, 68, 71, 88, 95, 100–2, 108,
   115, 145, 167, 168
Place de Bastille, 51
Place de Grève, 51
plagiarists, 53, 190 n. 66
planning, histories of, 12
Pluchonneau (*aîné*), 29
poetry, 30, 62, 160; *see also* literature
   epic, 162, 163, 164, 168
   romantic, 3, 107
policing, 45, 46, 49
political unrest, 51, 52, 164
Pontarlier, 142
potager pittoresque, 85
power bloc, 6, 61, 139, 152, 157, 159, 180
Préault, A., 107
Préfecture of the Seine, 17, 44, 46, 49, 52
press, 41, 46, 53, **57**, 60, 155; *see also*
   journalism
   expansion of, 33, 54–5, 59
   technology of, 54–5
private letters, 129, 139, 149, 151
Prix de Rome, 113
professionals, 6, 35, 41, 49, 71, 85, 86,
   102, 112, 115, 116, 120, 135, 137,
   139, 146, 152, 157, 176, 181
proletarian dreams, 7, 77, 164, 165; *also*
   artisans, working class
Promenades de Chailly, 100
prostitutes, 35, 40, 53
prostitution, 42, 46, 49, 50, 52, 55
provinces, 100, 105, 117, 158, 181
   cultural opposition from 116, 135, 142–